# CONSPIRACY JOURNAL READER
## The Deepest, Darkest Secrets
Selected by Timothy Green Beckley

Published in the United States of America By
Global Communications/Conspiracy Journal
Box 753 · New Brunswick, NJ 08903

**Staff Members**
Timothy G. Beckley, Publisher
Carol Ann Rodriguez, Assistant to the Publisher
Sean Casteel, General Associate Editor
Tim R. Swartz, Graphics and Editorial Consultant
William Kern, Editorial and Art Consultant

Sign Up On The Web For Our Free Weekly Newsletter
and Mail Order Version of Conspiracy Journal
and Bizarre Bazaar
www.ConspiracyJournal.com

r Hot Line: 1-732-602-3407
ıl: MrUFO8@hotmail.com

Covers by William Kern

# EXCERPTS FROM SOME OF THE POWERFUL REPORTS YOU'LL FIND IN THIS NEW CONSPIRACY JOURNAL BOOK:

An explanation for the UFO known as the "Black Triangle" may have been found. From 1982 to 1985 researchers from the Defense Advanced Research Projects Agency (DARPA) and NASA revived the notion of the Trans-Atmospheric Vehicle (TAV). This project became known as Copper Canyon. The objective was to find a replacement for the Lockheed SR-71 Blackbird which was retired from service in 1989. This was also around the time of the first "triangle" sightings.

From the numerous eye-witness reports of the triangle it became obvious that the vehicle is hypersonic rather than supersonic, as was the SR-71. The SR-71 was very capable of a Mach 3.5+ performance, and given the many advances in American military technology since the SR-71 was designed, it isn't unreasonable to assume that an aircraft capable of a Mach 5+ performance has been developed. However, the SR-71 was returned to service in 1996. It's replacement may have been the Advanced Stealth Technology Reconnaissance Aircraft (ASTRA), which has often been referred to, mistakenly, as Aurora.

## *Mystery of the American Black Triangle*

**CHRISTA TILTON** of Oklahoma claims she had an experience of missing time in July, 1987, when she had been abducted by two small grey aliens and transported in their craft to a hillside location where she encountered a man dressed in a red military-type jump suit. She was taken into a tunnel through computerized check-points displaying security cameras. She reports having been taken on a transit vehicle to another area where she stepped on a scale-like device facing a computer screen. After the computer issued her an identification card, she was told by her guide that they had just entered Level One of a seven-level underground facility. Christa goes on to relate how she was eventually taken down to Level Five, where she reports having seen alien craft and little grey alien entities in some of the areas she passed through.

## *Area 51 Breeding Tanks*

Beginning in 1983, residents of the Hudson Valley area of New York and nearby Connecticut started seeing strange UFOs described as larger than a football field with multicolored flashing lights. The object seems to take on a boomerang or triangle shape. Most witnesses reported the UFO was a solid object made up of some type of very dark, gun-grey material.

At the peak of its activity, the object was seen by at least five thousand witnesses which include police officers, scientists, and people from all walks of life. All indicate that the silent slow-moving UFO was something that they had never seen before and could not identify.

## *Secrets of the Black Triangles*

The Philadelphia Experiment, or Project Rainbow, was supposedly an experiment conducted in the Philadelphia Naval Yard in the early days of World War II. The ultimate goal was to make that ship invisible to enemy radar.

It is commonly believed that the mechanism involved was the generation of an incredibly intense magnetic field around the ship, that would cause refraction or bending of light or radar waves around the ship, much like a mirage created by heated air over a road on a summer day. The story goes on to say that the experiment was a success...except that the ship actually disappeared physically for a time, and then returned. They wanted to "cloak" the ship from view, but they got de-materialization, teleportation and possibly time travel instead.

## *Time Wars and the Philadelphia Experiment*

During my career in military intelligence I was privy to a lot of information that was deemed beyond top-secret. This information was so sensitive that no more than a handful of people at any given time were ever allowed access to it. At the time I didn't question the policies to keep this information from the general public, but as I got older, and maybe a little more wiser, I began to see that keeping such secrets was actually in direct violation to the pledge I took. More and more I saw that an elite few were using these secrets to gain power and profit off of the backs of the country's population. This kind of power grab made me extremely angry and disappointed. I was raised in a military family and was taught at a young age to be honest, noble and to work for the good of the people.

## *Confessions of a NWO Whistle Blower*

# The Deepest, Darkest Secrets

Selected By
Timothy Green Beckley

# Conspiracy Journal

## Reader

# CONTENTS

# Conspiracy Journal Reader

## The Deepest, Darkest Secrets

### Selected By Timothy Green Beckley

## THE AMERICAN BLACK TRIANGLE

First published in UFO Magazine

Black Triangle Spotted Over Belgium

An explanation for the UFO known as the "Black Triangle" may have been found. From 1982 to 1985 researchers from the Defense Advanced Research Projects Agency (DARPA) and NASA revived the notion of the Trans-Atmospheric Vehicle (TAV). This project became known as Copper Canyon. The objective was to find a replacement for the Lockheed SR-71 Blackbird which was retired from service in 1989. This was also around the time of the first "triangle" sightings.

From the numerous eye-witness reports of the triangle it became obvious that the vehicle is hypersonic rather than supersonic, as was the SR-71. The SR-71 was very capable of a Mach 3.5+ performance, and given the many advances in American military technology since the SR-71 was designed, it isn't unreasonable to assume that an aircraft capable of a Mach 5+ performance has been developed. However, the SR-71 was returned to service in 1996. It's replacement may have been the Advanced Stealth Technology Reconnaissance Aircraft (ASTRA), which has often been referred to, mistakenly, as Aurora.

On March 4th, 1997, the BBC in the United Kingdom ran a news item showing film footage which had been secret for nearly 20 years. The film showed a Hercules aircraft fitted with rocket boosters to the front, rear and undercarriage. The plane was able to take off almost vertically and be airborne in under five seconds.

The project's aim was to enable the aircraft to land on ground the size of a soccer pitch, pick up hostages in Iran and take off in less than a hundred yards. The project was started in the late June of 1980, abandoned in October of that year and cost $30 million. The reason for halting the project was, apparently, that on the first test flight the plane crashed on landing.

The BBC didn't actually tell the whole truth in their report of the incident. There was in fact three aircraft involved and it is strongly rumored that the project was a success.

Incidentally, the hostages were released three months later. The C-130 Hercules is the heaviest carrier in service in the Royal Air Force (RAF). If the project was successful and the technology applied to smaller fighter planes, the speed in which they could be airborne could rival the Harrier jump-jet.

Assuming the ASTRA has been in active service since 1989, what has DARPA and/ or NASA been developing and test-flying since then? This brings in the concept of Aurora. It has been suggested that Aurora's configuration resembles that of a pure delta ranging from 100-200 feet. If the Aurora has an advanced version of the Hercules rocket system giving it jump-jet capabilities and stealth technology it would be a formidable aircraft, a giant "triangle" that would be able to hover and depart at great speed. It is also suggested that the aircraft has an advanced form of vectored thrust and that the powerplant is a Pulse Detonation Wave Engine.

From the numerous worldwide reports it seems that the "Black Triangle" is a very real and advanced craft. To develop such a craft an advanced level of technology and a lot of money is required. The only country which could meet these standards is America, with Britain possibly as well.

A substantial amount of evidence has been collected on the "triangle" mystery and a strong connection with America has been identified. For example, examine the following report:

A group of six soldiers on maneuvers on Salisbury Plain encountered the "triangle" at approximately 2a.m. one morning. This event occured in the winter of 1989, again around the time of the first "triangle" sightings. According to one of the witnesses they came across a copse in a wood where they saw bright lights. Looking up the men saw a large black craft which suddenly beamed a powerful light into the copse. The size of the craft was estimated to be as big as a C-130 Hercules or bigger. The enormous craft hung motionless without sound then suddenly departed at an incredible speed, still silent.

Later during hypnotic regression, one of the soldiers recounted an amazing story.

He told how a beam of light had encircled the man paralysing him. At this time a man wearing a black zip-up flying suit appeared from the woods and spoke to them in an American accent. In the moments that follow we are told how the beam moves the man, making them shuffle along the edge of the woods. The witness then looks up and sees a black triangular craft, sort of wedge-shaped, with the beam of light coming from it's center. He then goes on to describe how the light pulsates with a humming noise.

The soldier then recalls how they found themselves 600 meters from where they should have been. Other details were disclosed in this account that lend weight to the conclusion of American involvement, such as the insignia worn by the American on the left chest area.

In light of this information - the Pulse Detonation Wave Engine, the advanced form of the Hercules rocket system and the witnesses' testimony - we can make the connection between the Triangle and America.

## AREA 51 BREEDING TANKS

by William Hamilton III

**CHRISTA TILTON** of Oklahoma claims she had an experience of missing time in July, 1987, when she had been abducted by two small grey aliens and transported in their craft to a hillside location where she encountered a man dressed in a red military-type jump suit. She was taken into a tunnel through computerized check-points displaying security cameras. She reports having been taken on a transit vehicle to another area where she stepped on a scale-like device facing a computer screen. After the computer issued her an identification card, she was told by her guide that they had just entered Level One of a seven-level underground facility. Christa goes on to relate how she was eventually taken down to Level Five, where she reports having seen alien craft and little grey alien entities in some of the areas she passed through.

In one large room she saw computerized gauges hooked to large tanks and large arms that extended from some tubing down into the tanks. She noticed a humming sound, smelled formaldehyde, and had the impression that a liquid was being stirred in the tanks. She was not shown the contents of those tanks. Christa has made drawings of much of what she claims to have witnessed during her abduction.

These tanks were also depicted in a set of controversial papers called the "Dulce Papers," which were allegedly stolen from the Dulce underground facility along with over 30 black and white photographs and a video tape. The mysterious security officer who took the papers claims to have worked at Dulce until 1979 when he decided that the time had come to part company with his employers.

In late 1979, Thomas C. could no longer cope with the awesome reality he had to confront. As a high-level security officer at the joint alien-U.S. Government underground base near Dulce, he had learned of and had seen disturbing things. After much inner conflict, he decided to desert the facility and take various items with him.

Using a small camera, he took over 30 photos of areas within the multi-level complex. He collected documents and removed a security video tape from the Control Center which showed various security camera views of the hallways, labs, aliens, and U. S. Government personnel to take with him. By shutting off the alarm and camera systems in one of the over 100 exits to the surface, he left the facility with the photos, video tapes and documents. The "originals" were hidden after five sets of copies were made.

Thomas was ready to go into hiding. But, when he went to pick up his wife and young son, he found a van and government agents waiting. His wife and child had been kidnapped. He had been betrayed by K. Lomas, a fellow worker. The agents wanted what Thomas had taken from the facility in order to get his wife and son back. When it became apparent to him that his wife and son would be used in biological experiments and were not going to be returned unharmed, he decided to get lost.

How did Thomas get involved in all this covert intrigue?

Thomas was in his mid-twenties when he received top secret training in photography at an underground facility in West Virginia. For seven years he worked in high security in the Air Force. In 1971, he left and went to work for the Rand Corporation in Santa Monica, California. In 1977 he was transferred to the Dulce facility. He bought a home in Santa Fe, New Mexico, and worked Monday through Friday. He communted to work via a deep underground tube-shuttle system.

At this time, a fellow researcher was working security in Santa Fe, and was privately investigating UFO sightings, animal mutilations, Masonic and Wicca groups in the area. Thomas had a mutual friend who came to Santa Fe in 1979 to visit both the researcher and Thomas. This visitor later viewed the photos, the video tape, and documents taken from the Dulce base. Drawings were made from what was seen and later circulated in the UFO research community as the "Dulce Papers."

Thomas alleges that there were over 18,000 short "greys" at the Dulce facility, and that he saw reptilian humanoids. A colleague had come face-to-face with a 6-foot tall Reptoid which had materialized in his house. The Reptoid showed an interest in research maps of New Mexico and Colorado which were on the wall. The maps were full of colored push-pins and markers to indiate sites of animal mutilations, caverns, locations of high UFO activity, repeated flight paths, abduction sites, ancient ruins, and suspected alien underground bases.

The multi-level facility at Dulce is reported to have a central HUB which is controlled by base security. The security level goes up as one descends to lower levels. Thomas had an ULTRA-7 clearance. He knew of seven sub-levels, but there may have been more. Most of the aliens supposedly are on levels 5, 6, and 7, with alien housing on level 5. The only sign in English was one over a tube shuttle station hallway which read "to Los Alamos." Connections go from Dulce to the Page, Arizona facility, then on to an underground base beneath Area 51 in Nevada. Tube shuttles go to and from Dulce to facilities below Taos, New Mexico; Datil, New Mexico; Colorado Springs, Colorado; Creed, Colorado; Sandia, then on to Carlsbad, New Mexico. There appears to be a vast network of tube shuttle connections under the U. S. which extends into a global system of tunnels and sub-cities.

At the Dulce Base, most signs on doors and hallways are in the alien symbol language and a universal symbol system understood by humans and aliens. Thomas stated that after the second level, everyone is weighed in the nude, then given a uniform. Visitors are given off-white uniforms; jump suits with a zipper. The weight of the person is put on a computer I.D. card each day. Any change in weight is noted; if over three pounds, a physical exam and X-ray is required.

Scales are located in front of all sensitive areas and are built into the floor near doorways and the door control panels. An individual places his computer I.D. card into the door slot, then enters a numerical code onto a keypad. The person's weight and code must match the card or the door will not open. Any discrepancy will summon security. No one is allowed to carry anything into the sensitive areas. All supplies are put onto a conveyer belt and X-rayed. The same method is used when leaving the sensitive areas.

All elevators are controlled magnetically; there are no elevator cables. The magnetic system is inside the walls of the elevator shaft. There are no normal electrical controls.

Everything is controlled by advanced magnetics, including lighting. There are no regular light bulbs and the tunnels are lighted by phosphorus units with broad, structureless emission bands. Some deep tunnels use a form of phosphorus pentoxide to temporarily illuminate certain areas. The aliens won't go near these areas for unknown reasons.

**Level 1** contains the garage for street maintenance. **Level 2** contains the garage for trains, shuttles, tunnel-boring machines, and disc maintenance.

The studies on **Level 4** include human-aura research, as well as all aspects of telepathy, hypnosis, and dreams. Thomas says that they know how to separate the bioplasmic body from the physical body and place an "alien entity" life-force matrix within a human body after removing the "soul" life-force-matrix of the human.

**Level 6** is privately called "Nightmare Hall." It holds the genetic labs where experiments are conducted on fish, seals, birds, and mice that are vastly altered from their original forms. There are multi-armed and multi-legged humans and several cages and vats of humanoid bat-like creatures as tall as seven feet. The aliens have taught the humans a lot about genetics; things both useful and dangerous.

The Grey and Reptoid species are highly analytical and technologially oriented. They have had ancient conflicts with the Nordic humans from other space societies, and may be staging here for a future conflict. Intensely into computing and bio-engineering sciences, they are led to conducting reckless experimentation without regard for what we consider to be ethical and empathetic conduct toward other living creatures.

Principal government organizations involved with mapping human genetics, the so-called genome projects, are within the Department of Energy (which has a heavy presence on the Nevada Test Site); the National Institute of Health; the National Science Foundation; the Howard Hughs Medical Institute; and, of course, the Dulce Underground Labs which are run by the DOE. Thomas has revealed that the chief of the genetic experiments for Los Alamos and Dulce is Larry Deaven.

According to Thomas, the alien androgynal breeder is capable of parthenogenesis. At Dulce, the common form of reproduction is polyembryony. Each embryo can, and does divide into 6 to 9 individual "cunne" (pronounced cooney, i.e.; siblings). The needed nutriment for the developing cunne is supplied by the 'formula," which usually consist of plasma, deoxyhemoglobin, albumin, lysozyme, cation, amniotic fluid and more.

The term 'genome" is used to describe the totality of the chromosomes unique to a particular organism (or any cell within the organism), as distinct from the genotype, which is the information contained within those chromosomes. The human genes are mapped to specific chromosomal locations. This is an ambitious project that will take years and a lot of computer power to accomplish.

Is the alien and human BIO-TECH being used to nurture and serve us, or is it being used to control and dominate us! Why have UFO abductees been used in genetic experiments?

It was when Thomas encountered humans in cages on Level 7 of the Dulce facility that things finally reached a climax for him. Row after row of thousands of humans, human-mixture remains, and embryos of humanoids were kept in cold storage. He says, "I frequently encountered humans in cages, usually dazed or drugged, but sometimes they cried and begged for help. We were told they were hopelessly insane, and involved in high-risk drug tests to cure insanity. We were told to never speak to them at all. At the beginning we believed that story. Finally in 1978 a small group of workers discovered the truth. That began the Dulce wars."

Thomas also says the aliens don't want the land, the gold, the minerals, or the water that we possess, nor even the human or animal life. What they do want is the magnetic power that surges on and through the Earth. The aliens harvest this magnetic power in a way unknown to us. Thomas says the aliens recognize this power as more valuable than any other commodity on our globe.

It may be unpalatable to digest or believe Thomas' story. In fact, it seems like part of a living nightmare. There is evidence that something strange does go on at Dulce. Does Thomas have the answer?

There may be a terrible truth hidden behind the continuing phenomena of UFO sightings, abductions, and animal mutilations. Our government intelligence agencies have had an ongoing watchful eye on all UFO activities for many decades now. This extraordinary phenomenon must have an extraordinary explanation. We may be only one outpost in a vast interstellar empire.

Recently, researcher John Anderson went to Dulce, New Mexico to see if there was any truth to the reported UFO activity. He says that as he arrived in town he saw a caravan of cars and a McDonnell Douglas mini-lab in a van going up a rural road near the town. He followed them to a fenced-in compound where he waited to see further developments. Suddenly, six UFOs descended rapidly over the compound, hovered long enough for him to snap one picture, then shot up and out of sight. When later stopping at a store, he told the owner of the UFO photo he had taken, the store owner listened and revealed how he had been a victim rancher of cattle mutes. Their conversation was interrupted by a phone call. The store owner told John to leave at once, then after John went to his car, closed the store. John saw a mysterious van drive up to the store and a man got out and went inside. John, deciding to leave Dulce, was followed by two men in a car as he left town.

Even more recently a research team has gone up to Archuleta Mesa to take soundings under the ground. Preliminary and tentative computer analysis of these soundings seem to indicate deep cavities under the mesa.

How long will the secret of Dulce, known to insiders as Section D, remain locked up inside the mute New Mexico mountains? Forever?


**TESLA TECHNOLOGY:**

**HAUNTING SECRETS OF THE BLACK TRIANGLE MYSTERY**

**SPECIAL REPORT**

by Tim Swartz

UFOs are reported in all kinds of different shapes and sizes from round, ball-like shapes, square boxes, flying cigars, to the traditional saucer. Out of all of these configurations, triangular shaped UFOs seem to be receiving more attention and publicity recently.

Beginning in the early 1980's many countries, including the United States have experienced mass-sightings of triangle UFOs, all with similar characteristics such as shape, sound, lighting and flight patterns. Seen with increasing frequency, several excellent photos and videos have been taken of these strange craft. Nevertheless, despite these photos, no good explanation has yet surfaced to account for the nature of these remarkable UFOs.

Many UFO researchers are certain that the flying triangles represent proof that the Earth is being visited by extraterrestrials. While the other side of the controversy says that these UFOs are in fact top secret, black budget military aircraft using technology that is years ahead of civilian science. There could, however, be another explanation that is so shocking and outrageous that those who have dared approach the subject soon find themselves caught up in a swirl of controversy that few have escaped from. The debate shows no sign of closure anytime soon.

### THE HUDSON VALLEY UFO FLAP

Beginning in 1983, residents of the Hudson Valley area of New York and nearby Connecticut started seeing strange UFOs described as larger than a football field with multicolored flashing lights. The object seems to take on a boomerang or triangle shape. Most witnesses reported the UFO was a solid object made up of some type of very dark, gun-grey material.

At the peak of its activity, the object was seen by at least five thousand witnesses which include police officers, scientists, and people from all walks of life. All indicate that the silent slow-moving UFO was something that they had never seen before and could not identify.

Most of the reports from that area at that time seem to support the idea that the flying triangle was very large, silent and very low. Most of the estimates place it around 500-800 feet above the ground. Local police were baffled by the sightings. State police told them that the sightings were caused by nothing more than a group of stunt planes flying in formation. The FAA official at Bradley International Airport would not confirm or deny if they had anything on radar, but insisted that the sightings were most likely a hoax with a hot air balloon. However, many people who saw the object say that the explanations don't fit. As one building inspector in the Hartford area said: "This thing about balloons and aircraft is a lot of crap."

### TRIANGLE UFOs AROUND THE WORLD

One of the most heralded cases of multiple black triangle sightings was the Belgian flap which began in November of 1989. The events of November 29 would be documented by no less than thirty different groups of witnesses, and three separate groups of police officers.

All of the reports related a large object flying at low altitudes. The craft was of a flat, triangular shape, with lights underneath. This giant craft made not a sound as it slowly, fearlessly, moved across the landscape of Belgium. There was free sharing of information as the Belgian populace tracked this craft as it moved from the town of Liege to the border of the Netherlands and Germany.

This first startling sighting would evolve into a wave over the next several months. On two occasions, a pair of F-16 fighters chased the mysterious object, but to no avail. On March 30, 1990, a frantic call to military headquarters came from a Belgian national police captain. He reported a giant flying triangle passing over, and simultaneously two ground radar stations were reporting an object of unknown origin on their screens. One of these bases was NATO controlled near the city of Glons, southeast of Brussels. After contacting other radar facilities, they learned that at least four other stations were also reporting the object on their screens. The object was moving across their screens slowly, and failed to send a transponder signal to identify itself.

Two F-16s were ordered to intercept and identify this phenomena, and one of the jet's radars locked the object in. It appeared as a small diamond on the pilot's screen. The pilot reported that only a few seconds after locking on the target the object began to pick up speed, quickly moving out of radar range. An hour long chase ensued, during which time the F-16s picked up the strange craft's signal two additional times, only to see it fade from view. The triangular craft seemed to be playing a cat and mouse game, and finally was lost in the night lights of Brussels. The pilots of the fighters reported that the UFO had made maneuvers at speeds beyond the capability of their technology, and once the radar showed the craft almost instantly drop from 10,000 to 500 feet in five seconds.

The extraordinary sightings continued for months as the triangular invader was witnessed more than 1,000 times, both day and night. The object dipped low enough to easily be seen with the naked eye, and the event became one of the biggest stories in the Belgian media.

One unusual occurrence associated with the Belgian flap, as well as other flying triangle sightings, was the inability to take a clear photograph of the UFO. Many observers had their cameras ready, and took what they thought would be clear images, but when the film was developed, the image was blurred, and the craft's outline was vague at best.

This anomaly was addressed by physics professor Auguste Meessen, who was employed by the Catholic University at Louvin. Meessen's investigation produced a theory that infrared light must be the reason that almost all the images were unclear. To put his theory to test, he exposed film to infrared, then photographed objects in regular light. The results were the same as the photographs of the triangle-shaped UFO.

## A RECENT PHENOMENA?

One reason that black triangles are considered to be manmade military aircraft is the mistaken impression that all sightings of these craft have been within the last twenty years. However, research on past UFO reports have uncovered a significant number of triangle-shaped UFOs dating as far back as the 1930's and possibly even before.

In 1933, Italian leader Benito Mussolini allegedly formed a top secret UFO study group to investigate a flap of flying triangle UFOs being sighted all over Italy at the time. Active until 1940, the Italian government organization compiled many documents and pictures that were kept secret.

Italian TV station RAI DUE interviewed two Italian ufologists who exhibited two 1933 teletype messages in which Mussolini ordered censorship of any information relating to "possible appearance of crafts of unknown origin or unknown phenomena—especially he notes that he forbids the spreading of information about some kind of triangle-shaped UFO landing near Milano."

Mussolini in 1941 gave a speech in which he warned the Allies that it should be more concerned about an attack from otherworldly civilizations than the mounting tensions that were occurring during that pre-World War II period. The television report added that the Italian leader's comments were not taken seriously at the time.

Another interesting report dated from September 1952 concerned the sighting of triangular-shaped UFOs seen during a NATO exercise called "Mainbrace." Significantly, UFOs witnessed by military personnel were reported throughout Mainbrace. This included a now famous encounter reported by half a dozen Royal Air Force personnel, stationed at RAF Topcliffe in Yorkshire, who saw a triangle shaped UFO operating near the airfield.

Interestingly enough, it was later stated by Edward J. Ruppelt (the one-time head of the U.S. Air Force's UFO study program, Project Blue Book) that it was the sightings reported throughout Mainbrace which caused the British Government to officially recognize the UFO mystery.

Barely one day into the exercise, at least two reports of encounters with triangular-shaped vehicles were filed with the authorities by naval personnel on board ships off the coast of Ireland. The first such encounter involved what was referred to as a "blue/green triangle" which was observed flying over the sea at a speed of 1,500 miles per hour; while later that same day, a triangular formation of lights emitting a "white light exhaust" was seen in the same vicinity.

In 1956 an incident was reported to the British Air Ministry by a Mr. W. Arnold of Greater Manchester. In a 1962 letter to the Air Ministry, Mr. Arnold wrote: "The recent UFO sighted over Manchester is not a new phenomenon, and one was sighted by myself in 1956 in the early hours of the morning. It was always my belief that this

aircraft was a British experimental plane. It carried no markings whatever and was of highly polished metal. If I am mistaken that this plane is British, then alternatively it could be a photo reconnaissance plane from source unknown and of an interesting design!''

Most remarkable of all, Arnold had included with his letter a hand drawn picture of the object he had viewed which looked like a cross between a triangle and the heel of a shoe. And it is perhaps notable that a number of witnesses to the reported UFO crash near Roswell in 1947 stated that rather than being saucer shaped, the crashed object was heel-like in design.

These early reports can only lead us to believe that at least some of the triangle-shaped UFOs cannot be secret aircraft of earthly origin. The technology possessed by most countries before and after WW II would preclude the possibility of such sightings being the result of secret testing of military aircraft. But, could there be another, more sinister explanation for the phenomena that involves both scenarios in a way only whispered by those unwilling to accept another explanation?

## INVESTIGATORS LOOK AT FLYING BLACK TRIANGLES

A just released study by the National Institute for Discovery Science (NIDS), based in Las Vegas, Nevada, sheds new light on the dark and mysterious craft.

NIDS researchers contend that Big Black Deltas, or BBDs, are U.S. Defense Department airships. They are so large they can carry massive payloads at low altitudes, cruising at speeds three to five times as fast as surface ships.

Among a range of NIDS observations, the group believes the BBDs are powered by electrokinetic/field drives, or airborne nuclear power units. These craft also fly at extreme altitudes, high above conventional aircraft and the pulsing of ground-based traffic control radar.

Electrokinetic propulsion means that no propellers or jets are used. A hybrid lighter-than-air craft would rely on aerostatic, lift gas, like a balloon. No helicopter-like downwash would be produced. Except for a slight humming from high-voltage control equipment — and in older BBD versions an occasional coronal discharge — a Big Black Delta makes no noise.

The BBDs most often reported are low-flying, silent, and appear to be about the size of a football field. They have been seen accelerating very rapidly from a hovering position. As one researcher noted: ''They can look as though they are leaping across the sky. Being silent, it's almost spooky.''

## THE LIFTERS: CLUES TO THE SECRET PROPULSION OF

## BLACK TRIANGLES

Tim Ventura, a UNIX programmer for AT&T Wireless, has been building unassuming devices he calls Lifters. Made from balsa wood, aluminum foil and 30-gauge magnet wire, when charged with a small amount of electrical power, they levitate, apparently able to resist Earth's gravitational forces.

Currently, the devices can only levitate themselves. But Ventura and others are working to convert electrical current into a force that can lift and move planes, trains and rocket ships. If that proves possible, the technology that powers lifters could extend the ability to explore space and drastically cut the use of fossil fuels on Earth.

Ventura uses an old Compaq computer display to power his lifters. Two wires come off the lifter, a positive power lead connected (PDF) via a high-voltage tap to the monitor's picture tube, which redirects electricity from the picture tube to the lifter, and a ground wire, also connected to the monitor.

Lifters seemingly do levitate and hover without standard propellants, but the problem is that no one is quite sure why. Some developers believe that electricity stimulates the electrons on the lifter's surface, providing propulsion. Other theories such as ion-wind currents or electromagnetic disturbance of the air around the lifter have also been proposed, but there has been little scientific testing.

One story is that the idea for lifters came from pieces of UFO wreckage taken from the Roswell site. A parcel of purported crash parts was sent by an unknown person to radio talk show host Art Bell in 1996. Bell sent them to a government researcher, whose investigations reportedly indicated that when electrical voltage was applied to the parts, they would move and in some cases levitate in much the same way as lifters do.

Could Lifter technology be the secret behind the mysterious flying triangles? Are Lifters primitive versions of sophisticated aircraft developed in secret at the turn of the century by a group of renegade scientists? New evidence compiled for the first time by UFO journalist Sean Casteel could shed some light on the secret origins of black triangle UFOs.

### THE TESLA/MARS CONNECTION

In his recent book: ***NIKOLA TESLA, JOURNEY TO MARS, ARE WE ALREADY THERE?***, (Published by Conspiracy Journal and Global Communications, 2002) Sean Casteel uncovers what could be the most incredible secret surrounding the life of electrical genius Nikola Tesla. A secret that he took with him to his grave, yet continues to haunt the world to this very day.

Casteel reveals in a series of fascinating interviews that a secret society located in the United States were the true inventors of heavier-than-air aircraft - aircraft that were seen, and widely reported in newspapers, as early as the 1850's.

The idea that a secret group of scientists was conducting experiments in flight years before the Wright brothers is truly amazing. However, the alleged source of the information used by this group borders on the fantastic, as it is thought the technical information was received from spirits during seances.

As incredible as it sounds, the instructions received were obviously accurate as airship sightings continued to increase in subsequent years, not only in the United States but in Europe as well. The air had been conquered by a group dedicated to scientific endeavors and strict secrecy. And while the original intentions of this secret group seemed to be benevolent, they were soon overtaken by others who were not interested in the betterment of mankind, but were instead interested in wealth and power.

In 1899, while conducting experiments at his lab in Colorado Springs, Colorado, the great scientist and inventor Nikola Tesla claimed to have received radio transmissions of a highly unusual nature. He would later write that he had the feeling he was the first man on Earth to hear a greeting "from one planet to another."

Soon after Tesla's story was released in the newspapers, he was approached by men who claimed to represent financial interests who were interested in backing Tesla on some of his pet projects. The only stipulation was that Tesla had to help them with a project so grandiose and impossible that Tesla thought he was dealing with madmen. But once Tesla was brought up to date on the accomplishments already achieved by this enigmatic group, he was all too willing to work on their grand scheme — A journey to the planet Mars in a ship built according to channeled instructions delivered through a spirit medium.

Does a secret society of scientists exist with their origins stretching back to the middle 1800's? Has this group been the real masters of the air years before the first motorized hops at Kitty Hawk? Could the mysterious black triangles be sophisticated, electrogravitic aircraft piloted by a secretive group whose intentions are known only to them?

These secrets have been kept under wraps for more than a century. It is now time for those who know what is really going on to come forward and admit the truth about black triangles and the haunting secret that surrounds them.

## TIME-WARS! BLACKOUT 2003

## AND THE PHILADELPHIA EXPERIMENT

By Commander X

The great blackout of August 2003 will undoubtedly go down in the history books for not only being the biggest power outage ever, but also for the way it caught the experts completely by surprise. The professionals who make their living by maintaining and monitoring the country's electrical grid were shocked by how quickly things went out of control that hot, summer afternoon. Some have admitted privately that what they observed that day defied normal explanation.

These same experts who watched the grid crash down in front of them are now challenged to discover the reason or reasons that the systems safeguards, built in to prevent blackouts from occurring in the first place, failed so spectacularly. This is a mystery that will have no easy answers.

At first glance, it may seem that the blackout was caused by simple mechanical and human error. However, the week the blackout occurred also held special significance with one of the biggest mysteries in conspiracy history - the infamous Philadelphia Experiment.

### The Philadelphia Experiment Redux

The Philadelphia Experiment, or Project Rainbow, was supposedly an experiment conducted in the Philadelphia Naval Yard upon a small ship in the early days of World War II. The ultimate goal was to make that ship invisible to enemy radar.

It is commonly believed that the mechanism involved was the generation of an incredibly intense magnetic field around the ship, that would cause refraction or bending of light or radar waves around the ship, much like a mirage created by heated air over a road on a summer day. The story goes on to say that the experiment was a success...except that the ship actually disappeared physically for a time, and then returned. They wanted to "cloak" the ship from view, but they got de-materialization, teleportation and possibly even time travel instead.

Researchers say that the experiments began in June of 1943, with the USS. Eldridge, DE (Destroyer Escort) 173, being fitted with tons of experimental electronic equipment. (It is debatable whether or not the USS. Eldridge was the actual ship used for Project Rainbow, but we won't get into that at this time.) According to one source this included two massive generators of 75 KVA each, mounted where the forward gun turret would have been, distributing their power through four magnetic coils mounted on the deck. Three RF transmitters (2 megawatt CW each, mounted on the deck), three thousand '6L6' power amplifier tubes (used to drive the field coils of the two generators), special synchronizing and modulation circuits, and a host of other specialized hardware were employed to generate massive electromagnetic fields which, when properly configured, would be able to bend light and radio waves around the ship, thus making it invisible to enemy observers.

On July 22nd, 1943, power to the generators was switched on, and the massive electromagnetic fields started to build up. A greenish fog was seen to slowly envelop the ship, concealing it from view. Then the fog itself is said to have disappeared, taking the Eldridge with it, leaving only undisturbed water where the ship had been anchored only moments before.

It seemed obvious to all involved that the ship and crew were not only invisible to radar but as an extra bonus, was invisible to the eye as well. Everything seemed to have worked as planned, and about fifteen minutes later they ordered the men to shut down the generators. The greenish fog slowly reappeared, and the Eldridge began to dematerialize as the fog disappeared.

When personnel from shore boarded the ship, the crew above deck was found to be disoriented and nauseous. The Navy removed the crew, and shortly after obtained another. In the end, the Navy decided that they only wanted radar invisibility, and the equipment was altered.

On the 28th of October in 1943, the final test on the Eldridge was performed. The modified electromagnetic field generators were turned on and the Eldridge became nearly invisible; only a faint outline of the hull remained visible in the water.

Everything seemed fine at first, but then, the ship suddenly vanished. Within seconds it reappeared miles away, in Norfolk, Virginia, and was seen for several minutes. The Eldridge then disappeared from Norfolk as mysteriously as it had arrived, and reappeared back in Philadelphia Naval Yard. This time the crew suffered horribly from the experiment. Most were violently sick. Some of the crew had disappeared, never to be seen again. Some went insane and had to be permanently institutionalized. But strangest of all, five men were physically fused into the metal of the ship's structure.

What had begun as an experiment in electronic camouflage, ended up as an accidental teleportation of an entire ship and crew through time and space all in a matter of minutes. The ripples from this experiment have stretched out across the decades since 1943, possibly culminating in a most unexpected way in the year 2003.

### Project Rainbow According to Al Bielek

Al Bielek, a retired electrical engineer says that he is one of the few survivors of the Philadelphia Experiment. In an interview with author Bill Knell, Bielek said that the days surrounding August 12, 2003 would be very important because of the anniversary date of one of the experiments.

Bielek insists that the crucial experiment in the Philadelphia Shipyard took place on August 12, 1943, and not October 28 as is often repeated in accounts of the experiments. The Navy had realized that a new and exciting technology had been discovered and weren't about to let it go. Not only had the project shown them that the use of controlled energy fields could produce the ability to move objects rapidly through time and space, but the fields produced an effect on the human mind. After some of the sailors from the 1943 sea trials went insane, the Navy wondered if that effect could be controlled and directed at friendly forces to make them fight fearlessly or at enemy forces to force their surrender?

Bielek has said that he began recalling disjointed, fragmentary memories of his involvement with the Philadelphia Experiment in 1986 after seeing the 1984 movie, *The Philadelphia Experiment*. According to Bielek, the Philadelphia Experiment is inextricably linked with another 'black' project involving time travel (and mind control) that was developed at an underground facility on Long Island, New York known as The Montauk Project.

Bielek claims that he and his brother were crewmen on the U.S.S. Eldridge and found themselves teleported to the Long Island facility in the year 1983, forty years in the future.

"We jumped over the side of the ship expecting to hit water," Bielek recalls. "We didn't hit water, instead we wound up in 1983, August 12. Now what was the nature of the problem that he finally came to grips with? It was rather basic. The ship came back to its point of reference because it had a Zero Time Generator and the reference system that brought it back. That remained intact; it was the generators that were destroyed, and certain other equipments that were destroyed, but that zero reference device brought the ship back to its original point of reference, even though it had shifted time slightly.

"Humans are born, or I should say not only born but at the time of conception, as he found out with his research, with their own time locks. Now you would have to go into some rather obscure physics, I'll leave out the math and try to make it simple. We're not living in a three dimensional universe. We're living in a five dimensional universe. The fourth and fifth dimensions are time. The fourth time dimension of course has been well alluded to as outlined by Einstein and others."

The brothers were given a briefing by an elderly Dr. John Van Neumann, the same senior scientist with whom they had been working in 1943 in preparation for the Eldridge invisibility experiment (albeit 40 years older).

Van Neumann told them they the Philadelphia Experiment had ripped open a dangerous 'hole' in the space-time continuum that needed to be sealed. Destroying the banks of power vacuum tubes aboard the Eldridge was the only way to shut down the shipboard equipment and return the ship to 1943.

"Von Neumann realized," Bielek said, "as it is known today by some physicists, that the fifth dimension is also time; it is a spinnor, a vector, rotating around the first primary vector which indicates the flow and direction of time. The flow is immaterial. We say that we are moving forward in time, that's because of our looking at it, and our reference. We don't sense time but it does flow at a fairly stable rate. And this other vector running around it is of no concern to us... normally.

"However every human at the time of conception is given a set of locks, if you will (it's part of the genetic structure), to the time point at which that individual is locked at conception, so that that individual flows with time and one born and lives a life out is referenced to everything around him which he comes to know all his friends, family, schooling, whatever, and doesn't slip in and out of time from the point of reference which he is used to. That is, normally."

Bielek says the two men were sent back to the deck of the Eldridge to smash the electronic equipment by walking through a time 'tunnel' created by a time machine that was developed at Montauk (the time machine being built with the help of extraterrestrial aliens with whom the government had made an agreement).

"Once the ship came back, is when the trouble started," Bielek said. "As long as it was in Hyperspace and the generators were going, they were all contained within the field. So far as I know, nobody else jumped overboard but the two of us.

"In retrospect, I wonder whether we ever should have, but nevertheless we did, and the events that took place, took place. When the fields collapsed, these individuals, having lost their time references right up to that point, who were held and contained within the field, started to drift. Some of them drifted totally out of reality, others drifted around, and were lucky if they got their feet on the deck, and some drifted and finally materialized, as happened, two on the deck, two in the bulkheads, and one with his hand in the wall, and that was because of the fact that they lost their time references, and they drifted, and they happened to drift back."

Al Bielek says that top Navy brass of 1943 insisted that August 12 was a "drop dead date" for running the invisibility experiment aboard the Eldridge. The experiment had to occur on that particular date. Bielek was later to find out that on August 12 - at forty and twenty-year intervals (E.g. 1903, 1943, 1983, 2003, etc) - the four principle "biorhythms" of the earth would lock up and match in phase with each other.

"Not only do humans have biofields that start at birth," Bielek says, "but planet Earth has its own set of biofields. This has been discovered rather recently, in the last decade roughly. Four of them, and they all four peak out once every twenty years. Guess what date? The 12th of August. 1943, 1963, 1983, 2003, you can go backwards or forwards, always twenty years. And this creates a very strange set of conditions on planet Earth, where there is a peak of energy, a peak of magnetic energies, and a capability of coupling, and this is what happened because of the culmination of dates of the two experiments, on August 12th, and the Earth's biofields peaking out at that time."

This phase 'lock-up' created a time window that would allow very unusual space-time phenomena to occur, but only on that date. Allegedly, extraterrestrials had manipulated the human planners of the Philadelphia Experiment to run the experiment on August 12 in order to allow large numbers of their ships to pour through the 'hole' in the space-time continuum and access our universe.

### The Importance of August 12, 13 and 14

During the first week in August 2003, Al Bielek predicted the failure of a major power grid sometime around August 12 in the United States. Bielek made this prediction on the nationally syndicated Coast to Coast radio show which features themes associated with the unexplained, paranormal and conspiracies. The 12th, 13th and 14th of August has long history of interesting events. Napoleon had his "mystical" experience on August the 12th, in the Kings Chamber, which even on his deathbed, he refused to fully relate, since he felt that people would not believe him anyway.

Similarly, the magician, scientist, head of the OTO (Ordo Templi Orientis, and founder of the Order of the Silver Star A:A), was inside the Great Pyramid, on August the 12th, when his wife received the book of the law, whose Cipher many UFO contactee's receive from their "Ashtars."

Furthermore, on August 12, 1923, Aleister Crowley does his first magickal time traveling experiment, opening a magical time portal to Orion and the "ancient ones." Then to culminate these two prior events, in 1943 on August the 12th, Aleister Crowley designed the Magickal basis for the Philadelphia Experiment that would link back to his experiment 20 years prior. The Phoenix and Montauk projects thus working in continued time travel and on August 12th 1983 and 2003 linking the time portals. August the 12th, 13th and 14th was the time that the Osiris Mysteries were shared and performed, the word Wizard comes from those who held the Staff of Power, which was called the WSR (Wassar). Osiris was the Life Force within creation, his backbone the Djed, or Djedhi.

Osiris was called SR, or ASR (Ausir), as well as Wassir. The Wasser staffs were electrical conductors of power, hence the Wizzards were Wassirs or Osiris' using WSR Wands for their Hex's (hexagon), in Egyptian Heku. So there is a very ancient lineage of traditions that have their Mysteries imparted on August the 12, 13 and 14.

These dates are the high point of Sirius. Nebiru (Neb Heru) in the sky. Nebiru is the sign of the cross within a cross. The cross of our solar system to the galaxy, to the star system of the cross, which is Neb Heru (Heru Ami Septeb, Horus of Sirius or Heru Sept, Horus of the Dog Star.

August the 14th is also the day when Quetzelcoatl was born, ruling the serpent of illumination, the fusion of bird with serPENT, Horus with Set's Sata snake, Gurudas with

Nagas. It is also the higher Venus cycles, the top of the pentagrams cycle of the order of Venus in our skies during one year. So August 12, 13 and 14 has a Venus-Sirius connection. The cycle of Sirius B is exactly 49 years cycle, alternating to 50 years. That is the Jubilee, so there is a Sirius/Isis Jubilee now.

It should also be noted that for many thousands of years the Schumann frequency (resonant frequency of earth) was 8,53 Hz with no variation. So it was constant. Since the eclipse of 1999 the frequency goes up to 9,05 Hz. The frequency will go up to a value about 13 HZ (in the fibonacci series after 8 there is 13). So for the first time in the last thousands years, we have values that are higher than 8,53 HZ.

In addition to this, the magnetic field of the earth, that was constant for thousands of years, is strongly decreasing. So on around August 12, 2003 for the first time we had this special combination: high Schumann frequency, low magnetic field and the earth cycle that repeats every 40 (20) years on August 12.

### The Great Blackout of 2003

It all started as a normal humid and hot summer day, but before it was over, the entire Northeast, including a large portion of Canada, was without power. This happened despite the fact that most of the East and Midwest was operating only at about 75 percent of capacity.

On Thursday, August 14 at 4:06 PM EDT the chief engineer on duty at the Albany New York complex, which is an Independent System Operator and the nerve center of the state's power grid, noticed something wrong. Reading indicated that there was unexpectedly a large amount of power flowing from New York toward Ontario through the transmission lines-underground and overhead cables. Seconds later, something happened that the engineer had never seen before - the 800-megawatt surge reversed course and began hurtling back toward New York, like some giant ectoplasmic monster on a rampage.

What wasn't known at the time was that hours before the blackout, several transmission lines in Ohio were carrying massive amounts of power "well above" emergency summer standards. American Electric Power couldn't offer any conclusions on the cause or source of the massive power surge.

The region where investigators suspect the eight-state blackout began had become a black hole, sucking electricity from generators and threatening to burn transmission lines because of the overload power company officials said.

"Something happened in the time leading up to the blackout," Pat Hemlepp, spokesman for Columbus, Ohio based American Electric Power. "Suddenly, the electrons destined for Columbus or Cincinnati or somewhere turned tail and headed north."

Generators from all over started to shut down to ward off the tremendous surge, which could overload and burn them out. Faster than most humans could respond, power grids across the region began "islanding" themselves, disconnecting automatically from the overloaded system. Generators clicked off in a cascade of shutdowns that darkened New York, Pennsylvania, the Midwest and much of Canada. In seconds, North America had suffered the worst blackout in its history. In about nine seconds, 61,800 megawatts were lost, and at 4:11 EDT, 50 million people were abruptly left without power.

According to the website http://enigma.elfrad.org/, the ELFRAD (Extremely Low Frequency Research And Development) worldwide system has been monitoring a strange radio transmission for several months. There is a signal burst in the ULF range from .5 to 4 hertz. The source at this time has not been identified.

What is interesting is that broadcasts on the day of the blackout suddenly stops at the time of the power disruption event. Usually these signals were regular, beginning daily around 12:00 noon EDT (1600 UTC) and stopping at 1:00 AM EDT. ELFRAD speculates that perhaps the source of this particular set of signal bursts was located somewhere in the area of the blackout.

### A Clash of Black Projects

A military scientist associated with the Wright-Patterson Air Force Base in Dayton, Ohio has said in a confidential report that the blackout was caused by a massive surge of electricity that originated from a top-secret project located at Wright-Patterson. This project was an attempt to hold open the wormhole in time that had been created by Project Rainbow in 1943.

According to the insiders information, the secret project at Wright-Patterson was an attempt to seize power from the Montauk Project located at the abandoned Camp Hero on Long Island, NY.

"The Montauk Project did not cease operations in 1983," the scientist said. "They suffered enormous set-backs after August 12, 1983 with the Phoenix III project — but those set-backs were only temporary. They have continued with their operations using the latest in technology and science to refine their capabilities. Their goal was to reopen the time warp created by Project Rainbow in 1943 and keep it open permanently. Their deadline was August 12, 2003 when the Earths biofields would peak. If they were successful, they would have power far beyond anything known today.

"The problem is," the whistle-blower continued, "is that the Montauk Operations have become so compartmentalized and self-contained that they were operating completely outside any responsibility to the military or the U.S. Government. They have become a very real and potent danger, but they have way too much power and influence for anyone to try and confront them directly."

There have been rumors for several years within military and intelligence circles that there was another black project group within the gray-zone of military and government contracted scientists who were attempting to build a operation similar to that at Montauk. This competitive group believed that the Montauk Project had gone rouge and was now a threat to national and global security.

Given the top-secret name Project Feedback and located in underground facilities deep within Wright-Patterson, this new group began a crash operation in 1998 to build their own generators, transmitters and a massive Delta-T antenna to create a time vortex to intercept the master vortex created originally in 1943.

The scientists with Project Feedback were certain that they could generate significant power using technology developed from research originating from the HAARP Project. They had already successfully opened "time-gates" using computers — a huge jump from the somewhat primitive methods used at Montauk with human subjects and the Montauk Chair.

The goal of Project Feedback was simple — using more power with advanced computers and superior technology — they would force the time-gate to open at their facility rather than at Montauk. Once this was done, the time-gate would be stabilized and permanently kept open. This would prevent the Montauk people from opening a time-gate and thus rendering them impotent.

The strange signal bursts monitored by ELFRAD in the ULF range from .5 to 4 hertz were originating from Wright-Patterson and were the results of frequency experiments using EM energies to hold a time-gate open.

Little is currently known on what happened in the days that followed August 12, 2003. After the blackout, information coming out of Project Feedback ceased. Considering the high-stakes that were involved in this project, the unexplained silence does not bode well for a successful outcome.

What is thought to have happened was that Project Feedback was successful in opening the master vortex and stabilizing the time-gate. That is until Thursday, August 14 when something obviously went terribly wrong. The powerful surge of electricity that was noticed by technicians in Ohio must have originated from Project Feedback. This surge could have been caused by an EMP (electromagnetic pulse) that radiated out of the time-gate in Dayton, Ohio, built up in the system and led to the complete collapse of the Northeast power grid.

With the information blackout that has come on the heels of the power blackout, we can only speculate on what happened with Project Feedback. Was the massive power surge the result of a successful stabilization of the time-gate, or its deadly collapse? Was Project Feedback successful in usurping the power base that the Montauk Project had built itself on? Or did the Montauk boys manage to destroy Project Feedback to continue their dominance in time travel?

For now, no one is talking. We may know someday what really happened on that hot August day in 2003 — that is unless time itself has been permanently altered to hide truth. After all, the winners are the ones who write history.

## CLOAK OF THE ILLUMINATI

by Sean Casteel

· Did the "Illumined Ones" of ancient times possess a cloak or garment that granted them supernatural powers and transformed them into Beings of Light?

· Does current military research being conducted at the Massachusetts Institute of Technology hold the key to the creation of such a 'power garment' today? Will the "super soldier suit of the future" also have spiritual uses that could forever change the human organism as we know it?

· The New Physics deals quite plainly with the possible existence of wormholes or "stargates." Were those portals to other worlds understood and used by the ancient gods and goddesses? Can we also learn to travel freely between Earth and the higher, heavenly realms?

Among those who take an interest in what is loosely called "Conspiracy Theory," there is general agreement that the name "Illuminati" carries with it many negative connotations, including the idea that the legendary secret society is behind an evil plot to enslave the Earth, even to the point of bringing the Antichrist to power and implementing the dreaded Mark of the Beast.

But author and lecturer William Henry begs to differ with that commonly accepted assessment. According to Henry, the name "Illuminati" means something quite different from a Satanic cabal working behind the scenes to carry out an organized yet mysterious wickedness.

"You find out," Henry told the Conspiracy Journal, "that when you look in Websters Dictionary, for instance, that the word Illuminati refers to a newly baptized Christian initiate. Which suggests, as Gnostic tradition upholds, that Jesus and John the Baptist and the Essenes [the ancient Israelite sect associated with the Dead Sea Scrolls] were drawing on mystery traditions that are traced back through ancient Egypt and then back into Sumerian times."

So with this understanding of "Illuminati" as the basis for his research, Henry explains further about why his take on the subject is different.

"What I'm primarily interested in," Henry said, "is, 'What does it do for me?' Absolutely nothing that I can discern. I can read all the conspiratorial books and I can't find any personal benefit that improves my being.

"I believe in the hypothesis," Henry went on, "the conjecture, that the Illuminati possess secrets for bumping an individual up the evolutionary ladder by ascertaining the mysteries of the body. By learning how to ignite enlightenment centers built into the body, and how to achieve, effectively, mastery over the body. So what I attempt to say is, what are those secrets?"

Along with his belief that the Illuminati are a basically benevolent force in the world, Henry does acknowledge that there remains an evil presence lurking in the shadows.

"I definitely believe," he said, "that there is the evil conspiracy; we'll call it evil. However you want to label the polarities. My research revealed that this goes all the way back to the early Sumerian myths of the conflict between two half-brothers. One that sought to uplift humanity, even to the level of the gods, and may have deposited knowledge for doing that within human DNA. And he's opposed by his half-brother, who seeks to keep humanity at the level of slaves and sex objects.

"So today we find that the same polarity exists within our world. You have the two forces: the forces of terror that seek to keep humanity imbued within a frequency of fear, and then you have the flipside of that, which are the forces of TARA. Its essentially the same word, but TARA means compassion and enlightenment."

Meanwhile, shining through the darkness and the "terror," there is still the Illuminati, who could potentially lead us back to the Garden of Eden, in Henry's belief system.

"That's what I think is the ultimate aim and the ultimate goal," Henry said. "The pathway is razor sharp and its filled with that duality. It seems that part of our quest is to escape that duality."

## The Cloak Of The Illuminati

An ally in the struggle against that duality is an ancient article of clothing Henry calls "The Cloak of the Illuminati," which is also the title of one of his books as well as a DVD that has just been released.

"I refer to it as the Cloak of the Illuminati," he explained, "because I'm tracing this garment that is worn by these initiates. Its a garment that ultimately transforms them into beings of light, which seems to be the goal of the mystery school traditions, and the aspiration of a lot of people that research this material today. But the way were going to achieve that garment of light in the near future is through a confluence of four of what I call 21st Century power tools through the application of our knowledge of genes, bits, neurons, and atoms. With this knowledge, we can remake the Earth matrix, and we can completely redesign the human body and change the human species in that way.

"And the question is, is that a good thing? Will they use this technology, these four power tools, as they have in the past? For control? Or will they use these four technologies to set us free, effectively? To effectively stop aging, to make us resistant to disease, to perhaps find a way to amplify our intelligence through the implantation of chips and through the tweaking of our DNA?"

The point of all that, Henry reaffirms, is the evolutionary progress of mankind.

"Again, it goes to the main thrust of my research," he said, "which is how do we accentuate our abilities as humans and raise up to the next level? Which we might call homo angelus or homo christos, the next model of human. That's been the driving force of humanity ever since we were evicted, so to speak, from the Garden of Eden. It appears that we're right now living with one foot in this new Atlantis, ready to embrace this future."

Henry's unique use of language in his work is another controversial aspect of an already undeniably original worldview. The puns and loose associations between various words fly thick and fast when Henry lectures.

"What I'm applying there," he said, "is called The Language of the Birds. It's a punning, mythological language that uses word plays and the sound of words to connect seemingly unrelated objects or concepts. This is a language system that scholars absolutely despise. I've been in catfights with scholars that say, God, you can't even believe this William Henry guy. The guy talks with birds. And they think it's literal. My response to them is, do you really think that Elijah was talking with a literal bird? Do you think that the dove that represents the Holy Spirit of Jesus is an actual bird? Are you nuts? This is the approach these scholars take, and I'm saying these are not birds.

"This is a specific reference to a language system," Henry went on, "that was used by the prophets of the past, by the Illumined Ones of the past. It's a language of the subconscious that's very dreamlike, that's very poetic, and ultimately is designed to connect us with the concept of the One Mind. There was at one time One Language, an original pre-Flood language, which was spoken by humanity in the Garden of Eden. But this language was lost, and it was lost during the Tower of Babel episode, when King Nimrod attempted to rebuild the Babel Tower."

Henry's version of the Tower of Babel story is, like nearly everything he presents, quite different from the usual telling of the tale.

"It's very interesting," he said, "because the word Babel originally meant Gate, and after the Hebrew God Yahweh destroyed our gate, which linked us with the heavens, his scribes changed the meaning of the word Babel from Gate, as in gate to God, to the word confusion, and humanity was separated by language. The Illumined Ones of the past, the mystery schools, have attempted to reclaim that original language of humanity, which is the language of the Gate and the knowledge of the gate returning us into the heavens."

Having made his point regarding the Language of the Birds, Henry returned to his concept of the "Cloak of the Illuminati."

"I make it my business," he said, "to investigate as many of the gateway stories as possible. Myth and scripture are loaded with references to gods and goddesses who come and go between the Earth plane and the heavenly realms through these gates. I would find a common thread that was woven through many of those gateway stories, and that was that, preparatory to that experience, they put on a cloak or a garment. This garment, in many of the stories, had supernatural power associated with it. So that when the god or goddess put on this garment, as did Elijah for example, as did Jesus before his crucifixion, as did the goddess Mary before traveling into the underworld, they accumulated this spiritual power.

"They appeared to have a temporary effect of beaming them up, if you will, into a higher spiritual vibration before they entered these gateways. And then, of course, their priesthoods or priestesshoods followed on them and preserved the secrets and legends of these cloaks. They were power garments of some kind. Do they exist today? Well, they're probably preserved in certain places, but what I look for is the way that they have been recreated in modern science."

Recreated in modern science? Henry explained.

"The example I cite," he said, "is that of the super, nano-technology, soldier suit that MIT is building right now for the United States military. This suit has some phenomenal powers associated with it. When the soldier of the future—and I'm talking near future here, the next ten years—puts on this cloak, he's going to be resistant to ballistic attack. You can't shoot this figure. He'll be resistant to chemical attack. The suit will have a charge built into its heels so that the soldier can leap 20 feet into the air, if need be. It's going to have one incredibly special feature, and that is a cloaking device, a nano-technological cloaking device, so that the soldier will have a chameleon-like quality. They can literally be standing next to me in my office right here and I wouldn't see the figure because he would blend in with the environment of my office."

Henry immediately perceived a link with ancient mythology.

"I said, well, wait a minute. As I read about this, I see now [the Greek goddess] Athena, before she went into battle, she put on her helmet of invisibility, and she put on her robe of power. I'm wondering, is it possible that the scientists at MIT were taking a cue from the ancient world? They tell me they're not. I've called up there and talked with them, and they say they don't see a connection between modern technology and the ancient power cloaks. But I definitely see one in human consciousness where this is an archetypal garment that is being recreated."

Which quickly leads to more questions for Henry.

"Are there spiritual applications for this technology?" he asked. "In other words, wouldn't it be nice if you never caught a cold again? In this age of AIDS, what if you could become resistant to that kind of virus? What if there was a specific tone or frequency, like for example they research at Stanford, that could be beamed into you so that 24/7 you're bathed within the frequency or tone of life that keeps your cells continually regenerating? Wouldn't that, thereby, give you a form of immortality, prolonging your lifespan by, lets say, a hundred years? What if you had that technology available? Would you become this part human, part cyborg machine that, for example, the Terminator movies warned us about? These are the kinds of questions that I think all of us are going to have to be answering within the next five to ten years because this technology is coming online so fast. Of course, it's the military that's leading the way, but there are other applications for these devices."

### Wormholes

From the latest research into military defense technology and its potential spiritual uses, Henry next moved on to an area that currently receives much interest from the practitioners of the New Physics: the existence of "stargates" or "wormholes."

"A stargate or wormhole," he explained, "is a tunnel that connects Point A on Earth with Point B elsewhere in the universe. It can even be on Earth or somewhere else in our solar system. One of the things I noticed in my search of the ancient world, again with those gateway myths, is that very often these gates were symbolized by the bulls eye or the concentric rings. This is an important symbol that you find, for example, in the ascension and transfiguration scenes of Jesus. You find numerous savior figures and other gods and goddesses that are poised in front of these concentric rings or bulls eyes. And they're always wearing what I call the Cloak of the Illuminati when they're standing in front of these bulls eyes.

"So I saw that as key symbol to look for," Henry continued. "When you follow the stories of these gates, they refer to the god being or the priest or priestess who is entering this gate and going into a higher, finer realm. I recognize that it's a leap for some to say, well, the ancient gods traveled in stargates or wormholes.

"Today, when physicists talk about creating these wormholes, they say that they're going to be constructed of an exotic matter that unfortunately can be harmful to humans. So as part of their criteria, they're looking for a manner in which they can line the tube of these wormholes to protect the humans while they're traveling through them. What I found in my search was that the ancients weren't too concerned with transforming the wormholes or stargates. They were more concerned about transforming the human being who was going through that experience. This transformation was undergone on the mental, the spiritual, the physical and the emotional level."

Which is essentially the same process Henry described earlier, with Homo sapiens transformed into a more highly evolved kind of "homo angelus."

"The emphasis was on the in here, on the human body as the stargate or wormhole, rather than on the creation of a transportation system out there. That's the primary difference and change that I think the physicists need to begin to incorporate as they start to design these stargates or wormholes.

"Ultimately, what were looking for," Henry said, "is the means to transform or transmute the human element. But the problem is, you can't have a planet full of Christs running around because they're unmanageable and they don't pay taxes. This is what the issue has been in terms of educating humanity to bring out the god within. The concept of god-making has been demonized, but that is the secret possessed by the Illuminati."

## ARE THESE CONCENTRATION CAMPS?

It seems impossible to go on the worldwide web without finding bold...some might say outrageous... statements concerning a possible roundup and incarceration of American citizens who do not accept a full-fledged take over by the New World Order or Secret Government.

One posted dispatch with the banner CONCENTRATION CAMPS, tells the following *seemingly* incredible story: "There are over 600 prison camps now in the United States, all fully operational and ready to receive prisoners. They are all staffed and even surrounded by full time guards, but they are all empty. These camps are to be operated by FEMA (Federal Emergency Management Agency) should Martial Law need to be implemented."

The posting explains that, "The camps all have railroad facilities as well as roads leading to and from the detention sites. Many also have airports nearby. The majority of the camps can house a population of twenty thousand prisoners. Currently, the largest of these facilities is just outside Fairbanks, Alaska. It is a massive mental health prison and can hold approximately two million inmates."

A commercial commuter pilot whose route is over Arizona recently claimed he did a double take when he flew his route and noticed that inside one restricted military base there were "white boxcars and rows of prisoners with hands secured behind their backs lined up in rows waiting to enter the boxcars." A source in Texas says that in another closed, restricted access military base, multinational forces were seen practicing for URBAN WARFARE of a chemical/biological nature. He noted that the predominant nationalities who were training were Russian and German soldiers

One individual, identified as Terry Kings, maintains that he discovered three "detention centers" in southern California. "At one site near Glendale, there were new;y constructed fences (all outfitted with new concertina wire that points inward). The fences surrounded a dry reservoir. There are also new buildings situated in the area. We questioned the idea that there were four armed military personnel walking the park. Since when does a public park need armed guards? At another location, police cars were constantly patrolling an area that housed new gray military-looking buildings and a landing strip."

A likely area for one huge concentration camp is the area surrounding... and even beneath... Denver's International Airport. One source says that there are huge underground "concrete corridors with sprinklers all along the ceiling."

There are even supposedly five buildings that are over 150 feet tall that could hold thousands if necessary. Furthermore, the "luggage transport vehicles move on a full-sized, double lane highway, and along this highway are chain-linked areas that could be used for holding pens." Some even claim that the big-eyed Greys and the Reptilians are connected with all of this...sort of field reps for the New World Order.

Actually, those "in the know" say that the evidence is all around you as you walk through the terminals. "There are massive symbols representing various Secret Societies throughout the place, and paintings that have all sorts of sinister, "hidden" meanings if you look closely enough."

In a public lecture, the past chairman of the Conservative National Committee of Washington, D.C., said government agents have admitted to him that they use National Security as a shield against disclosing their darker activities. He says that the U.S. is like the Titanic and will sink beneath the waves sometime in the next five years, and that those who control the nation will do anything...including harrassing honest citizens... to prevent this from happening.

Are concentration camps already a reality, or is this all the ramblings of "conspiracy crackpots?" Only time will tell, and there are those who are certain *we have little time left!*

## CONFESSIONS OF A NWO WHISTLE BLOWER

### by Commander X

**Question:** Why is it so important to keep your identity a closely guarded secret?

**Answer:** My entire adult life was dedicated to upholding the oath I took in service for this great country of ours. My pledge was to protect the rights and freedoms of the citizens of the United States at all costs.

During my career in military intelligence I was privy to a lot of information that was deemed beyond top-secret. This information was so sensitive that no more than a handful of people at any given time were ever allowed access to it. At the time I didn't question the policies to keep this information from the general public, but as I got older, and maybe a little more wiser, I began to see that keeping such secrets was actually in direct violation to the pledge I took.

More and more I saw that an elite few were using these secrets to gain power and profit off of the backs of the country's population. This kind of power grab made me extremely angry and disappointed. I was raised in a military family and was taught at a young age to be honest, noble and to work for the good of the people.

The very people that I had been taught to admire and respect were instead using sensitive information for their own personal gain. This revelation led me to reexamine the oath that I took to God and country. Let me tell you that I spent many a sleepless night working this problem over in my head.

I finally came to the correct conclusion that my allegiance was to the United States and its citizens, not to the people who were in positions of power. Nowadays those in control want us to think that our allegiance to the country is with the government, some political party or group of rich corporate elites. Well it's not! The government is not the country. We are the country. The government owes its allegiance to us.

When I realized this truth, I swore that there would be no more secrets. Everyone has the right to know what is really going on — and as long as I live, I will do my best to bring these secrets out into the light for all to see. This of course has not endeared me to those in power. They want these secrets to be kept all to themselves.

Due to the fact that over the last sixty years many people have had access to these secrets, it is almost impossible to pinpoint who the whistleblower or whistleblowers actually are. It also helps that there are others out there with the same backgrounds that are assisting me in getting the truth out.

So to be sure that I can continue to spread the gospel of truth, and to protect the lives of my family and friends, it is important that I remain anonymous. It is extremely risky, but I think it's worthwhile considering what will happen to the country and ultimately the world if I remain silent.

**Question:** What do you say to people who say your credentials are not what you claim?

**Answer:** It's impossible to seriously debate these questions concerning my credentials. It wouldn't matter if I came forward with all of my service records, personal background, and golf scores whathaveyou. There would still be people who would be skeptical and insist it was all a lie.

It happens all of the time. Look at what happened to my good friend Col. Philip Corso. Here was a man who truly believed in God and country and had an unblemished career in the military. Yet, when he published in his book "The Day After Roswell" the fact that he was involved with farming out unknown technology acquired from a crashed UFO to various laboratories across the country, he was branded a charlatan and was ostracized by the very people who at one time praised him.

This is what happens to those who dare go up against the secret government. It's not like the movies where thugs take you out and make it look like suicide, (even though it does happen to those not in the public eye). Instead the norm is character assassination.

You see it happen time and again to those who attempt to wake up the sleeping public. It can happen in all kinds of ways: you could simply be branded a nut and a whacko and people just stop listening to you. Or it can be as extreme as arrested on some trumped up charge. It doesn't matter how it happens because the results are always the same, your credibility is forever ruined. I instead chose to take the more cautious route and make it all about the message and not the messenger.

People instinctively know the truth when they hear it. This is why my books, and now the video of one of my secret lectures, resonate so much with the public. They know it is the truth.

**Question:** It was alleged at one point that you were really Jim Keith or even Wild Bill Cooper. They have both passed so that allegations can't be true, but it must tickle you to know there is a guessing game going on in Conspiracy Land.

**Answer:** It seems to be a favorite hobby of some people to eternally speculate on who Commander X really is. Some of the guesses have been extremely funny on how far off the mark they actually are.

Once again though some people are missing the point about all of this as they are focusing on me and not the message that is being put forth. But I suppose that this is human nature and there is nothing I can do about it.

I can say, however, that so far none of the guesses have even come close. I am still very much alive and continue to write. Even if my true name was revealed, it wouldn't matter - I am not someone who is, or ever has been in the public eye. I am no one special. What is special is what I have been telling you all of these years. Listen to that.

**Question:** Maybe some of our readers still do not realize that you speak from first hand experience in a lot of instances. For example, you have revealed that you were employed inside Area 51. What exactly did you do there? And what did you see?

**Answer:** I was never a full-time employee of Area 51, but I have been there a number of times over the years for various duties that had been assigned to me. Most were routine assignments dealing with security. However, I was also called out to Area 51 several times to lend my expertise in trying to uncover the secrets surrounding some very interesting things that were being kept at the facility.

You see I was a participant of a top-secret remote-viewing research project that covered over twenty years of my career. Every branch of the military had such a project going on from time to time, as well as the CIA and NSA. Despite what you have read, these groups are still very active today and are an important part of modern military and intelligence strategy.

What most people don't understand is that the Area 51 complex is a lot more than just the aircraft facilities that are shown in the satellite photos. The Area 51 complex covers hundreds of miles of the mountains and desert of Nevada. There are top-secret areas known as Dreamland, S4, the Papoose Lake facility, and many others with names that have never been made public. The research and development that takes place in these remote locations would have your head swimming trying to understand the science that was involved.

I was ordered to Area 51 on several occasions to use my remote-viewing abilities to try and ascertain the function of various types of devices that were being studied in some of the secret laboratories hidden on the complex. Nothing was ever said to me as to where this technology was from, but I was left with the clear impression that it was not of this planet.

Even though I felt that my reports were vague and uncertain as to the origins and purposes of those bits of machinery, those who had commissioned me obviously felt that I was worth inviting back for an even more interesting experiment.

**Question:** Wasn't there a time when you actually flew a UFO through the use of your telekinetic powers?

**Answer:** Yes. My story is detailed in my book: Teleportation: From Star Trek to Tesla. But to briefly summarize — a few years after my attempts to remote-view technology that was said to be from captured UFOs — I was invited back to a different facility located at the base of a mountain and camouflaged to look like the surrounding rocks.

Inside this hangar was a craft that looked just like a traditional UFO, or flying saucer. It was metallic and so pristine it looked brand new. I didn't ask if this was an actual captured UFO or a manmade aircraft, and my handlers never volunteered any information other than what was necessary for my project.

The interior of this craft was surprisingly bare. In the middle of the floor was an obviously manmade chair that had been crudely bolted to the floor. My job was really very simple. I was to sit inside this craft and just wait for something to happen. I wasn't supposed to touch or do anything. Just sit.

After days of sitting with nothing happening I got sleepy and my mind started to drift. At that moment I could feel an abrupt change in the air as the ship came to life. Later I learned how to control it with my mind, it was if the craft had become a part of me and I could will it to go anywhere I wanted. Just like you will your hand to pick something up, I could will this ship to move.

I would love to know for certain whether this was an actual captured alien space-craft, or something that we built, maybe using technology obtained from a crashed UFO. The truth of the matter is that I don't know — there are only the rumors.

**Question:** What other projects did you know about that are underway there now?

**Answer:** I am certain that by now there are top-secret aircraft operating out of Area 51 that use propulsion systems that we would call antigravity. Much of the "black-triangle" UFO reports coming from around the world are sightings of these manmade aircraft. In fact, this technology may have been in use as far back as the early 1980's — so by now I am positive the technology has been perfected.

There is also continuing experiments in time/space/dimensional travel that had its earlier origins with the Montauk Projects at Camp Hero on Long Island. The Montauk Projects were eventually shut down because of the corruption among the projects leaders who saw the time travel/mind control experiments as a way to gain ultimate power. Many of those men were liquidated by the military under charges of treason.

I have been told that the Area 51 experiments are to try and understand the historical changes that the Montauk Projects caused and whether or not they are fixable. We are apparently living in a time line that was created by the Montauk Projects interference with human history. This interference created a branching effect in time and we are now on one of these branches - away from our original timeline.

Some of this timeline interference may have come from a group of UFO creatures that are now known as the greys. These beings, along with several other "races" of alleged outer space creatures, have told us that our warlike ways are causing problems on their home worlds across the galaxy. To help us grow more spiritually, the greys have not only been actively altering our DNA through selective breeding, but they have been responsible for feeding us the techniques of time travel with the purpose of changing our timeline.

**Question:** Do the greys still have breeding chambers there and do they still walk around down at the lower levels?

**Answer:** I don't really know if they were ever there or not. It may have just been a clever disinformation ploy to hide what is really going on with UFOs and the alleged aliens that fly them.

I used to believe absolutely the stories about the secret underground bases filled with greys. I even knew people who swore to God that they had actually seen one of these secret bases. And I heard the stories in the halls of the Pentagon long before the tales made it out into the UFO community. So I still think that there is probably some truth to the stories.

Over the years I have come to realize that the actual truth is far more complicated than a simple cover-up of extraterrestrials zooming around in spaceships. The truth has become so muddied over the years with disinformation, rumors and downright lies that the truth on what is really going on is completely obscured. I suppose we need to start completely over and get rid of our past perceptions and look at the UFO problem from a different viewpoint.

**Question:** Why have you decided to break your code of silence at this point with your new video?

**Answer:** I have been giving secret lectures for several years now. These lectures have been by invitation only with the location being revealed only hours before the lecture begins. It is a nerve-wracking experience and despite our best precautions, we have almost been caught several times by those who want to keep us quiet.

I decided finally to allow a video camera to record one of these lectures in an effort to find a new audience that may have never read any of my books, but are still open to learning the truth and questioning what they have been taught over the years.

**Question:** Obviously you must think there is urgency because of the expanding tactics of the NWO?

**Answer:** The secret government, run by the New World Order, has been around for a long time. We are talking about something that is generational, passed down from father to son for many decades. They have long-term goals that go way beyond our petty political squabbles of liberals and conservatives, or even from country to country, ideology to ideology.

This relatively small group of people, royalty, old-money elites, political and military figures, controls the world like a puppeteer controls a marionette. They know what strings to pull to make something on the planet jump.

The New World Orders plans were severely disrupted apparently sometime in the 1930's when the first solid evidence of extraterrestrials was uncovered by Nazi Germany. Using spiritual mediums, leaders in the Nazi Party came into contact with beings that claimed to be from planets outside of the solar system.

These claims were somewhat authenticated when the Nazis recovered a crashed UFO using information given to them from the channeled aliens. The Nazis used this craft, as well as the channeled messages, to develop a new technology that eventually led to the development of the world's first manmade flying saucers.

The New World Order was left in a quandary. They knew how to control the population with money, food, and sex. What they didn't know was how to control was the UFOs and the alleged aliens that flew them. This was the beginning of a new direction for the New World Order. If they couldn't control UFOs, then they could certainly control the population's perception of them.

Our current world political and economic situation is the result of this new direction taken by the New World Order.

**Question:** I understand that the video presentation started out as a broadband Internet broadcast to military, scientists and government personnel who had been out of the loop. Do you know who might have attended in cyberland?

**Answer:** This video presentation, like my live lectures, was by invitation to those we knew would be open to learning the truth. It is ultimately up to them to decide what to believe. However, we know that everyone invited to that special presentation had openly expressed doubt on what was being told to them by their superiors, bosses or leaders. They were open to new information and we were there to give it.

Some of the greatest minds on the planet watched our presentation and we know that they will find their own ways to bring this information out to the rest of the planet. It will take time, and it won't be easy, but we have started a new era of truth and openness.

No matter what they do, the secret government won't be able to hide behind their trumped up wars, terrorism attacks or economic turmoil's. The truth will come out with the fact that we are being controlled and we will finally be able to do something about it.

**Question:** What do you cover on the video?

**Answer:** I cover what is really going on in the world today. I show how for years the New World Order has controlled our lives using politics, greed, religious yearnings, bigotry and terrorism.

I talk about how the NWO uses mind control techniques to create living monsters and quiet sheep to be led to the slaughter. I show how secret scientific research has broken not only the barrier of space, but also the gates of time and other dimensions.

I also reveal the ultimate secret of UFOs, their connection with the Nazi party, the United States and the New World Order.

These are just a few of the many subjects that I cover on this tape and I invite anyone who is interested in finally thinking for themselves to view it and open your mind to new possibilities.

We have a great chance, given to us by God, to make a difference and reshape the world to be the paradise that it was meant to be. It all can start now with one small step and the willingness to question what has been presented to us as the truth for all these years.

**Question:** Thank you very much for your time.

**Commander X:** My pleasure. You're welcome.

**COSMIC DECEPTION:**

**LET THE CITIZEN BEWARE**

Steven M. Greer MD

Director, The Disclosure Project

http://www.disclosureproject.org

Imagine this: It is the summer of 2001, and someone presents you with a script for a movie or book that tells how a diabolical terrorist plot unfolds wherein both 110 story World Trade Center towers and part of the Pentagon are destroyed by commercial jets hijacked and flown into those structures.

Of course you would laugh, and if you were a movie mogul or book editor, reject it out of hand as ridiculous and implausible, even for a fictional novel or movie. After all, how could a commercial jet, being tracked on radar after two jets had already hit the World Trade towers, make it through our air defenses, into the most sensitive airspace in the world, and in broad daylight on a crystal clear day, slam into the Pentagon! And this in a country that spends over $ 1 billion a day to defend itself! Absurd, illogical - nobody would swallow it!

Unfortunately, there are some of us who have seen these scripts - and of far worse things to come - and we are not laughing.

One of the few silver linings to these recent tragedies it that maybe -just maybe - people will take seriously, however far-fetched it may seem at first, the prospect that a shadowy, para-governmental and transnational entity exists that has kept UFOs secret - and is planning a deception and tragedy that will dwarf the events of 9/11.

The testimony of hundreds of government, military and corporate insiders has established this: That UFOs are real, that some are built by our secret 'black' shadowy government projects and some are from extraterrestrial civilizations, and that a group has kept this secret so that the technology behind the UFO can be withheld - until the right time. This technology can - and eventually will - replace the need for oil, gas, coal, ionizing nuclear power and other centralized and highly destructive energy systems.

This 5 trillion dollar industry - energy and transportation - is currently highly centralized, metered and lucrative. It is the stuff that runs the entire industrialized world. It is the mother of all special interests. It is not about money as you and I think of it, but about geo-political power - the very centralized power on which the current order in the world runs. The world is kept in a state of roiling wars, endless poverty for most of Earth's denizens and global environmental ruin, just to prop up this evil world order.

As immense as that game is, there is a bigger one: Control through fear. As Werner

Von Braun related to Dr. Carol Rosin, his spokesperson for the last 4 years of his life, a maniacal machine - the military, industrial, intelligence, laboratory complex - would go from Cold War, to Rogue Nations, to Global Terrorism (the stage we find ourselves at today) to the ultimate trump card: A hoaxed threat from space.

To justify eventually spending trillions of dollars on space weapons, the world would be deceived about a threat from outer space, thus uniting the world in fear, in militarism and in war.

Since 1992 I have seen this script unveiled to me by at least a dozen well-placed insiders. Of course, initially I laughed, thinking this just too absurd and far-fetched. Dr. Rosin gave her testimony to the Disclosure Project before 9/11. And yet others told me explicitly that things that looked like UFOs but that are built and under the control of deeply secretive 'black' projects, were being used to simulate - hoax -ET-appearing events, including some abductions and cattle mutilations, to sow the early seeds of cultural fear regarding life in outer space. And that at some point after global terrorism, events would unfold that would utilize the now-revealed Alien Reproduction Vehicles (ARVs, or reversed-engineered UFOs made by humans by studying actual ET craft -see the book 'Disclosure' by the same author) to hoax an attack on Earth.

Like the movie Independence Day, an attempt to unite the world through militarism would unfold using ET as the new cosmic scapegoat (think Jews during the Third Reich).

None of this is new to me or other insiders: The report from Iron Mountain, NY, written in the 1960s, described the need to demonize life in outer space so we could have a new enemy. An enemy off-planet that could unite humans (in fear and war) and that would prove to be the ultimate prop for the trillion dollar military-industrial complex that conservative Republican President and five star general Eisenhower warned us about in 1961 (no one was listening then, either...).

So here is the post-9/11 script - one that will be played out unless enough people are informed and the plan can be foiled because they will be unable to fool a sufficient number of citizens and leaders:

After a period of terrorism - a period during which the detonation of nuclear devices will be threatened and possibly actuated, thus justifying expanding the weaponization of space - an effort will ramp up to present the public with information about a threat from outer space. Not just asteroids hitting the Earth, but other threats. An extraterrestrial threat.

Over the past 40 years, UFOlogy, as it is called, combined with a mighty media machine, has increasingly demonized ETs via fearsome movies like Independence Day, and pseudo-science that presents alien kidnappings and abuse as a fact (in some circles) of modern life. That some humans have had contact with ETs I have no doubt; that the real ET contact has been subsumed in an ocean of hoaxed accounts I am certain.

That is, real ET events are seldom reported out to the public. The Machine ensures that the hoaxed, frightening and intrinsically xenophobic accounts are the ones seen and read by millions. This mental conditioning to fear ET has been subtly reinforced for decades, in preparation for future deceptions. Deceptions that will make 9/11 look trivial.

I write this now because I have recently been contacted by several highly placed media and intelligence sources that have made it clear to me that hoaxed events and story-lines are imminent that will attempt to further ramp up the fear machine regarding UFOs and ET s. After all, to have an enemy, you must make the people hate and fear a person, a group of people, or in this case an entire category of beings.

To be clear: the maniacal covert programs controlling UFO secrecy, ARVs and related technologies - including those technologies that can simulate ET events, ET abductions and the like - plan to hijack Disclosure, spin it into the fire of fear, and roll out events that will eventually present ETs as a new enemy. Do not be deceived.

This hogwash, already the stuff of countless books, videos, movies, documentaries and the like, will attempt to glom onto the facts, evidence and first-hand insider testimony of The Disclosure Project, and on its coattails, deliver to the world the cosmic deception that falsely portrays ETs as a threat from space. Do not be deceived.

By commingling fact with fiction, and by hoaxing UFO events that can look terrifying, the Plan is to eventually create a new, sustainable, off-planet enemy. And who will be the wiser?

You will. Because now you know that after 60 years, trillions of dollars and the best scientific minds in the world pressed into action, a secretive, shadowy group - a government within the government and at once fully outside the government as we know it - has mastered the technologies, the art of deception and the capability to launch an attack on Earth, and make it look like ET s did it. In 1997, I brought a man to Washington to brief members of Congress and others about this plan. Our entire team at the time met this man. He had been present at planning sessions when ARVs - things built by Lockheed, Northrup et al, and housed in secretive locations around the world - would be used to simulate an attack on certain assets, making leaders and citizens alike believe that there was a threat from space, when there is none. (Before he could testify, his handlers spirited him away to a secret location in Virginia until the briefing was over...) Sound familiar? Werner von Braun warned of such a hoax, as a pretext for putting war in space. And many others have warned of the same.

Space based weapons are already in place - part of a secret parallel space program that has been operating since the 1960s. ARVs are built and ready to go (see the book 'Disclosure' and the chapter with the testimony of Mark McCandlish et al). Space holographic deception technologies are in place, tested and ready to fire. And the Big Media is a pawn, now taking dictation from the right hand of the king.

I know this all sounds like science fiction. Absurd. Impossible. Just like 9/11 would have sounded before 9/11. But the unthinkable happened and may happen again, unless we are vigilant.

Combine all of this with the current atmosphere of fear and manipulation and there is a real risk of suspending our collective judgment and our constitution.

But know this: If there was a threat from outer space, we would have known about it as soon as humans started exploding nuclear weapons and going into space with manned travel. That we are still breathing the free air of Earth, given the galacticly stupid and reckless actions of an out of control, illegal, secret group, is abundant testimony to the restraint and peaceful intentions of these visitors. The threat is wholly human. And it is we who must address this threat, rein it in and transform the current situation of war, destruction and secret manipulation to one of true Disclosure and an era of sustained peace.

War in space, to replace war on Earth, is not evolution, but cosmic madness. A world thus united in fear is worse than one divided by ignorance. It is now time for the great leap into the future, a leap that moves us out of fear and ignorance and into an unbroken era of universal peace. Know that this is our destiny. And it will be ours just as soon as we choose it.

© Steven M. Greer MD

Director, The Disclosure Project

Albemarle County Virginia

The Disclosure Project

PO Box 2365

Charlottesville VA 22902

(434) 245-5006

http://www.disclosureproject.org


## DOORWAYS TO THE PAST

by Commander X

Time is a funny thing. We never seem to have enough time — yet there is an infinite amount. Time slips through moment upon second, into eternity past, yet present to begin the future.

We tend to think of time as unstoppable in its relentless push toward the future. We perceive ourselves as bound up in time as an insect in amber. Forever imprisoned and forced to reconcile with the regularity and inevitability of change. The past is gone — the present, fleeting — and the future is unknown.

Or is it?

If you were to ask a Merseyside policeman by the name of Frank, he may have an entirely different opinion on the subject of time.

On a sunny Saturday afternoon in July of 1996, Frank and his wife, Carol were visiting Liverpool's Bold Street area for some shopping. At Central Station, the pair split up, Carol went to Dillons Bookshop and Frank went to HMV to look for a CD he wanted. As he walked up the incline near the Lyceum Post Office/CafÈ building that leads onto Bold Street, Frank suddenly noticed he had entered a strange "oasis of quietness."

Suddenly, a small box van that looked like something out of the 1950s sped across his path, honking its horn as it narrowly missed him. Frank noticed the name on the van's side: Caplan's. When he looked down, the confused policeman saw that he was unexpectedly standing in the road. The off-duty policeman crossed the road and saw that Dillons Book Store now had Cripps over its entrances. More confused, he looked in to see not books, but women's handbags and shoes.

Looking around, Frank realized people were dressed in clothes that appeared to be from the 1940s. Suddenly, he spotted a young girl in her early 20's dressed in a lime-colored sleeveless top. The handbag she was carrying had a popular brand name on it, which reassured the policeman that maybe he was still partly in 1996. It was a paradox, but he was relieved, and he followed the girl into Cripps.

As the pair went inside, Frank watched in amazement as the interior of the building completely changed in a flash to that of Dillons Bookshop of 1996. The girl turned to leave and Frank lightly grasped the girl's arm to attract attention and said, "Did you see that?"

She replied, "Yeah! I thought it was a clothing shop. I was going to look around, but it's a bookshop."

It was later determined that Cripps and Caplan's were businesses based in Liverpool during the 1950s. Whether these businesses were based in the locations specified in the story has not been confirmed.

Franks experience is not that unusual in the realm of strange phenomenon. There is even a name given to such events — time slips.

A time slip is an event where it appears that some other era has briefly intruded on the present. A time slip seems to be spontaneous in nature and localization, but there are places on the planet that seem to be more prone than others to time slip events. As well, some people may be more inclined to experience time slips than others. If time then is the unmovable force that physicists say it is, why do some people have experiences that seem to flaunt this concept?

### TWO SIDES OF THE SAME COIN

Time travel, according to modern scientific theory, may still be beyond our grasp. Yet for a number of people who have had unusual time slip experiences, time may be easier to circumnavigate than expected.

A classic example of a time slip can be seen in a note from Lyn in Australia. Lyn had read the book, Time Travel: A How-To Insiders Guide and thought her experience was similar to others featured in the book.

In 1997 Lyn lived in a small outback town that was built in 1947 and had changed little since that time.

"I was driving toward the main intersection of the town, when suddenly I felt a change in the air. It wasn't the classic colder feeling, but a change, like a shift in atmosphere. The air felt denser somehow. As I slowed at the intersection, I seemed to be suddenly transported back in time to approximately 1950. The road was dirt, the trees were gone and coming toward me to cross the intersection was an old black car, something like a Vanguard or old FJ Holden. As the car passed through the intersection the driver was looking back at me in total astonishment before he accelerated. From what I could see he was dressed in similar 1950s fashion, complete with hat.

"This whole episode lasted perhaps 20 seconds and was repeated at least 5 times during my time there, always at the exact spot. I tried to make out the registration plate number but the car was covered in dust."

Lyn wondered if there is someone out there still living who remembers seeing a strange sight at the intersection back in the 50s...of a weird car with a bug-eyed woman at the wheel.

Derek E. tells another interesting story. When he was a child, his father was a taxi driver in Glasgow, Scotland. One day in the late 1960s, Derek's father was driving in the north of the city along Maryhill Road near Queen's Cross, one of the older parts of town and once its own separate community outside the city.

"One minute it was now," Derek wrote, "cars, buses, modern clothes, tarmac roads etc. - and the next thing my dad knew he was in some earlier time. It was certainly pre-Victorian given the clothes he described people wearing, horses, rough road, lower buildings, people in rough clothes and bonnets etc. It lasted as long as it took him to be aware of it and then it vanished and he was back in 'now.'"

Derek also reported that in the 1980's, he and his wife were on a driving holiday in the North York Moors in England. They went to a tiny coastal village called Staithes, which had a steep winding and narrowing road down to the harbor, with the entrance to the houses and narrow footway at a higher level of three or four feet.

"We parked at the top of the village, hamlet really, where the tourist buses and cars had to stop and made our way down on foot. What I remember is a brilliantly sunny day with lots of other people around, but as we made our way down, it just suddenly seemed as if no one else were there but my wife and me. An old woman appeared on the footway opposite us. It became cooler and duller. She asked, in what seemed to me an old-fashioned and very polite way, what year it was. Now lots of old people get confused and it could have been that, but what I remember vividly is her black clothes ñ hand-made, rough and with hand-sewn buttons ñ really big compared with modern ones. Her shoes were very old fashioned with much higher and chunkier heels than you'd see an older person wearing nowadays. In the time it took me to turn to my wife and say, 'Did you see that?' she was gone. The sun was back and so were all the people. My wife had also seen the same old woman and felt the same chill."

Derek's experience seems strikingly similar to traditional ghost stories. Many ghost sightings are readily explained as individuals who appear out of their normal location or time; but often the ghost also seems to change the surroundings of the witness, giving the impression of a time slip. What is open to question is whether these are glimpses into another time or does the witness or the ghost actually travel in time? Perhaps it is simply different sides of the same coin.

## THE NATURE OF TIME

Much of the philosophy of ancient Greek was concerned with understanding the concept of eternity, and the subject of time is central to all the world's religions and cultures. Can the flow of time be stopped or slowed? Certainly some mystics thought so. Angelus Silesius, a sixth-century philosopher and poet, thought the flow of time could be suspended by mental powers:

Time is of your own making;

its clock ticks in your head.

The moment you stop thought

time too stops dead.

The line between science and mysticism sometimes grows thin. Today physicists would agree that time is one of the strangest properties of our universe. The question that needs to be asked is are time slips a natural occurrence, or the result of manmade time travel experiments that are now rebounding across time and space?

Secret military experiments in time travel (the Rainbow Project and Project Phoenix) that were conducted at the Montauk Air Force Base on Long Island New York, may have caused ripples in space-time that have created doorways that open briefly to other times and places. Government whistle-blowers who claim inside knowledge of these experiments say that the year 2003 will see an increase in time slips and bizarre, almost supernatural events due to the nature of the original time experiments that took place in Philadelphia in 1943.

Writer Richard Boylan says that a reliable ex-NSA consultant told him that government scientists working at Los Alamos "Nuclear" Laboratory, NM have succeeded in generating a holographic portal. They have used this portal to travel across space-time, and possibly interdimensionally.

Boylan's contact said that the government considers time travel research a "dangerous technology."

This research would be a follow-on to previous secret government successful research into time travel and teleportation, Los Alamos physicist Robert Lazar told about the government's Project Galileo research into time travel, which he was briefed on when he worked at the S-4 Base south of Area 51.

The secret of time travel may be close to being revealed once and for all if these events do come to pass. The government may finally be forced to admit that working time machines have been built and are now under the control of the United States military.

* For more information on the secrets of time travel, see the book: TIME TRAVEL: A How-To Insiders Guide by Commander X and Tim Swartz

## ZULU SHAMAN, CREDO MUTWA, EXPOSES

## UNDERGROUND LAIR OF THE REPTILIANS

## — HENCHMEN OF THE ILLUMINATI

by Sean Casteel

Credo Mutwa is a genuine Zulu shaman, known more precisely among his tribe as a "Sanusi." During his life, this highly articulate tribal elder has had numerous encounters with various species of aliens. He is also living proof that the UFO occupants do not hesitate to cross all racial boundaries in terms of who they abduct and interact with. Credo, who is now 80-years-old, has an endless supply of stories to tell about African "experiencers" as well as a plethora of personal experiences to relate, many of which are more shocking than the stories we hear in the West, but which nevertheless have the unmistakable feel of literal "truth."

## CREDO'S BACKGROUND

Harvard psychiatrist Dr. John Mack devotes a chapter to Credo in his book "Passport To The Cosmos" (Crown Publishers, 1999), and provides some fascinating biographical background on Credo.

"Credo was born in the South African province of Natal on July 21, 1921," Mack writes. "His father was a Roman Catholic catechism instructor during Credo's childhood, and converted to Christian Science when Credo was fourteen. His mother was the daughter of Ziko Shezi, a Zulu shaman and warrior. According to Credo, this grandfather was a great healer and played an important part in his training to become a medicine man."

Credo attended a mission school and advanced rapidly upward through the grades. He also "learned a great deal about Western civilization and ways in this school," Mack writes.

Credo's parents were unwed, which resulted in him being shunned "as a bastard, a thing born out of marriage." This did not cause any acute loneliness for Credo, however, because he was always in the company of "little people," according to Mack, "strange companions" who used to tell Credo things having to do with his schoolwork, which sometimes led to his knowing more than his teachers. Credo regards the creatures of his childhood as friendly, quite unlike the grays and reptilians he would deal with later as an adult.

One result of Credo having been educated in Western ways is that, when he refers to the aliens, he feels "caught between, on the one hand, Western thought, including the Christian religion, and African thought, which accepts these things without question."

Credo would eventually become not only a shaman and a healer, but also a successful author, painter and sculptor, as well as an eloquent spokesman for his native Africa as it struggles to survive continual internal strife and warfare and an AIDS epidemic that shows no signs of relenting. But it is his experiences with aliens, more specifically reptilian aliens, which interest us here.

## SHARED LEGACY OF THE REPTILIANS

In an exclusive interview with the publication SPECTRUM, Credo speaks at length to interviewer Rick Martin about a group of reptilians who are able to change shape at will and have secretly been in control of our planet for eons without our consent or knowledge.

Credo begins by giving SPECTRUM reporter Rick Martin some of the history of his African brothers' interaction with aliens from ancient times.

"The people of Rwanda," Credo tells Martin, "the Hutu people, as well as the Watusi people, state, and they are not the only people in Africa who state this, that their very oldest ancestors were a race of beings whom they called the *Imanujela*, which means 'the Lords who have come.' And some tribes in West Africa, such as the Bambara people, also say the same thing. They say that they came from the sky, many, many generations ago, a race of highly advanced and fearsome creatures who looked like men, and they call them *Zishwezi*. The word *Zishwesi* means the dival or the glidal-creatures, that can glide down from the sky or glide through water."

Credo said the legend extends to other tribes as well, including the Dogon people who astonished many in the West with their apparent advanced knowledge of astronomy and their ability to accurately chart the heavens.

"Everybody, sir, has heard about the Dogon people in Western Africa," Credo said, "who all say that they were given culture by the normal beings, but they are not—the Dogon people are but ONE of many, many peoples in Africa who claim that their tribe or their king were first founded by the supernatural creatures that came from the sky.

"The Zulu people," Credo continued, "are famous as a warrior people, the people to whom King Shaka Zulu, of the last century, belonged. When you ask a South African white anthropologist what the name Zulu means, he will say it means 'the sky,' and therefore the Zulu call themselves 'people of the sky.' That, sir, is nonsense. In the Zulu language, our name for the sky, the blue sky, is *sibakabaka* . Our name for interplanetary space, however, is *izulu* and the *weduzulu*, which means 'interplanetary space, the dark sky that you see with stars in it every night,' and also has to do with traveling, sir. The Zulu word for traveling at random, like a nomad or a gypsy, is *izual*.

"Now, you can see," Credo went on, "that the Zulu people in South Africa were aware of the fact that you can travel through space—not through the sky like a bird—but you can travel through space, and the Zulus claim that many, many thousands of years ago there arrived, out of the skies, a race of people who were like lizards, people who could change shape at will. And people who married their daughters to a walking extra-terrestrial, and produced a power race of Kings and tribal Chiefs. There are hundreds of fairy tales, sir, in which a lizard female assumes the identity of a human princess and poses as her and gets married to a Zulu Prince."

Again, the shapeshifting reptiles are spread throughout Africa, according to Credo.

"Amongst many tribes," he said, "you'll find stories of these amazing creatures who are capable of changing from reptile to human being, and from reptile to any other animal of their choice. And these creatures, sir, do really exist. No matter where you go throughout Southern, Eastern, Western and Central Africa, you'll find that the description of these creatures is the same. Even amongst tribes which never, throughout their long history, had contact with each other at all.

"So there ARE such creatures," Credo said. "Where they come from, I will never claim to know, sir. But they are associated with certain stars in the sky, and one of these stars is a large group of stars which is part of the Milky Way, which our people call *Ingiyab*, which means 'The Great Serpent.' And there is a red star, a reddish star, near the tip of this huge rim of stars, which our people call *IsoneNkanyamba*. Now, this star called *IsoneNkanyamba*, I managed to find its English name. It is the star called Alpha Centauri, in English. Now, this, sir, is something that is worth investigating. Why is it that well over 500 tribes in parts of Africa which I've visited in the last 40 or 50 years or so, all of them describe similar creatures?"

## REPTILES PREY ON HUMANKIND

The creatures don't exactly sound like they're friendly, however, and you wouldn't want to be around one when he's hungry.

"It is said that these creatures," Credo explained, "feed on us human beings; that they, at one time, challenged God Himself to war, because they wanted full control of the universe. And God fought a terrible battle against them and He defeated them, injured them, and forced them to hide in cities underground.

"They hide in deep cavities underground," he continued, "because they are always feeling cold. In these cavities, we are told, there are huge fires which are kept going by slaves, human, zombie-like slaves. And, it is further said that these *Zuswazi*, these *Imbulu*, or whatever you choose to call them, are not capable of eating solid food. They either eat human blood, or they eat that power, the energy that is generated when human beings, on the surface of the Earth, are fighting and killing each other in large numbers.

"I met people who have fled from the early Masaki in Rwanda, from years ago, and these people were horrified by what was happening in their country. They said the slaughter of the Hutus by the Watusi, and the Watusi by the Hutus, is actually feeding the Imanujela, monsters. Because the Imanujela like to inhale the energy that is generated by masses of people being terrified or being killed by other people."

## THE COMING OF THE CHITAULI

Credo pointed out that there are many words the Africans have in common with other peoples of the world.

"If you study the languages of all African peoples," he said, "you find within the languages of our people words which are similar to Oriental, Middle-Eastern, and even Native American words. And the word *Imanujela* means 'the Lord who came.' A word that anyone can discover in Rwanda, amongst the Rwandan Hutu and Watusi people, is very similar to the Hebrew word *Immanuel*, which means 'the Lord is with us.' *Imanujela*, 'the ones who came, the Lords who are here.'

"Our people believe," Credo went on, "that we, the people of this Earth, are not masters of our own lives, really, although we are made to think that we are. Our people say, that is, black people of all tribes, all of the initiated ones, all of the shamans everywhere in Africa, when they get to trust you and share their deepest secrets with you, they say that with the *Imanujela*, there is Imbulu. And there is another name by which these creatures are known. This name is Chitauli. Now the word Chitauli means 'the dictators, the ones who tell us the law.' In other words, 'they who tell us, secretly, what we are to do.' Now it is said that these Chitauli did a number of things to us when they came to this planet."

The arrival of the Chitauli to Africa sounds very much like a full-scale alien invasion from a 1950s science-fiction movie, complete with ships and a plentitude of special effects.

"When the Chitauli came to Earth," Credo began, "they arrived in terrible vessels which flew through the air, vessels which were shaped like great bowls and which made a terrible noise and a terrible fire in the sky. And the Chitauli told human beings, whom they gathered together by force with whips of lightning, that they were great gods from the sky and that from now on they would receive a number of great gifts from the gods. These so-called gods, who were like human beings, but very tall, with a long tail, and with terrible burning eyes, some of them had two eyes—yellow, bright eyes— some had three eyes, the red, round eye being in the center of their forehead. These creatures then took away the great powers that human beings had: the power of speaking through the mind only, the power of moving objects with their mind only, the power of seeing into the future and into their past, and the power to travel, spiritually, to different worlds.

"All of these great powers the Chitauli took away from human beings," Credo told SPECTRUM's Rick Martin, "and they gave humans a new power, now, the power of speech. But human beings found, to their horror, that the power of speech divided human beings, instead of uniting them, because the Chitauli cunningly created different languages, and they caused a great quarrel among people. Also, the Chitauli did something that has never been done before: they gave human beings people to rule over them and they said, 'These are your kings, these are your chiefs. They have our blood in them. They are our children, and you must listen to these people because they will speak on our behalf. If you don't, we are going to punish you very terribly.'

There were still even more dramatic changes meted out by the Reptilians from outer space.

"And then, human beings were given strange new feelings by the Chitauli," Credo went on. "Human beings started to feel unsafe, and so they started making villages with very strong fences of wood around them. Human beings started becoming country makers. In other words, they started creating tribes and tribal lands, which had borders, which they defended against any possible enemy. Human beings became ambitious and greedy and they wanted to acquire wealth in the form of cattle and seashells.

"And another thing the Chitauli forced human beings to do, they forced human beings to mine into the Earth. The Chitauli activated human women and made them to discover minerals and metals of certain types. Woman discovered copper; women discovered gold; women discovered silver. And, eventually, they were guided by the Chitauli to alloy these metals and to create new metals which had never existed in nature before, metals such as bronze and brass and others."

While it may seem like the Chitauli were a "civilizing force" there in Africa, one cannot help but wonder what an Eden it must have been like before the indigenous people were given all the knowledge that would so change their lives.

Credo spoke of another myth regarding the Chitauli.

"The Chitauli told our people," he said, "that we human beings are here on Earth to change the Earth and to make it suitable for 'God' to come down one day and dwell in it. And it is said that they who work to change this Earth and make it safe for the serpent god, the Chitauli, to come and dwell in it, will be rewarded with great power and with great wealth."

Credo again spoke of the fundamental reality of the serpent race he has been describing.

"There ARE such creatures," he said, "and the sooner skeptics amongst us face up to this fact, the better it shall be. Why is humankind not progressing? Why are we running around in a great circle of self-destruction and mutual-destruction? People are basically good; I believe this. People don't want to start wars. People don't want to destroy the world in which they stay, but there are creatures, or there is power that is driving we human beings toward self-annihilation. And the sooner we recognize this, the better."

### EATING WELL IS THE BEST REVENGE

In the second half of his interview with Rick Martin, Credo dropped quite a bombshell into the conversation.

"Far too many people," Credo said, "fall into the temptation of looking upon these 'aliens' as supernatural creatures. They are just solid creatures, sir. They are like us; and furthermore, I'm going to make a statement here which will come as a surprise: the Gray aliens, sir, are edible.

"Their flesh is protein," he continued, "just as animal flesh on Earth is, but anyone who ingests Gray alien flesh comes very, very close to death. I nearly did."

Credo described how the alien flesh came into his hands.

"You see," he said, "in Lesotho there is a mountain called Laribe; it is called the

Crying Stone Mountain. On several occasions, in the last 50 years or so, alien craft have crashed against this mountain. One such incident was reported in the newspapers not so long ago. An African who believes that these creatures are gods, when they find the corpse of a dead Gray alien, they take it, put it in a bag, and drag it into the bush, where they dismember it and ritually eat it. But some of them die as a result of ingesting that thing."

Credo said that a friend of his from Lesotho gave him the flesh from what the friend called a "sky god."

"I was skeptical," Credo said. "He gave me a small lump of gray, rather dry stuff, which he said was the flesh. And he and I and his wife ritually ate this thing one night."

A great many surprising results were to follow quickly on the heels of their otherworldly "dinner." To find out more, send for the tapes advertised in this catalogue, which will "flesh out" Credo Mutwa and his amazing stories much more completely than is possible in the space available here.

No matter what Credo discloses it is bound to be sensationalistic. His ongoing confrontations with aliens, and his visit to and subsequent escape from an underground lair of the serpent race (Dero?), are bound to curl the toes of even the most jaded reader of conspiracy inspired material.

But he really hits a home run when he confirms one of the pet theories of mentor David Icke. The theory is that many global leaders are really shapeshifting reptilians—we're talking the likes of the Queen, George Bush, Bill Clinton, and all the other elitist rulers who have long been associated with the bloodline of the Illuminati, said to be in charge of politics and money matters worldwide.

When pressed for more information on the subject, Credo seems uneasy, as if there might be a big "price to pay" for talking about such things. But talk he does on the three recently released REPTILIAN AGENDA videos now stocked by "Conspiracy Journal."

The text of the above article is based primarily upon a lengthy interview conducted by Rick Martin for The Spectrum.

www.TheSpectrumNews.org

### DARK MIGRATION: NAZIS IN SOUTH AMERICA
### TALES OF HITLER'S ESCAPE, GERMAN MADE UFOS,
### AND UNDERGROUND RACES STILL ABOUND

By Scott Corrales

© 2004

Ordinarily one would have suspected that Germany would have had little interest in Latin America, on the other side of the world for practical purposes, yet modern Venezuela had been turned over to the German banking family of the Welsers by Charles V in the 16th century as collateral for his loans. Since then, immigration from the German mainland to Latin America had been slow and steady. By 1896, there were at least half a million Latin Americans of German descent and the German Empire's investments in the region were in excess of four hundred million dollars—a considerable sum a hundred years ago—while international trade reached the amount of one hundred forty-six million.

However, political interest in the Spanish-speaking Americas had been slim until the very late 19th century, when the Kaiser's navy began to draw up a military strategy that would alarm the United States, a budding hegemonic power at the time. Both countries, lacking any apparent animus, had come to loggerheads in Manila Bay in 1898 and had almost gone to war over Samoa and the Caroline Islands as well in 1889. When the German High Command witnessed the collapse of the Spanish Empire's last few remaining possessions in the Caribbean and the Pacific, and the sudden windfall earned by a United States bent on expansion, the decision was reached to increase the size and power of the Imperial Navy—and a plan to wrest these possessions from the Americans.

It was Admiral Tirpitz who saw the need for acquiring coaling stations and bases in the Caribbean in order to project imperial power. The islands of Curacao and St. Thomas—modern tourists destinations that hardly evoke strategic value—were eyed as possibilities. Admiral Von Knorr took this interest a step further by stating that trade from the Gulf of Mexico and the Panama Canal, which was under construction at the time, could be readily intercepted from either of these Dutch or Danish possessions, which were ripe for the taking, whether by purchase or by force. The pretext for any intervention (for military action always requires a pretext) would be the need to protect the considerable German investment in the Caribbean coffee-growing regions and the steamship lines that handled the traffic between northern Europe and the Caribbean. In any event, the Imperial Navy had already intervened quite handily in two incidents, once in Haiti (1897) and once in Guatemala (1902).

From any of these dreamed-of Caribbean bases, speculated the war planners, it would be possible to launch an attack on the American mainland. Vice-Admiral Thomsen suggested that one of the islands—Puerto Rico—would be of great value as a staging ground for any such operations.

María Eugenia Estades, author of La presencia militar de Estados Unidos en Puerto Rico, 1898-1918 (The U.S. Military Presence in Puerto Rico, 1898-1918), describes one of these war plans as follows:

Based on this initial work, the German Admiralty formulated the first *advance plan* in 1899 for use in a possible war against the United States. The attack route envisioned a stop in the Azores to collect coal prior to proceeding the journey toward the Puerto Rico, if the attack took place in winter, or directly toward the final goal—the United States—if the invasion occurred during the summer (p.71)

But reality has a way of tampering with the best-laid war plans. Kaiser Wilhelm II was the first to realize that his high command had conjured up a pipe dream: at least fifty thousand men would be required to seize either Cuba or Puerto Rico, and another hundred thousand would be required for the attack on Boston and New York. Even this human steamroller would be unable to penetrate very deep into the American heartland by more than a few miles. In 1903, Vice-Admiral Büchsel, the new commander-in-chief of the Admiralty, came to the Kaiser with a new plan: the main goal of German strategy should consist in drawing the U.S. fleet into a battle far from its home waters, again, by occupying Puerto Rico. German interest would soon shift from the Caribbean islands—stepping-stones toward the Spanish-speaking mainland—to a number of countries including Mexico, Brazil and Argentina: an interest that would continue halfway into the 20th century.

## HITLER DIED IN BARILOCHE, YOU KNOW?

On Sunday, July 11, 2004, a Chilean newspaper, Las Ultimas Noticias, published a brief interview with an author whose recent book created a stir throughout South America. Abel Basti's **Bariloche Nazi** openly suggested that the Fuhrer had not only not died in a Berlin bunker, but had managed to follow the escape route to South America in the company of his mistress Eva Braun. Both spent their last days in the Argentinean mountain resort of San Carlos de Bariloche in the Andes. Hitler died in 1960; no date for Braun's death has been put forth. One of the locations singled out as *hideaways* for Hitler on his sojourn in Argentina is the San Ramón estancia or ranch, owned by the German principality of Schaumburg-Lippe; another is the Inalco Mansion on the shores of Lake Nahuel Huapi.

The San Ramón ranch, Hitler's first home away from home, had a rather illustrious past, haivng been the place where Admiral Canaris, the head of German Intelligence, had been sheltered in 1915 after escaping from Chile and braving the Andes on foot to reach neutral Argentina. Hitler's days in Argentina were apparently uneventful, as he went for long hikes along the shores of Nahuel Huapi and took in the clean Andean air.

His trademark mustache gone and his hair gone gray, the architect of the death of millions had settled down as a householder.

Basti states that in the late summer of 1945, two former crewmen of the battleship *Graf Spee*—scuttled in the city of Montevideo to keep it from being captured by the British Navy—had gone to an undisclosed location in Patagonia, possibly the gulfs of San Matías or San Jorge, to rendezvous with a submarine carrying some very important exiles from the shattered Third Reich. It must be remembered that the British Admiralty had issued a command to all German submarines in the high seas, after the fall of Germany, advising them to hoist a black flag or emblem after surfacing and an order to turn themselves in at the nearest port. This directly countermanded coded message 0953/4, the Nazi fleet's last official communication, which advised U-boat commanders of the surrender and directed that their vessels be scuttled before falling into enemy hands. As of May 29, 1945, the seas were believed to have been cleared of the dreaded *wolf packs* of Nazi subs, until one of them pulled into the Portuguese port of Leixoes, causing the Allied Command to believe that Hitler had in fact made good his escape aboard one of his subs. A few weeks later, the U.S Navy reported that four or five U-boats remained unaccounted for.

Hunted and running out of fuel, it was a matter of time before the *dead-enders* turned up. But where? On July 10, the Argentinean submarine base at Mar del Plata was surprised by the arrival of the U-530, commanded by lieutenant commander Otto Vermouth. A month later, the U-977, under the command of Heinz Schaeffer, surfaced off the Argentinean coast and surrendered to two coastal patrol vessels engaged in exercises. Could there be more rogue submarines somewhere in the South Atlantic Ocean?

But back to Basti and his story: "The sailors," he writes, "say that they slept in a Patagonian ranch and in the early morning hours were on hand to receive the submarines. They brought trucks and loaded baggage and people onto them. One researcher spoke with the sailors—now deceased—and they confirmed the story. On the other hand, we have the proof of the evacuation and on the other, the discovery of the sunken subs." The convoy of Kriegsmarine U-boats consisted of 10 vessels carrying at least sixty passengers each—Adolf Hitler among them. According to the author, the sailors went public with their story in 1950.

Allied forces managed to reconstruct the trajectory of the U-977 from its departure from Norway on May 2, 1945 to its arrival in Argentinean territorial waters in August of that year thanks to the U-boat's log. Captain Schaeffer and his crew had sailed underwater from Bergen to the South Atlantic without surfacing. Had the submarine formed part of the 10-ship convoy that the nameless sailors of the *Graf Spee* had received in Patagonia?

A book written in 1956 by Jochen Brennecke, another crewman of the *Graf Spee*, described having loaded half a dozen trucks with a series of boxes stamped geheime

Reichssache, which had been unloaded from submarines off the Argentine coast, and later taken to an estancia or ranch deep in Patagonia. Other authors have suggested that these boxes contained the nearly ninety kilos of platinum and two thousand kilos of gold and precious jewels that formed part of the Waffen-S.S.'s treasure—enough to finance a war of resistance from a hidden location.

Stories like this one, or their variants, have been told for the past fifty years. The Fuhrer and his closest advisors board a submarine (the Baltic port of Kiel is often mentioned as the point of departure) and take off for parts unknown, usually Antarctica or some South American location—Brazil, Paraguay, Argentina or perhaps even Chile—from which the Reich could reorganize and strike back at the world. Some versions posit that advanced technology in the form of *flying saucers* was brought along during the escape, and that the blond haired, blue-eyed saucernauts were perfect Aryans achieved through advanced genetic engineering.

But what Abel Basti probably doesn't know—and what many Nazi history buffs have probably overlooked—is that Hitler had cast a predatory eye on Latin America long before the rise of the thousand-year Reich. According to an article by William F. Wertz, Jr. appearing in Executive Intelligence Review and titled **The Nazi-Instigated National Synarchist Union of Mexico**, the Fuhrer's greater geopolitical strategy for the planet Earth included Latin America as a fertile and very enticing part of the world to be brought to heel.

According to Wertz, Hitler believed that the Mexican Republic was "the best and richest country in the world, with the laziest and most dissipated population under the sun; a country that cries for a capable master. With the treasure of Mexican soil, Germany could be rich and great!" The source of this quote is none other than Hermann Rauschning, the governor of Danzig who left the Nazi cause in 1936 and who is better known in conspiracy and paranormal circles as the source of Hitler's contacts with extrahuman forces that would leave him quaking in terror.

Yet unlike "Kaiser Bill," Hitler did not envision hundreds of thousands of infantrymen and mechanized divisions crossing the Atlantic to win this prize. His plan was to make use of the German nationals living in Latin American countries as forces already on the ground, subverting the local political process with the assistance of the German industrial and economic presence in Latin America. It isn't clear, though, if he ever saw himself having to take refuge in the lands he once saw as ripe for the taking.

### IN THE SHADOW OF THE SWASTIKA

Politically, Argentina had remained neutral throughout World War II, although it was no secret that there was a strong pro-Axis sentiment in the country. The Secretary of War at the time was Juan Domingo Perón—the legendary strongman immortalized by a Broadway musical—countermanded an initial order given to the Argentinean Navy to intercept the Kriegsmarine elements attempting to round Cape Horn and escape into the Pacific Ocean, presumably toward Axis Japan. The Argentinean fleet was instructed to return to its base at Port Belgrano; that very spring, Peron's wife, the glamorous María Eva ("Evita") Duarte, had received considerable deposits in her name from the Transatlantic German Bank, the Banco Germánico and the Tornquist Bank. A year later, Evita Perón visited Genoa to play an instrumental role in getting Martin Bormann into Argentina.

The long, hot summer of 1945 had been a busy one indeed: Gestapo chief Heinrich Miller had emerged from a submarine at Orense Beach in southern Buenos Aires province while other U-boats were reportedly seen at Claromecó and Reta. Writing in his book ODESSA al Sur (The Southern Odessa), Jorge Camarasa states: "Someone had told me that Heinrich Miller had come ashore at Orense in 1945, and that the trawler *Ottolenghi* had transferred him to Necochea, from where he headed to [the town of] Coronel Pringles to organize the escape of sailors from the *Graf Spee* who were interned in the old Sierra de la Ventana hotel." Could some of these sailors have formed part of Hitler's welcoming committee, as described in Bariloche Nazi?

Camarasa has worked closely with the Simon Wiesenthal Center in Buenos Aires on the extradition of Nazi war criminals and his research has turned up some fascinating information, such as obtaining over fifty documents from Argentina's naval authorities regarding a dozen reports of Kriegsmarine U-boats on the Patagonian littoral in a forty-day period, such as landing in Quequén, and multiple sightings off the coastal tows of Comodoro Rivadavia, Ingeniero White and San Antonio Oeste.

Camarasa believes that another landing occurred near the current location of Villa Gessell, where small numbers of personnel debarked bringing along boxes of unknown content. It is believed that they remained at this location for a certain time before leaving to other destinations, perhaps elsewhere in South America. In the 1990s the World Jewish Congress pressured then-president Carlos Menem to declassify all information regarding the presence of Nazi war criminals in Argentina, but it would not be until May 2003 that President Néstor Kirchner ordered this Ministry of the Interior to look into the "dark migration" of war criminals to his country, a task which started with the opening of that department's files.

Entry cards for one Helmut Gregor (an alias employed by "Doctor Death", Josef Mengele), for example, report his arrival in Buenos Aires in 1949 aboard a Panamanian freighter, describing him as a 38 year-old Catholic lathe operator from Germany. No further remarks are evident.

Another investigative journalist, Uki Goñi, unearthed more leads on the Nazi migration southward and the complicity of government functionaries in allowing the entry not only of former Gestapo, SS and military personnel, but also members of the Croatian Ustasche (at least fifteen war criminals among a total of seven thousand immigrants).

Two to four years after the U-boat landings, "superstars" like Adolf Eichmann and Erich Priebke began to arrive in Argentina, allegedly aided by members of the Catholic clergy, particularly an Italian bishop who facilitated their escape through the port city of Genoa.

In his book ***Historias de la Aeronàutica que Nos Hicieron Creer en OVNIS*** (Aeronautical Stories that Made Us Believe in UFOs) (Spain: Tetragrammaton, 2000), Spanish author Francisco Mañez reports that a number former Luftwaffe pilots, such as Adolf Galland and Hans Ulrich Rudel, had formed part of the military migration from the fallen Third Reich to Argentina. Nor were engineers in short supply: Reimar Horten, designer of the flying wing, and Kurt Tank, a well-known aviator and director of Focke-Wolfe Aviation, soon found a dictator willing to employ their services: the charismatic and ambitious Juan Domingo Perón, the former Minister of War who had ordered his Navy not to intercept the German submarines.

But something more interesting than advanced technology aircraft was taking place at Isla Huemul. In 1952, one of Argentina's foremost physicists, Jose Antonio Balseiro, teamed up with Ronald Richter, a scientist who had offered his skills to the Reich and had later sought refuge in the Southern Cone, to carry out the "Huemul Project", an effort at obtaining nuclear reactions through fusion rather than fission. The German scientist had convinced President Perón that his country could beat both the Americans and the Soviets to unlocking the wonders of fusion.

Peron's ego was gratified no end by this offer, and money began to flow from the government's coffers. The project was installed in the island of Huemul on Lake Nahuel Huapi, famous for its lake monster. It was José Balseiro's hard-nosed report on the futility of achieving nuclear fusion that ultimately brought the project to an end, and he went on to head a nuclear physics institute that has played a vital role in training his country's nuclear engineers

"The winds of silence," writes Máñez, "still blow over Huemul. One can play the tourist and visit the facilities which sheltered the Axis scientists and their mysterious work, but we cannot even cast a glance at the classified papers of Richter or his collaborators—Beck, Haffke, Ehrenberg, Seelman-Eggebert, Greinel, Abele and Pinardi..."

## CHILDREN OF THE REICH

In 1956, a land purchase took place in the Chilean locality of La Parra, some 400 km south of Santiago de Chile. The buyer was a man named Paul Shafer, who quickly established the ***Sociedad Benefactora y Educacional Dignidad*** as a settlement for a small knot of European emigrés. Before long, the tiny settlement had evolved into a major center of activity complete with an airstrip, several factories, filling stations, trucks, schools and its own power station. It would soon become known as "Colonia Dignidad" and become the focus of Nazi activity in Chile, playing a major role in aiding the Pinochet dictatorship.

While this may come as a surprise to may, it was simply one of the many moves in a process that had been taking place for decades. According to Chilean historian Victor Farías, the first National Socialist organization in Chile was established in the town of Osorno in April 1931, becoming instrumental in promoting the spread of Nazism throughout the country thanks to a military man, General Faupel. In eight years, the Chilean Nazi Party had over a thousand card-carrying members, most of them influential figures from the spheres of business and politics.

In his book *Los nazis en Chile* (Spain: Seix Barral, 2000) Farías delves into the contempt in which the Nazis and their supporters held the local Chilean population. The locals were considered a "bastard race" of European and native ancestry and intermarriage with them was strictly forbidden. The historian makes a more daring charge: that Nazi militants had made use of 468 children and young men between the ages of six and eighteen for purposes of "racial study."

Chile is also the home of one of the most notorious proponent of what has been described as esoteric Hitlerism, former diplomat and author Miguel Serrano, whose career brought him into contact with Indian traditions while he served as his country's ambassador to India in the 1950s, also soaking in the same Tibetan lore and wisdom that had so fascinated European nazis. He later went on to hold a number of prestigious positions with the United Nations.

Serrano's works occult fascism have appeared as a trilogy whose first book bears the title *Adolfo Hitler, el último avatara* (1984)(Hitler, the last avatar) and tries to establish a link between Nazism and the Germanic mystical tradition, the Knights Templar, the ancient Aryans and the belief in underground civilizations of supermen like Aghartha. In Serrano's viewpoint, his ideology seeks to perform the holy task of keeping the world safe from a Zionist-Masonic plot for world domination and enshrine the sacred teachings handed down from the hidden realm presided by the "King of the World."

## DR. LEONARD HOROWITZ

## ON UFOs AND STAR WARS WEAPONS

by Sean Casteel

Along with his brave effort to expose various New World Order medical conspiracies, Dr. Leonard Horowitz also holds some interesting opinions on the always relevant topics of UFOs and Star Wars space-based weaponry. First, his take on UFOs.

"I'm not an expert in that field," Horowitz cautioned, "and I've shied away largely because I don't want to project my ignorance. The fact of the matter is though that, just as a thinking human being, I cannot conceive that we would be the only forms of life in this expansive universe.

Humanity has been "dumbed down," according to Horowitz, by those in control of the economic and political structures ofthe planet.

"But if conceivably," he said "among the probably dozens of other forms of life in the universe, there would be a culture, a civilization, which was NOT engaged in dumbing down their populations, but lovingly facilitating their development and growth, it would seem to me that those people would be appalled at what they are seeing on Planet Earth, and that they would probably do their best to work on spiritual and physical levels to attempt to facilitate the paradigm shift that I've just articulated.

"So that's the extent to which I'm aware of an alien phenomenon," Horowitz continued. "It just makes sense to me. I can say that I've seen UFOs, you know. Do I know them to be absolutely certain? No, I don't. Was I ever taken into a spaceship, like some people say they have? I don't know.

"I can say one thing, though, that's very clear; that the alien phenomenon itself is a political agenda. Whether or not it exists is a whole other question. The fact of the matter is that it's being promoted and projected to accomplish a nefarious mind control, population control outcome. That's what's disturbing about it from my perspective. You begin to realize that there's probably something more going on. Why would these people want us to fret about alien visitations and debate those issues and fear planets colliding with Earth and all of these things?"

Horowitz answered his own question by saying that it was a ruse being used by the New World Order governors, super- governors and "banksters" to give humanity the false assurance that it was being "protected" by space-based weaponry.

"Another tie-in," he explained, "is where the satellite technology armed with laser and frequency radiation capabilities will be the great protectors of our poor little planet. I think that is a gross manipulation. Whether this type of threat actually exists, to me it's a moot point. If I have full faith and trust that I'm doing everything I can right here right now, to serve humanity in a meaningful way, and express my divine connection and my destiny and purpose in life, which is to help humanity, then I'm not even going to worry about what's going to happen next week, let alone the next minute."

However, Horowitz did allow that he had an interest in recent statements made by Representative Dennis Kucinich (D-Ohio).

"Kucinich exposed the fact that they've launched space-based weaponry," Horowitz said, "capable of psychotronic warfare and frequency emanations delivered at human beings' minds, and they have the capacity to control everything from thoughts to moods to behavior. And ultimately, now, with the understanding of genetic predispositions for diseases, they can resonate a certain gene sequence. It's not at all farfetched to conceive of this; that they have been developing technologies that have allowed this capability for the last 20 years now.

"They could resonate a certain gene sequence," he went on, "because they know the specific frequencies, the specific structures, that are associated with it. Theoretically they could shatter a certain gene, creating a cancer or disease predisposition in a certain targeted population."

Horowitz said he had taken no small amount of flak from the right wing patriot community for supporting Congressman Dennis Kucinich, because many in thal rather extreme political faction consider Kucinich to be a globalist himself.

"But my litmus test on it," Horowitz said, summing it all up, "is to ask,'What would the messiah do?' or 'What would the Creator do if he were here right now? Would he be voting in favor of space-based weaponry! Or being opposed to it?' My feeling is that probably both the messiah and the Creator would be opposed to it, so that is why I've chosen to support Dennis Kucinich in this effort."

## THE EVE OF DESTRUCTION

On a spring day in 2004, two linked events made news. The first was spectacular and horrifying. The second was surprising, irritating to some —and ominous to others. Both happened exactly 911 days after the 9/11 attacks on the World Trade Center and the Pentagon.

The first was the brutal attack on Madrid's rail system which left almost 200 dead and over a thousand injured. Dubbed Europe's 9/11, it was an alleged al-Qaida bid to shock Spain into departing from George Bush's Iraq coalition.

Those terror bombs struck Madrid on Tuesday, 11th March, 2004 —exactly 911 days after the 9/11 attacks of 2001.

The second event that day was the unexpected announcement that three investors involved in buying the World Trade Center complex just seven weeks before the total destruction of it's twin 110 story towers, had just bought the last of the USA's 110 story skyscrapers —Sears Tower, in Chicago.

A trio of reclusive New York landlords had just paid Metlife close to $850 million for the third remaining 110 story tower. The Chicago skyscraper used to have a spooky pre-9/11 valuation of exactly $911 million. News of the purchase was announced on the same morning as Madrid's carnage —exactly 911 days after 9/11.

The irritating part was that potential competing bidders for the Sears Tower never had a chance to make a better offer. Metlife closed the deal with the New York buyers so quickly, that real estate experts were left scratching their heads as to why.

Some saluted the resolve of the new investors, who clearly were either undaunted by terror risks —or else well protected by accomodating insurers willing to underwrite the risk.

The Sears Tower management had worked hard to show its total commitment to security and its conviction that the building was as terror-proof as humanly possible.

Most existing and potential tenants had been reassured. With perhaps one notable exception. For whatever reason, Goldman Sachs are set to leave the Tower —despite a lease which secured their tenancy until 2011.

Sears Tower was not the only deal going down in town. Real estate analysts say the Chicago market had been buzzing since the start of 2004 —making it the third most active market in the U.S.

So, that day, March 11th, 2004 saw a 9/11-style attack —911 days after 9/11, and the purchase of a 110 story tower valued at $911 million dollars prior to 9/11 —by investors who had seen their two 110 story towers crumble to the ground within weeks of purchase, on 9/11.

No wonder some people sat up and took notice. Things had gotten curious. And the ominous part is that they get even curiouser. The references to 911 and 110 which cropped up on March 11th are scheduled to intersect again very soon:

On April 19th, 2004 it will be the 110th day of the year. The day will begin at midnight, when it will be EXACTLY 911 hours since the midnight after the Madrid bombings. (38 days X 24 hours = 912 hours, minus 1 hour for daylight savings = exactly 911 hours in 38 days.)

On April 19th, 2004, it will also be 9 and 11 years respectively since two of the darkest moments in modern American history: the Oklahoma Murrah Building blast on April 19th, 1995; and the related mass incineration of David Koresh's followers on April 19th 1993, at Waco, Texas..

Propping up these gloomy resonances are a host of further esoteric indications which point to April 19th and the Sears Tower, as detailed in the articles below.

And it is against this inauspicious backdrop that in recent days have come media reports of questionable origin.

These reports are based on murky intelligence contacts touting a claimed transcript of the interrogation of a terror suspect.

Under breathless headlines like "Sears Tower Was Terror Target," articles have been popping up on news pages around the world over the last few weeks.

The supposed interrogation transcript say that Sears Tower was/is a prime target for the "terrorists" who perpetrated 9/11. But everyone knows this anyway. After all, on the day of 9/11, the Sears Tower was immediately evacuated as a blindingly obvious precaution.

Those reports are basically, old news. Or maybe, they are not.

Maybe theose media reports are signs that world media are being carefully primed to pin the blame in the "right" places —should anything happen to the Sears Tower.

Perhaps the very same people who brought you Waco, Oklahoma and 9/11 are about to unleash more of their brutal brand of socio-political manipulation.

And, I'm not talking about terrorists here. Consider this a blindingly obvious pre-caution.

Fintan Dunne April 8th, 2004

**PART 2**

**By Danny**

**THE SEARS TIMEWAVE**

Dear Fintan and Alex, I was intrigued by your recent show, where Fintan prophesied that the next major 'terror attack' will take place on the Sears Tower on the 19th April 2004.

Are you familiar with Terrence McKenna's Timewave Zero theory?

Basically, this prophetic system, based on the i-Ching, graphs the ups and downs of 'novelty' in the course of human and world affairs.

Times of severe novelty are marked by a sharp 'downward' spike in the graph.

Curious as to what the Timewave graph would say about this numerological theory pertaining to 911, Madrid and the Sears Tower, I casually entered the programme (which is still available in DOS format) and keyed in the date 19th April 2004.

Guess when the next major downward spike in 'novelty' is due? Yes, you guessed it - the 19th April 2004 !!!

I've attached a screenprint of McKenna's Timewave Zero graph. It shows the period 24th March — 24th April, 2004.

Refer to the graph — the target date is self-explanatory: It's the 19th April. and it is illustrated on the novelty graph by a vertical purple line.

Could this be the next 911 on the Sears Towers, as foretold by the mainstream press [Washington Times] and foreshadowing the onset of the 'military government' spoken of by Tommy Franks? Could this be the starting point for the next phase in the 'war on terror' - a new and no holds barred escalation?

I have been going around for the past year boring the pants off people, telling them to watch out for a MAJOR event coming up in April 2004 which will be AS BIG, if not bigger, than 911. Well, if a new 911 occurred, that would certainly settle the US election wouldn't it? Unlike in Spain, it is likely to be cancelled altogether!

When you 'pull back' the timeframe to a larger canvas of 5 years, see how just after April 19th, there is a much greater major downward spike on 19th May 2004.

The two purple vertical lines close together mark April 19th and May 19th. From the 19th May, the novelty graph falls steeply until 28 September 2004. The extent of the May 19th fall makes our April 19th spike look tiny by comparison.

Now see the single purple line at left which marks 11th September, 2001. Notice how the graph does not immediately fall on 9/11. Novelty may be like a big ship —it takes a while to respond. Click the Graphs to open larger version in a new window. Make the window smaller and you can read the text while viewing the graphs.

When you pull the timewave timeframe further back to about 31 years, you can see the bigger picture, all the fluctuations of novelty up and down over that period.

There are markers at Sept 2001; September 2004 —roughly the end of the novelty event which began in April and May of 2004.

And in August of 2008 there's another drastic downward spike in novelty that might correlate with the start of a possible WW3.

Like the year 2006 which was mooted in The Bible Code as the possible year of an armageddon even, 2008 has also been mooted at an apocalyptic date in many prophecies and end times traditions. Following that event, it's all pretty much downhill the rest of the way, as they say. Basically, when the graph is running downwards, things are just getting more and more novel until the reach Terrence McKenna's zero point of 2012, beyond which is anyone's guess.

It is clear that between now and 2012 there are two major downward spikes - one coming up in 2004 and the second coming in 2008, before we just trend downwards all the way to the bottom of the graph on 21st December, 2012.

## FEMA AND THE HIDDEN UNDERGROUND GOVERNMENT

by Steven Osgood

Feb. 20, 1998

If you still believe that the entire government of the United States is for the people, you may be surprised to know that the elite heads of our government do not demonstrate those same views. The federal agency known as FEMA (Federal Emergency Management Agency) is propagandized as being an emergency relief agency, whose primary responsibilities are to assist the citizens of America during times of crises, such as war or natural disasters (hurricanes, tornadoes, floods, droughts, etc.).And, while this scenario is partially true, it is by no means the primary responsibility of this powerful arm of America's secret government.

# CONSPIRACY JOURNAL READER: THE DEEPEST, DAARKEST SECRETS

While the administrative headquarters of FEMA is located in Atlanta, Georgia, with various branch offices across America, the tactical headquarters are located in a gigantic underground facility near Bluemont Virginia. This site is called Mt. Weather, and has also been referred to as the Western Virginia Office of Controlled Conflict Operations, a name that will appear more accurately descriptive as you read on.

The federal government took control of the land in 1903 and used it for various projects until 1936. This is when the U.S. Bureau of Mines started a major digging and construction project that wound up being a literal underground city! It is complete with streets and sidewalks, private apartments, cafeterias, hospitals, supply stores and even it's own mass transit system! Furthermore, it has a water purification system, fed by lakes and underground springs and of course, it's own power plant and sewage disposal system. This is quite a contrast to the visible, above ground structures, which give the appearance of an innocent complex of a dozen or so well kept government communication-type office buildings with antennas and microwave relay systems. All this is located on a beautiful landscape and shows no resemblance of anything really strange.

Beneath the unsuspecting ground-level complex is what is often called the "Doomsday Hideaway", this huge mystery mountain of secrecy has gone virtually unnoticed by the public, and even most members of congress are unaware or very unfamiliar with it. It is a self contained, fully equipped and operational headquarters for the "hidden parallel government" of the United states and more!

Here is a list of some of the departments and agencies that are housed within the heavily protected mountain: the departments of Agriculture; Commerce; Health, Education and Welfare; Housing and Urban Development; Interior; Labor; State; Transportation; and Treasury. Some of the federal agencies located within are: the FCC, Selective Service, the Veterans Administration, the Federal Power Commission, the U.S. Postal Service, and the Federal Reserve (which by the way, is not controlled by the federal government). Another little know fact is that the headquarters for the World Bank is located in this safe haven!

FEMA, who also heads up the Multi-jurisdictional Task Force (a national and international military/police force, which is a story within itself) is the commanding agency over the Mt. Weather operations. In the event of a national crises, which nowadays may be anything the president decides it to be, FEMA takes full control of the executive branch of government and rules the nation with all the powers of martial law!

Each of the federal and private agencies located within the Mt. Weather complex is under the control of a single individual. The person in control of each agency or department is not elected by the people, but are appointed by the president.

They have their own staff or cabinet members who are also appointed and answer directly to the powerful cabinet head. It is a duplicate of our federal government, but without the consent or even knowledge of the taxpayers who fund it. The other fundamental difference is that cabinet members and cabinet heads of each duplicate government department are not trained to be a democratic government in waiting. They are, however, a well trained dictatorship in waiting, not to serve the public, but rather to help administrate control over the public, while FEMA directs the execution of military/police operations against the citizens of America.

FEMA has been in charge of a military police force for several years. This multi-jurisdictional task force (mentioned above) has been actively conducting training operations across America (mostly in larger cities) under the guise of an anti-terrorist training operation.

The real purpose of these illegally performed training operations known as MOUT (military operations in urban terrain) are actually for preparing these teams to take control of major population centers, disarming American citizens and crushing any rebellious or anti-government groups who attempt to resist the military takeover.

These so-called anti-terrorist training missions, MOUT, are scheduled to increase in 1999. These unsuspecting maneuvers (assaults) around the nation are illegal, because they are being conducted without the required permission from most state governors and city officials.

Members of the public have been terrified in cities where these operations have occurred. Unmarked helicopters and black hooded, armed troops descending on unsuspecting American mass population centers is one of the most gross and infringing violations of governmental and military authority ever perpetrated on the U.S. citizenry. But this is mild compared to what it will be like when the training stops and real implementation begins!

Yes, indeed, FEMA is definitely an emergency management agency, and when the president decides there is a national emergency, FEMA will certainly do the "managing"!

Now, getting back to FEMA's underground headquarters and some of their other functions. FEMA, as you would suspect, has the most advanced communication and data compiling technology available. Their massive data bank includes information on practically every citizen in the U.S. It also has lists of nearly all organizations or groups. Especially those whom they consider subversive or militant.

This basically includes every group, organization, and many individuals who actively oppose the goals, aims and objectives of our increasingly imperial American government. Your name may very well be on this list.

However, there is another list of names kept by FEMA, and I bet your name is not on it. This is a list of approximately 10,000 people, in addition to the president and his selected staff, who are considered "essential" people to insure the rebirth and continued survival of the country after a nuclear war wipes out the rest of us. Mt. Weather will be their luxurious safe haven in such a catastrophe.

It's probably reassuring to know, however, that FEMA didn't leave the protection of the rest of us out. They print a brochure that tells us we can construct make-shift protection shelters out of book shelves, various furniture and such. Wow, I feel much better now, don't you?

Since Mt. Weather's secret hiding place is not as secret as it once was, FEMA also has alternative safety measures for its "essential" citizens. As previously mentioned, this vast underground city has, among other amenities, a mass transit system.

Why? Well, you see, Mt. Weather is the main hub of a network of about 100 other underground facilities! Connector routes to and fro allow for quick relocation of personnel and "residents" of underworld America. When imminent danger exists in one location, the mass transit system can transfer people out of harm's way and keep any potential enemy thoroughly baffled.

I don't believe that hiding under a stack of furniture will yield the same results, but isn't it nice to know that our tax money will be protecting this "essential" group of imperial elitist, whose main objective is to control and enslave all of us worker bees who, except for serving the wealthy power mongers, are of little or no importance?

## IDLING AT TANNHAUSER GATE

By Midori Severi

The mothership is on standby power at the entrance to the wormhole known as Tannhauser Gate. Scoutships have been deployed to Earth; others bivouac on the dark side of the moon. The sneaky little greylings are staging for an invasion of Hertha, the third rock from the sun.

As a distraction, the offworld halflings have implanted the thought into the minds of several Earthers the notion that they should go forth in the dead of night to stomp enigmatic circles into the surrounding corn fields.

The first step in a covert operation is to create a diversion. Get everyone looking at the ground so they don't notice what's coming through that hole in the sky. It seems to be working. Next, the greylings implant into the minds of a large number of humans the odd belief that they have been abducted and taken aboard spaceships to be examined, prodded and probed in the most intimate of locations. It seems to be working. Humans begin experiencing vivid, disturbing dreams. Prophetic dreams. Cataclysmic dreams. And the dreams come true.

Ivan Ilych, as he lay dying, cried out, *"Leave me alone!"*

(*The Death of Ivan Ilych*; Leo Tolstoy)

Ivan blamed everyone but himself for his misfortunes.

Humans blame their madness on greylings and anti-grav lightships somewhere out there beyond the gate, but rarely on themselves. And as long as we humans look outside ourselves for the solutions to our many problems, they will forever remain unresolved.

Ivan, at least, had the momentary clarity of mind to understand that people should leave him alone long enough for him to die without listening to their hysterical nonsense. I suspect most UFOnauts do not have the same clarity of mind when it comes to believing in phantom ships and grey halflings who slip through the hole in the sky to invade their dreams. To them, all such stuff is real and, what's more, they don't even question it.

Which is inordinate madness.

The conspiracy theorists claim that something mysterious fell to earth at Roswell, New Mexico in the earth year 1947. In nearly 60 years, the aliens who sent it there have been unable to invade and conquer this planet, which failure speaks volumes about their lack of efficiency and resolve. Does it not strike you as remarkable in the extreme that a race of beings who have managed to make their way to this isolated little rock from somewhere across the galaxy have been unable or unwilling to do anything to exploit their great discovery? Can it be that, even after over half a century, the off-worlders are still puzzling about what they should do with us, or to us, or if they should do anything at all? This is irresolute ambivilance carried to abnormal lengths (for us, at least).

But, say the conspiracists, the alien agenda is now, and will be forever, unknowable to us. We cannot now or at any time in the future fathom the alien mind because they have implanted in our own minds the idea that they mean us no harm. They are not after our oil, our gold, our worthless paper money. They don't need our saltwater oceans or any of the creatures that dwell within or without. They don't even want the corn in the fields they have vandalized. They just want our women to produce their little hybrid babies.

Oh, give me a break!

So what's the deal? If we are being visited by off world beings, might it not be to their advantage to let us in on it? After all, if you watch television for more than thirty seconds a day, you'll clearly see that there are women out there who would gladly carry an alien child to term and then just as gladly give it away if they thought there was something in it for them at the end and if the birthing of the child was, as is claimed, without trauma or memory. But where are they?

I'm a skeptic, you see. Or, perhaps, it would be safer and more appropriate to claim that I am a cautious believer. If there are underground bases in the southwest desert where scads of greylings reside while they plan the conquest of Earth, show me them. Let me see some paperwork proving the claim. If lightships are orbiting Earth why cannot the Air Force see them or, at least, detect them? If thousands of humans have been abducted by alien beings, why are there no outward signs to prove it? Where are the tens of thousands of halfling children? Where? Where?

And where have they parked their massive lightships while all this nonsense is going on?

Okay, there may be something else at work here. Perhaps humans have not been abducted; only been prompted to believe they have. Perhaps no one has ever actually seen a UFO; only been prompted to believe they have. Perhaps corn circles are just the products of canny hucksters (no pun intended) and have absolutely nothing to do with scout ships and anti-grav/anti-matter drives or zero point energy.

*"There is some kind of intelligence that we are connecting with,"* says John Mack. *"It's not simply the imagination of people. This experience shatters people's constricted worldviews, which can then connect them to a larger reality. It opens their pores to the divine, to home, to source, to what we once called God."*

That intelligence seems obsessed with our present ecological situation, as if it were a galactic feedback loop kicking in as the world comes apart like a cheap suit, breaking through our scientific materialism as waking dreams, truck-stop myth, and supernatural anomaly. Greylings are the new elemental heralds, the elves and ogres of a decaying forest. And while encounters with them are often traumatic, John Mack and others believe they can transform us all.

Transform us into what? I submit that no good could come of global transformation of the human psyche. Someone will slip through the matrix and run around screaming that we are deluded and being subordinated by invisible aliens. We'll either die laughing or we'll kill all the madmen who will try to warn us of the plot.

Or the advanced aliens will do it for us. No good, you see.

Still, given all that we think we know about ETs, UFOs, global mind control, and the agenda of the invaders sailing about in their zero point energy lightships, it would be nice to have one of the little buggers land in the back yard and the occupants come in for a cup of Sassafras tea beside a cozy hearth. Until that happens—and I strongly suspect it never will—I will simply tell the conspiracists the same thing Ivan told the people who were lurking at his bedside, waiting (and hoping) for him to croak.

*"Leave me alone! Let me go in peace."*

## LOST WORLDS AND UNDERGROUND MYSTERIES OF THE FAR EAST

Introduction

By Timothy Green Beckley

I have been fascinated with lost civilizations and ancient mysteries since I was a kid. When I was about nine or ten, I remember seeing an ad for a company that put out intriguing sounding booklets for the price of a Coke. I waited probably two months for the arrival of several titles that you couldn't find in your bookstore (much like our titles today, except there were no web sites or Amazon.com to order from).

One of these was a 40-page pamphlet—complete with rusted staples and tiny print—the title of which had originally caught my attention in the back of a Batman comic. *Lost Civilizations of South America* was written by Harold T. Wilkins, a researcher who spoke about dinosaurs he claimed still existed along the banks of the Amazon River in Brazil, as well as other monsters that should have been extinct a million or more years ago.

Wilkins had a way with words that had me thirsting for additional information. But there was little else that covered the subject matter that was available in my school library, or anywhere else in our tiny town for that matter. Sure, there was King Kong and a few other "big ape" movies, but it was hardly the same thing.

About this time I happened to come across a copy of a magazine called MYSTIC which was edited by Ray Palmer, the original co-publisher of FATE, a digest sized magazine devoted to the unexplained which is still available today. Palmer was a slick pulp writer who knew how to turn a word.

I became fascinated and utterly intrigued by the supposedly true stories that he was spinning in regard to a civilization that existed beneath our feet in huge caverns that stretched toward the center of the earth.

Another writer, Richard S. Shaver, supported Palmer's contention that we were co-inhabitants of the same planet with an unknown race, or races, of beings. For years Shaver said that he had been fending off the negative advances of a group of subterranean dwellers known as the Dero. The Dero were a mentally degenerate group who for eons has had the utter destruction of humankind in mind.

Shaver claimed the Dero had been forced underground thousands of years ago when the lost continent of Lemuria sank beneath the sea. In addition, Palmer said that the planet Earth was hollow, had its own central sun at the planet's core and could by visited by taking a journey through vast openings that existed at both the North and South Poles.

Shortly after reading numerous episodes of this type by Palmer and Shaver, I began collecting data of my own, supporting their theories, and put it together into book form. The Shaver Mystery and the Inner Earth was the beginning of my career in the controversial area of what we could loosely call "conspiracy journalism."

At the tender age of 16 Gray Barker thus published my first book, which is now in its seventh printing by my own Inner Light Publications under the title SUBTERRANEAN WORLDS INSIDE EARTH. Some long time readers may realize that for a couple of years I came to write regular columns for Ray Palmer's magazines SEARCH and FLYING SAUCERS. I also began a very lengthy correspondence with Shaver who had moved from Pennsylvania to Arkansas in order to get away from the Dero.

Every week he would send me a letter and a box of rocks collected from his backyard in which he claimed he could see a pictorial of the earth's past that had literally been imprinted in the core of these stones for researchers to rediscover in this day and time.

Somewhere along the line, I also picked up a book by John Keel called JADOO that dealt with the mysteries of the Far East such as the controversial Indian rope trick and holy men who could levitate and fly through the air. Was Keel putting us on, or were all such "fantasies" possibly true?

It was all so bold and all so "far out," and it definitely changed my life. Getting into publishing on my own, I eventually began to come across other manuscripts that dealt with topics of a "fringe nature." There were books on Atlantis, on the builders of the Great Pyramid. There were dusty volumes on Tibet and on the wonders of China and Mexico. Most amazing was the fact that these works contained highly "disputed" information that ordinary texts had edited so as not to disturb fellow academicians.

What I have found is that from time to time a "lost manuscript" will resurface at a moment in history when it is better understood or welcomed than when it was originally published. The book you are now holding is one such rarity written in the early 1930's by Mr. M. Paul Dare, News Editor of the Times of India, a very prestigious daily in its heyday.

Upon finding and thumbing through a first edition of this literary wonder far back in the basement of a used bookstore, I knew I was going to reissue it for a contemporary audience as it dealt with a part of the world that is in the headlines almost every day—but whose culture remains enshrouded in mystery as it was centuries ago. Well written and well researched, this long out of print book proves that sometimes myths and legends can be all too true.

## FREEDOM LOST: Mind Control in the 21st Century

by Tim Swartz

"Do people ever stop to think there may be a dark, hidden plan to control their freedom? Do people stop to think that if there was such a plan, would they ever know it even existed?"

These are the first words of Kai Bashir in her self-published book: *Mind Control Within the United States*. Bashir recounts years of mental harassment and torture at the hands of unknown assailants who had seemingly picked Bashir at a young age for some kind of bizarre experiment.

In this fascinating self-published book, Ms. Bashir reveals the devious and hidden controls that she says threaten to enslave all humanity through electronic mind control methods. For Kai Bashir, her problems started when she was a child when she began to experience strange sensations akin to electric shocks that ran throughout her body. These shocks were soon replaced by disturbing thoughts that seemed to originate outside of her mind.

"I found that there were thoughts to steal, thoughts on war and patriotism, thoughts to tell a lie, thoughts to change beliefs on religion, thoughts that were not my own."

Kai Bashir is not alone in her beliefs. Thousands of people across the globe claim that they are under mental attack by outside forces. There are of course different kinds of mental illnesses where sufferers imagine that tormenters are "beaming" messages into their brains. However, there are just as many people claiming to be under mental attack who appear to be perfectly sane, despite their horrifying ordeals.

Can the government, or some secret black project intelligence organization, read your thoughts? Even worse, can they implant thoughts into your head? Would that be the ultimate mind control, if they could control what you actually think and yet, you could never even detect it?

There is overwhelming evidence to suggest this is the case. More and more these days we hear about mass-murderers quoted as saying "I hear voices in my head" or "A voice told me to do it". Is this a mass phenomenon, a coincidence? Or is it the result of years of research and work by some secret group into electronic methods of mind control?

Mind control comes in many forms. Poisoning of our food supply, pharmaceutical and hard drugs, sexual abuse, electronic and personality imprinting. Electronic mind control may be the most effective, in that it is practically invisible and not easily detected. We are constantly surrounded by electromagnetic energies with antennas broadcasting everything from cell phones, radio and TV signals, to power plants and electrical grids and power lines.

Electronics and sound come together when you are dealing with frequency. You can create an electronic device to produce specific frequencies. Frequencies, by themselves, can shatter glass, explode an object, including a person, and affect the nature of energies already present at various locations. Frequencies combined with particular oscillation rates can do things that seem straight out of science fiction.

### Early Experiments in Remote Mind Control

The CIA's experiments in radio control of the brain are based on the development of the EEG in the 1920's. In 1934, doctor's Chaffee and Light published a pivotal monograph, A Method for Remote Control of Electrical Stimulation of the Nervous System. Work along the same lines allowed Dr. Jose Delgado of Cordoba, Spain to climb into bull-ring and, with the push of a button, trigger an electrode in the head of a charging bull and stop the beast in it's tracks.

L.L. Vasiliev, the famed Russian Physiologist in Critical Evaluation of the Hypnogenic Method, made further groundbreaking advances. The article detailed the experiments of Dr. I.F. Tomashevsky in remote radio control of the brain "at a distance of one or more rooms and under conditions that the participant would not know or suspect that she would be experimented with. One such experiment was carried out in a park at a distance," Vasiliev reported, and "a post-hypnotic mental suggestion to go to sleep was complied with within a minute."

By 1956, Curtiss Shafer, an electrical engineer for the Norden - Ketay Corporation, detailed the possibilities at the National Electronics Conference in Chicago.

"The ultimate achievement of bio-control may be man himself," Shafer said, "The controlled subjects would never be permitted to think as individuals. A few months after birth, a surgeon would equip each child with a socket mounted under the scalp and electrodes reaching selected areas of brain tissue. Sensory perceptions and muscular activity could either be modified or completely controlled by bioelectric signals radiating from state-controlled transmitters." (From The Hidden Persuaders - Vance Packard, David McKay, 1957)

The CIA had nefarious plans of their own with the founding of an experimental mind control clinic in Montreal, directed by the notorious Dr. Ewen Cameron, M.D. Allen Memorial was housed in a limestone mansion atop Mount Royal, donated by Sir Hugh Allen and staffed with psychiatrists fresh from war-torn Europe.

In 1992, Retired Colonel L. Fletcher Prouty, formerly a Pentagon liaison to the CIA, told author Dick Russell that Allen Memorial "was pretty well organized." Prouty wrote "If you get a hold of a directory for the American Psychiatric Association in around 1956 or 1957, you'll be surprised to find that an enormous percentage of the individuals listed are foreign-born. Mostly they came out of Germany and Eastern Europe in a big wave. They were all called "technical specialists", but really they were psychiatrists. They went into jobs at universities mostly - but many were working on these 'unconventional' mind control programs for U.S. intelligence...These would go to people like Dr. Cameron in Canada."

The psychotronic heart of Dr. Cameron's laboratory was the Grid Room. The subject was strapped into a chair by force, his head bristling with electrodes and transducers. Any resistance was met with a paralyzing dose of curare. The subject's brainwaves were beamed to a nearby reception room filled with voice analyzers, a wire recorder and radio receivers. The systematic annihilation or "depatterning" of a subjects mind and memory was accomplished with overdoses of LSD, barbiturate sleep for 65 days at a stretch and ECT shocks at 75 times the recommended dosage. Psychic driving, the repetition of a recorded message for 16 hours a day, programmed the empty mind. Fragile patients referred to Allen Memorial for help were thus turned into carbuncular jellyfish. (From The Experiments of Dr. D. Ewen Cameron by David Remnick, Washington Post 7-28-85, and reprinted in the Congressional Record 8-1-85)

Encouraged by the progress shown at Allen Memorial, the CIA published a secret manual in 1962 on the electronic wizardry of Radio-Hypnotic Intracerebral Control (RHIC), originally developed by the Pentagon. According to a 1975 issue of Modern People: "When a part of your brain receives a tiny electrical impulse from outside sources, such as vision, hearing, etc., an emotion is produced — anger at the sight of a gang of boys beating an old woman for example. The same emotions of anger can be created by artificial radio signals sent to your brain by a controller. You could instantly feel the same white hot anger without any apparent reason."

The objective of the CIA's umbrella remote mind control program in the 1950's (Project ARTICHOKE) was the creation of a "Manchurian" killer-puppet with a revolver and a memory like a steel sieve, both emptied by electrical stimulation. This technology existed by the early 1960's according former FBI agent Lincoln Lawrence (an alias) and researcher Art Ford in the classic investigation of CIA mind control ops: Were We Controlled? The writers contend that Lee Harvey Oswald was a Hypnogenic Assassin - with an electrical implant in his head.

In 1965, the New York Times learned of obscure electronic experiments quietly funded by the government, and went tabloid with the front-page headline "MIND CONTROL COMING, SCIENTIST WARNS."

In the article, Dr. David Krech, a psychology professor at the University of California, warned that "our research may carry with it even more serious implications than the awful, in both senses of the word, achievements of the atomic physicists." When leaks to the press exposed the horror stories, he said: "let us not find ourselves in the position of being caught foolishly surprised, naively perplexed and touchingly full of publicly displayed guilt."

## Microwaves and the "Zapping of America"

In 1965, upon discovering that the Russians were dousing the American Embassy in Moscow with microwaves, the DoD's secretive Advanced Research Projects Agency (ARPA) set up a laboratory at the Walter Reed Army Institute of Research in Washington D.C. to study the effects that radio waves had on the human brain. Dr. Jose Delgado (whose work with radio waves was underwritten by the CIA and Navy) thought that these invisible weapons were "more dangerous than atomic destruction."

With knowledge of the brain, he said, "we may transform, we may shape, direct Robotize man. I think the great danger of the future is... that we will have robotized human beings who are not aware that they have been robotized."

The Moscow Signal, however, remained a puzzle to scientists. Officials of the intelligence community consulted experts on the biological effects of the radiation. Dr. Milton Zaret, a leading microwave scientist, recalls that the CIA inquired: "whether I thought electromagnetic radiation beamed at the brain from a distance could affect the way a person might act," and "could microwaves be used to facilitate brainwashing or to break down prisoners under investigation."

The State Department chose to keep the Signal a secret from embassy employees - and studied the side effects instead. Ambassador Stoessel's office was situated in the beam's center. He fell prey to a blood disease, bleeding eyes, nausea, and eventually lymphoma. Two other State Department employees, Charles Bohlen and Llewellyn Thompson have been stricken with cancer. The existence of the Soviet beam was only acknowledged in the U.S. in 1976, in response to a Jack Anderson column.

CIA researchers, meanwhile, explored other bands of the EM spectrum. Dr. Jose Delgado blasted the brains of four of his patients with radio waves. He reported that they experienced differing emotions, sensations, and "colored visions."

At UCLA, Dr. Ross Adey (who worked closely with émigré Nazi technicians after WWII) rigged the brains of lab animals to transmit to a radio receiver, which shot signals back to a device that sparked any behavior desired by the researcher. (From Mind Control - by Larry Collins, Playboy, Jan. 1990 P. 204)

In The Controllers, Martin Cannon argues that the brain transmitters and "stimoceivers" of the 1960's were "similar to those now viewed in (UFO) Abductee MRI scans." The press ceased coverage of brain telemetry experiments in the mid-seventies. But Cannon's study of abduction accounts led him to conclude that effects of brain stimulation "can now be elicited with microwaves and other forms of electromagnetic radiation, with and without electrodes".

## Voices From the Sky

The next logical step in mind control would be to incorporate this technology into

71

satellite communications. Since other countries are known to have similar capabilities, there could occur a situation in which electronic mind control warfare is waged against a civilian population, receiving conflicting mental manipulation from both sides.

A meeting sponsored by Defense & Foreign Affairs and the International Strategic Studies Association was held in Washington DC in 1983. High-level officials from many countries met for this conference. They discussed psychological strategies related to government and policymaking. A summary of the agenda reads: "The group will be discussing the essence of future policymaking, for it must be increasingly clear to all that the most effective tool of government and strategy is the mind. If it's any consolation to the weapons-oriented among defense policymakers, the new technologies of communications—satellites, television, radio, and mind control beams—are 'systems' which are more tangible than the more philosophically based psychological strategies and operations.

"But we should make no mistake; it will be the 'psychologically based' systems which determine the world's fate in coming years. And we should not ignore the fact that the USSR is working on electronic systems to beam messages directly into the brain. What good, then, are conventional systems if these types of weapons are not countered? And, on a more basic level, what good is a weapon system if public opinion or political constraints prohibit its deployment?"

On July 21, 1994, the U.S. Department of Defense proposed that non-lethal weapons be used not only against declared enemies, but against anyone engaged in activities that the DOD opposed. That could include almost anybody and anything. Note that the mind-control technology is classified under non-lethal weapons.

A 1998 news item states that U.S. Air Force General John Jumper "predicts that the military will have the tools to make potential enemies see, hear, and believe things that do not exist" and that "The same idea was contained in a 15-volume study by the USAF Scientific Advisory Board, issued in 1996, on how to maintain U.S. air and space superiority on the battlefields of the 21st century." (Aviation Week, March 9, 1998)

It is thought that the NSA's (National Security Agency) Signals Intelligence group can remotely monitor information from human brains by decoding the evoked potentials (3.50HZ, 5 milliwatt) emitted by the brain. Prisoners who were experimented on in Gothenburg, Sweden and Vienna, Austria have been found to have evident brain lesions. Diminished blood circulation and lack of oxygen in the right temporal frontal lobes can result where brain implants are usually operative. A Finnish victim of mind control experiments experienced brain atrophy and intermittent attacks of unconsciousness due to lack of oxygen.

Such history brings us back to the situation today, where there seems to be a dramatic increase in the number of "wavies," those who feel they are experiencing bombardment by ELF, VLF, SHF microwaves, magnetic waves and other radiation of the electromagnetic spectrum which can be modulated so that voices can be heard inside the head, without implants, without speakers. Most of them have been diagnosed as being "Paranoid Schizophrenic."

Mind control techniques can be used for political purposes. The goal of mind controllers today is to induce the targeted persons or groups to act against his or her own convictions and best interests. Zombified individuals can even be programmed to murder and remember nothing of their crime afterward.

It is believed that this "silent war" is being conducted against unknowing civilians and soldiers by military and intelligence agencies. Since 1980, electronic stimulation of the brain (ESB) is suspected to have been secretly used to control people targeted without their knowledge or consent. All international human rights agreements forbid nonconsensual manipulation of human beings; even in prisons, not to speak of civilian populations.

On March 15 1995, two patients of New Orleans therapist Valerie Wolf testified before the Advisory Committee on Human Radiation Experiments. Although this was outside the purview of the Committee, they were permitted to testify because some of the names of CIA-connected researchers they mentioned were already familiar to the Committee. These two women remembered sessions when they were around eight years old that involved electric shocks, hypnosis, shots with needles, x-rays, sexual abuse, and even training in intelligence tradecraft. One case occurred from 1972-1976 and the other in 1958. The media did not cover this testimony.

Under an initiative of U.S. Senator John Glenn, continuing discussions commenced in January 1997 about the dangers of radiating civilian populations. Targeting people's brain functions with electromagnetic fields and beams (from helicopters and airplanes, satellites, from parked vans, neighboring houses, telephone poles, electrical appliances, mobile phones, TV, radio, etc.) is part of the radiation problem that should be addressed in democratically elected government bodies.

One reason this technology has remained a state secret is the widespread prestige of the psychiatric Diagnostic Statistical Manual IV produced by the U.S. American Psychiatric Association (APA) and printed in 18 languages. Psychiatrists working for U.S. intelligence agencies no doubt participated in writing and revising this manual. This psychiatric "bible" covers up the secret development of MC technologies by labeling some of their effects as symptoms of paranoid schizophrenia.

Victims of mind control experimentation are thus routinely diagnosed, knee-jerk fashion, as mentally ill by doctors who learned the DSM "symptom" list in medical school. Physicians have not been schooled that patients may be telling the truth when they report being targeted against their will or being used as guinea pigs for electronic, chemical and bacteriological forms of psychological warfare.

There is a growing concern that the U.S. government is stepping up its secret mind control operations. It is believed the first steps have been taken to turn the United States, and later the rest of the world, into a police state. The War on Terrorism is more than likely a ploy to frighten the population into allowing the government and military to suspend the Constitution and remove all rights and freedoms.

The next wave of terrorists to strike this country may actually be mind controlled "sleepers" sent out by secret forces within certain political parties whose goal is ultimate control and power. These pre-programmed victims of mind control have no idea what they have been secretly programmed to do. Given the proper stimulus, such as a command by radio wave sent directly into their brains, these agents of destruction could be sent out to commit mass murder, assassinations, terrorism, etc. Thus terrifying the population into allowing the government to enact more and more draconian laws and destroying democracy in this country forever.

These disturbing acts of terrorism will continue until each and every individual begins to accept the reality of this human rights atrocity. When the majority of people eventually acknowledges and accepts the reality of this truth, only then will we be able to stop this cowardly, authoritarian and brutal mentality of the power elite and their quest to covertly manipulate and dominate our society.

## WHO WAS CARLOS ALLENDE?

### by Commander X

It is hard to believe that what we now know today about the Philadelphia Experiment had its humble beginnings in a series of odd letters sent to UFO author Morris K. Jessup. Even though the legend of the Philadelphia Experiment has continued to grow and evolve over the years with such remarkable additions as the Montauk Project and alleged first-hand accounts from Al Bielek and others, the original source of information, a man by the name of Carlos Allende, has been almost forgotten.

The story of the Philadelphia Experiment begins with the 1955 publication of a book called The Case of the UFO by Morris K. Jessup, a Washington, D.C. auto parts salesman who once did graduate work in astronomy at the University of Michigan. The book proved to be a remarkable success and Jessup found a receptive audience who were fascinated by the idea that UFOs could be visitors from other planets.

In July of 1955, the Chief of the Office of Naval Research in Washington, D.C received a copy of The Case for the UFO. The odd thing about the book was that it had been heavily annotated in the margins, either by three different writers or by one writer using three pens with different colors of ink and disguising his handwriting to make it appear that three writers were involved.

The annotation writers seemed to know all about UFOs, writing in a rambling way about "magnetic nets," "vortices," home ships," "statis fields," and also about a 1943 U.S. Navy experiment at the Philadelphia Naval Yards in which a Navy ship was supposedly made to disappear.

On January 13, 1956, Jessup received a letter from a man who called himself both Carl M. Allen and Carlos Miguel Allende. The letter, whose return address was New Kensington, Pennsylvania, but was actually postmarked Gainesville, Texas, scolded Jessup for suggesting continued research into UFT. Allende claimed that in October 1943 the United States navy had used Einstein's theories in an experiment that not only rendered a destroyer totally invisible but also caused it to be teleported from the Philadelphia dock to the Norfolk-Newport News-Portsmouth area and back again in a matter of minutes.

As "proof" of these fantastic claims, Allende referred vaguely to articles in unnamed regional papers and listed a few names of persons with whom he supposedly witnessed this grand experiment while aboard the Matson Lines Liberty ship, the S.S. Andrew Furuseth.

Jessup, who at first had ignored Allende's letters, gradually became obsessed with them and began an investigation into their claims. In 1958, he turned over much of his material, including a copy of the Varo edition of The Case for the UFO with Jessup's own annotations of the annotations, to his good friend and fellow researcher, Dr Ivan T. Sanderson.

Jessup commented privately to friends on a strange pattern of coincidences that disturbed him greatly. In 1958, after visiting publishers and several friends in New York, he disappeared after he said he was going to visit his old home in Indiana. After many inquiries were made, Jessup was finally found dead in a car outside of his home in Coral Gables, Florida in what was officially claimed to be a suicide.

None of Jessup's true friends accepted this and inquiries into the official investigation left many unanswered questions. The obvious conclusion by some investigators was that he was murdered.

The Philadelphia Experiment legend has since grown into numerous books and two movies. It has also attracted a steady following of supporters. In fact, it can even be considered that the Philadelphia Experiment legend has reached epic proportions if you consider it all began with a few strange letters from the mysterious Carlos Allende.

In October 1980, writer Robert A. Goerman published an article in Fate Magazine entitled: Alias Carlos Allende. In his article, Goerman revealed how he had discovered the true identity of Allende whose family still lived in New Kensington, Pennsylvania.

Carlos Allende was actually Carl Meredith Allen who was described by his family as a "master leg-puller" and "an outcast by his own choice." However, Allen had indeed served in the Navy during WWII, but his family was unable to tell Goerman whether Allens claims of witnessing the Philadelphia Experiment were true or not.

Carl M. Allen faded into obscurity, just another forgotten chapter in the annals of UFO history. But Allen refused to go down without feeding the fire of controversy with one last log.

In an obscure newspaper called "THE NEWS of Colorado Centennial Country," (published weekly by Old Weldpress, Inc., John J. Dugan Jr, Editor and Publisher, Volume 2, Number 31, dated August 22nd, 1986,) Carl Allen tells reporter Jim Frazier in his article: Mystery Man Offers Death Bed Statement, that "the Philadelphia Experiment was real, and that it worked!"

"Einstein and his team were using the Navy for their research. Steinmetz wound the coils on the beam generator. It was based on the work of Nikola Tesla, but only Steinmetz could make the winding. That little drawf — a hunchback — was the world's best researcher.

What Einstein really was working on was a starship propulsion system. You have to realize that this was before rockets. This was before NASA's space program. This was Einstein's test of space travel - starship drive at faster than light.

"What Einstein proved was that invisibility is a precursor to propulsion beyond the speed of light. Invisibility is nothing more than the precondition to a practical utilization of the magnetic field related to the Einstein Tunnel Propulsion system. There is nothing to be afraid of with invisibility. Of the many combinations of human blood type, bone type and flesh type, there is only one that remains invisible for life. Others are not affected adversely. This means that the door is open for star travel for all Americans. We must do it. We must proceed. This is the future."

Carl M. Allen has since passed away. But the legend he created lives on.

## PINE GAP

by Sean Casteel

Has the United States virtually taken over the defense and emergency infrastructure in Australia, staging a covert coup of sorts to protect American interests?

According to an anonymous report received by THE CONSPIRACY JOURNAL, aliens work together with token humans in a series of underground bases in Australia. Are the Strategic Defense Initiative (Star Wars) and the HAARP transmitter in Alaska the result of technology shared by the aliens?

Another anonymous report claims that there is a nefarious human group behind much of what is currently taken to be "alien activity." Is there a neo-Nazi conspiracy afoot to bring about the enslavement of mankind and implement the dreaded Mark of the Beast?

· In the ongoing search for the truth in the murky territory of conspiracy, one is often forced to sift through reams of material in order to get to the bottom of many of the classified subjects that intrigue us and keep us up at night. Sometimes the information we have to go on is "speculative" in nature, and there are many unproven assertions about the nature of the New World Order and its many secret machinations that are frequently difficult for even the hardiest of souls to sort out. One of those capable of going "behind the scenes" to get at the nitty gritty is THE CONSPIRACY JOURNAL's own Commander X, author of numerous "underground" classics.

Commander X recently organized and edited A GUIDE TO INCREDIBLE CONSPIRACIES, with contributions by some of the leading conspiracy researchers of our time. One of the most exciting disclosures you will find in this volume concerns startling revelations about an underground base very similar to Dulce or Area 51, except that this one is located in Australia. Shortly before the book was published, I was forwarded the section concerning the Top-Secret Installation at Australia's Pine Gap and asked to condense the findings that were being revealed for the first time in the U.S.

## INFORMATION FROM AN AUSTRALIAN GOVERNMENT INSIDER

Here is what I learned from this manuscript: an Internet news site called the Rumor Mill News recently posted an informative summary of secret activities being carried on in Australia that it claims was submitted by a former Australian government insider who cautiously has decided to remain anonymous. The insider begins by describing how emergency services in Australia were brought under an umbrella of American and international control. "In 1989," the report states, "Australian emergency services began to be upgraded and the National Safety Council was started. Police, fire and ambulance services are now under one roof, and sold to a company called *Intergraph, Inc.,* which is a specialized American communications company said to be closely connected to the U.S. National Security Agency."

Which means that the emergency services infrastructure in Australia is now under foreign control and being overseen by what are supposedly private corporations.

"The machinery of a police state is now in place," the report declares, "and total military control could be established in a few hours."

America's own tight grip on Australia has even been admitted to by Jim Cairns, the Deputy Prime Minister there, who is quoted as saying that the Americans would mount a violent overthrow of the government there if they did not succeed by clandestine means.

"I believe there is a strong chance the Americans will try to do to us," Cairns said, "what they have just done in Chile. We could all be killed in the process."

With that kind of deadly threat hanging over their heads, it isn't hard to understand why the U.S. gets the kind of cooperation it demands.

### UNDERGROUND BASE AT PINE GAP

A scientist among Australia's elite in a key position revealed that there are at least ten top-secret American facilities in Australia with the so-called "Joint Defence Space Research Facility" at Pine Gap being the most important.

The Pine Gap base was built by American workers flown in for that purpose on a shift basis. The base became operational after two years.

"Large underground facilities are rumored to extend some twelve miles below the base," the report continues. "Long tunnels are laid out in a pattern similar to the spokes of a wheel, and extend several miles from the center of the base. In a deep, shielded underground chamber, a secret nuclear reactor similar in size to those used to power submarines was installed to drive large AC and DC generators. Reportedly, extending some 20,000 feet below the base is a borehole containing an ultra-low frequency antenna that is apparently used for secret experiments supposedly related to Nikola Tesla's resonance theories as well as low-frequency communications throughout the world.

"Pine Gap is a multi-billion dollar operation of great importance to the American government," the report says.

### UFO SIGHTINGS ARE A PART OF THE PICTURE

In the aftermath of the construction of the secret underground facility at Pine Gap, the number of UFO sightings in the area has increased to epic proportions. One such incident, in 1989, involved three hunters who were on an all-night shooting trip in the hills near Pine Gap.

"At around 4:30 AM," the anonymous source narrates, "they observed a large camouflaged door open on the side of a low hill inside the security compound and a metallic, circular disc appear from the gaping black hole. The disc tipped on its edge and disappeared vertically at tremendous speed. The door then slowly shut, and everything returned to normal. The camouflage was so good that from their vantage point they were unable to observe anything unusual about the area after the door closed."

Another incident with a camouflaged door was also recorded.

"Another camouflaged door case occurred when two members of the Northern

Territory Police," the report said, "who were taking part in a search for a missing Alice Springs child, watched as three "bathtub-shaped" objects flew slowly over the base and then one by one disappeared into an oblong black hole in a hillside. This also occurred during the early hours of the morning. As the two police officers had arranged to meet other members of the search party, they left without seeing the door close."

The report also describes other UFO sightings at the Pine Gap underground base, all of which point to a conspiracy between secret military forces and some of the many alien races who are said to be visiting the Earth and carrying out their own agenda, an agenda our governments may be helpless to do anything about.

## A HISTORY OF ALIEN CONTACT

According to the Australian government insider, as many as nine different alien groups are said to be visiting the planet, and secret official research dating from the 1950s indicated that several of these groups appeared to be preparing a huge worldwide military operation or police action against the Earth, so friendly cooperation with at least some of the groups became even more crucial.

"In return for our governments allowing these aliens secret exploitation of the planet and the human race," the report continues, "they would provide the technical know-how to prevent further major wars and stop any other interested extraterrestrials from invading the planet. It has been said with some authority that they are the brains behind the Strategic Defense Initiative (Star Wars), the extension of which is HAARP, which is aimed at creating an electromagnetic shield around the world to prevent an attack from outer space.

"The Russians have actively cooperated since its inception. Such advanced defense systems required worldwide coverage involving operational centers in secure areas in several countries. Australia is used for this purpose, including Pine Gap."

But Pine Gap is also the location of an even more sinister kind of activity beyond its use as a communications center for SDI and other military operations.

"Though its communications functions are important," the report says, "its research and development sections situated below the surface are considered vital to the future of the planet. Here extraterrestrials conduct their work in partial cooperation with human scientists. They live in special conditions in virtual isolation, and come and go as they please."

## REPORTERS STUMBLE ONTO A SECRET

While such activities are obviously among the most highly guarded secrets of all the nations involved, occasional leaks do happen. The report describes an incident that took place at a major UFO research facility located at a Royal Australian Air Force base in Victoria.

"Four people from a TV station attended the opening of a new building at the base. A large hangar had two side doors open so they decided to take a look inside. Towards the rear of the hangar was a large metallic gray disc-like object standing on three short legs. It was about sixty feet in diameter with a central height of about eighteen to twenty feet. Scaffolding was arranged around its right hand side with a platform extending to what looked like a curved doorway situated near the top of the object.

"They also noticed what appeared to be small square windows on each side of the doorway and evenly spaced around the top of the object. They videoed it, noticing surface markings similar to Korean script. There was an elderly man talking to two smaller men, the size of five-year-old children, in the center of the office area. They were looking at drawings on a small table and didn't notice the cameramen.

"The tall man looked up and appeared puzzled by the two cameramen. He walked to the door and asked them if HQ needed more pictures and why hadn't they called him about it. The TV men replied that they had nothing to do with HQ. The man's expression was one of absolute horror. The intruders were met by four guards who confiscated the videotape."

One can only wonder what would have happened had the TV crew made it out of the area with their videotape intact. Would the public have at last been let in on the secrets that surround so much government-military-alien collusion?

## CONSPIRACIES OF THE HUMAN KIND

Another report brought to the attention of *THE CONSPIRACY JOURNAL* also comes from an anonymous source. In this case, the author puts more of the blame for the secrecy surrounding the UFO phenomenon on human conspirators as opposed to aliens from the great unknown. A lot of this information is attributed to researcher Vladimir Terziski, former head of the American Academy of Dissident Sciences, whom we have quoted many times, and whose various video lectures we have made available. (See issue #13 of THE CONSPIRACY JOURNAL for a list.)

"Terziski believes," the report begins, "that in spite of all the descriptions of 'aliens' given by abductees, that there are also craft constructed by 'the Illuminati' which are taking advantage of the 'alien' question by attempting to pass off their own black projects as 'alien technology'."

Although Terziski is uncertain as to the existence of the so-called "grays", he does admit his belief in an ancient human-like society that possesses antigravity craft. Terziski states that whether or not "the grays" exist, the New World Order may be using the external alien threat as a means to bring about world unity after the fall of Russia while "at the same time, hundreds of valid but undesirable E.T. contacts with more advanced races are debunked or ignored by the government."

## CONSPIRACY JOURNAL READER: THE DEEPEST, DAARKEST SECRETS

The anonymous author lists the various members of what he calls "Bavarian Intelligence," which are said to include the Illuminati's Skull and Bones Society, the Thule Society's Nazi Empire, and the CIA-NSA network that was "german-ated" from within the Bavarian Illuminati and Bavarian Thule Societies. The Bavarian Intelligence group is alleged to be working with the grays in secret. This Bavarian group not only controls the United Nations, but is reportedly tied in with the reptilian gray empire in such a way that resistance to them is simply futile. A phony war intended to keep the human race in a state of disorder, chaos, confusion and fear is necessary to the group achieving its final goal, what the author calls an "absolute electronic dictatorship in which every human being will be "tagged" and branded like cattle with an electronic chip implant which will make them the absolute spiritual, mental and physical slaves of the New World Order. Multitudes may be deceived into receiving this "mark" of the Beast, and in doing so will have relinquished the greatest thing that they possess, their *free agency*, and with it their soul."

There is a lot more to tell about these and other complex subjects, which you can read about in greater detail in *A GUIDE TO INCREDIBLE CONSPIRACIES*, published by Inner Light and Global Communications.

## MICKEY MOUSE SYNDROME

by Robert S. Newport, Jr.

Hollywood animator Paul Scarzo is the latest victim of what has become known as the "Mickey Mouse Syndrome", which has hit countless animators and filmmakers who have been laid off their jobs by Walt Disney Co., Warner Bros., and other movie studios. The studios have shipped thousands of jobs overseas to China, devastating the once-thriving community of animators and other technicians.

Scarzo, an animation artist, appears to have become a victim of this "syndrome", which manifests as depression, despair, and a feeling of hopelessness. Scarzo was laid off his job as an animator about 3 years ago, according to his friends in Burbank, California. He found some part-time work, but there are few jobs left in the industry, and when his money ran out he lost his house and his wife filed for divorce. He had recently found a new girl friend, but when a small argument turned in to a major dispute, Scarzo allegedly "flipped out" and threatened to shoot his girlfriend and take his own life. His terrified girlfriend managed to escape and notify police, who launched a search for the hapless artist.

Accounts have it that Scarzo grabbed his girlfriend's little cats, threw them in his car with a pistol and took off. Burbank police spotted him and pulled him over at about 9:30 on a July evening, but he jumped back in his car and sped off, leading police and California Highway Patrol on an hour-long chase over L.A. freeways. The cat-napper

81

eventually got off the freeway system in Redondo Beach where he crashed into some parked cars. He jumped out and ran for blocks with police in pursuit. A standoff then ensued, with Scarzo pointing a gun to his own head and threatening to kill himself. Police, wary of the oft-used technique of "suicide by cop" eventually managed to tackle him and wrest the gun away. He was reported to be in L.A. County Jail.

The cats, though terrified after the non-stop joyride and crash, were unhurt and returned to their owner. Animal rights activists were outraged about the incident. "This is horrible", said one woman, "these nuts are now holding little helpless kittens hostage". But a local cracker-barrel pop-psychologist, whom we fondly call "Dr. Jack", has another theory. "Dr. Jack", has been researching job loss -related disorders. "These unemployed animators and artists have what I call the "Mickey Mouse Syndrome," said Dr. Jack. " They develop a deep-seated hatred for mice and rats because of their bad experience and layoff from Disney. I think that Mr. Scarzo actually took the cats with him for protection. He subconsciously had an overwhelming fear of being attacked by rats, and in his demented state of mind, the cats would protect him and ward off any such aggressors."

One of Scarzo's friends, Bob, who works in a Burbank Bookshop, said that "Paul was complaining for years about these bad dreams he was having, dreams of armies of mice attacking him. I guess he finally flipped out."

As well as being an animator, Scarzo was also a well-known local parapsychologist and documentary filmmaker. His most famous ghost hunting episode took place on the old Queen Mary ship in Long Beach. Scarzo joined Richard Senate and a team of researchers who were trying to capture some of the ship's ghosts on film. Scarzo's plan was to use a stereoscopic camera to take the pictures. That way, any ghost or apparition would appear on two pieces of film at once, proving it was real and not just a mark on a piece of film or just some chemical blotch on the negative. The whole adventure was filmed by Hollywood's "Sightings" television show, and was broadcast on September 17, 1995.

Scarzo has also written a graphic novel, entitled "The Counterfeit Order". This was, in effect, a storyboard for a planned film. The subject matter is taken from captured WW2 records and underground legends about a secret Nazi polar base in the Antarctic. This Nazi base, built before WW2 began, was called Neues-Schwabenland. The diehard Nazis fled there via submarine upon losing the war, and they remained in an underground facility, while spreading business tentacles throughout South America and the world. Admiral Byrd led an expedition to root them out in the 1950's, but was beaten back, as the Nazis still had some working prototypes of their "flying saucer" type craft. An interesting theory, and Scarzo had planned a movie based on this information.

Only 100 copies of his graphics oriented book were printed, each signed by Paul Scarzo. A few are left and can be purchased from Global Communications. The book sells for $35. Scarzo also has made several documentary films. One film on ghosts was just about to be released when this tragic incident occurred, so it is currently not available.

Another documentary, about 2 hours long, is entitled **"Hitler's Secret Flying Saucer Program"**. This film is a lengthy exploration of the case of William Lyne, who claimed to have found documents in a New Mexico salvage yard that referred to the U.S. Government's secret program to reverse-engineer saucer craft pioneered in Nazi Germany. A very interesting video!

The strange situation about this whole case was pointed out by one of Scarzo's associates, bookshop owner Paul Hunt, proprietor of Atlantis Book Shop in Burbank, California. Hunt claims that this entire incident of the "police chase and car chase" is totally out of character to Scarzo. Hunt describes Scarzo as a very "nice guy, a mild mannered Asian American fellow, who was always smiling and very low key." Several of Scarzo's other friends made similar comments, and all were shocked when they heard about the car chase. Hunt also pointed out some other mysterious events that have recently taken place.

According to Hunt, Scarzo was living in Glendale, California up until about 6 months ago. During this time Scarzo was trying to "market" his storyboard idea for a movie based on the book "The Counterfeit Order" an action-adventure relating to the previously mentioned secret Nazi base in the Antarctic.

Scarzo told Hunt that he was receiving "threats" that he believed were related to the movie project and to his work on documenting UFO activity and the connection between the U.S. Government secret technology acquisition and the former Nazi scientists from "Operation Paperclip".

Shortly after that, Scarzo was physically attacked and assaulted while coming out of his Glendale duplex late one night. A neighbor called police and Glendale Police immediately responded and apprehended the attackers, who turned out to be two cops from Vernon, California, another city about 50 miles from Glendale. The two Vernon cops claimed they were serving Scarzo with a legal paper, which turned out to be a document that was from his divorce proceeding a year previous, and his divorce had meanwhile been finalized.

"It was one of the weirdest things I have ever heard of", said Hunt. "City cops are never allowed to serve any legal papers, this is the job of the L.A. County Sheriff's Department or the Marshall's office. I have never heard of a traffic cop, a motorcycle officer and an off duty detective driving outside the city limits of their own city to serve an outdated piece of paper on a case that was already settled many months before. It was obvious that something else was behind the assault, the paper document was just a cover."

Scarzo was taken into custody that night by Glendale Police, who probably just wanted to figure out what was going on. He was released the next morning, with no charges, as he was certainly the victim in the incident. Hunt said that Scarzo would not be intimidated. He filed a claim against the City of Vernon for damages, and talked about filing a Civil Rights lawsuit if the claim was denied.

Shortly after the assault, Scarzo decided to go "underground" and lay low for a while, and try to figure out who or what organization was behind the threats, and their connection to the Vernon Police Dept. among others. Could it be a secret Nazi organization upset about the UFO video? Or agents of a U.S. alphabet-soup group trying to cover up the Operation Paperclip conspiracy? And further, since the entire recent incident of the police chase was so out of character, what set him off? Was he the victim of a drugging or a mind-control operation?

It is known that the government possesses equipment that can be used to remotely beam mind control messages targeting almost any individual. Or, did he fall prey to the "Mickey Mouse Syndrome", and succumb to the pressure of losing his job and then his family life? We may never know. The Scarzo case remains a mystery wrapped in an enigma. Mr. Scarzo, although only 45 years old, has indeed accomplished a lot during his career. He worked on several television animated shows, including "Exosquad" and "The Greatest Fear", and was a guest at the huge San Diego Comic Book Convention in 1999. It is indeed a shame that his career has come to at least a temporary end. He was an innovative, talented artist, a documentary filmmaker and animation artist, but possibly ran afoul of a little "mouse",..... you know the one!

## NIKOLA TESLA: SECRET TIME TRAVEL EXPERIMENTS

By Commander X

I have long been an admirer of the great inventor Nikola Tesla. That should come to no surprise to anyone who has read some of my previous books. Here was a man whose genius was far beyond the great minds of his day. He had an intellect that at times seemed almost unearthly. I suppose this is why some have speculated that such a remarkable individual could not have sprung from the bosom of mother Earth, but instead was the product of extraterrestrial intervention. I must admit that for a while the idea that Nikola Tesla was not of this planet held a certain appeal to me. It would certainly answer a lot of questions about this enigmatic man – but of course it would also create even more questions that would be impossible to answer in my lifetime. So I was finally left with the simplest explanation on the true origins of Nikola Tesla. I have concluded he was an extraordinary human the likes we so rarely see. My primary schooling was bereft of any education of Tesla or his great achievements. His name, in its absence, spoke of dark conspiracies and downright thievery.

In public, only the Tesla-coil stands out in honor of its namesake, but few know of the person for whom it is christened. Textbooks held no place between its pages for this great man, and teachers rarely uttered his name. Thankfully, some have come to recognize the great injustice that has been done to Tesla and have found a place in some classrooms to teach his history. I think it would be safe to say that Nikola Tesla was the man who invented the 20th Century. But a mystery remains. A mystery that has been diabolical in its treachery not only to Nikola Tesla, but to humanity as a whole.

We know that the United State Patent Office granted patents to many of Tesla's inventions. These were inventions that Tesla and his investors saw as potentially profitable – the AC motor is an excellent example of one of Tesla's inventions that changed the world.

However, Tesla also invented an unknown number of other items that were never patented for one reason or another.

Tesla had a keen sense of what would garner financial interest, but he also worked on and developed technology that was simply for his own curiosity. Of these inventions, we know practically nothing. Remarkable by any standard, Tesla's patents illuminate only his most purposive, practical work. As he often lamented, there just wasn't enough time to tame the racing of ideas in his head; so much had to be left incomplete. Some of the projects— achieving an ultrahigh vacuum, a rocket engine design, experiments in directed beams and solar power—simply don't fit into the early 20th Century. Frequently he was content to publish his findings without regard to priority or patentability: he introduced in this way the therapeutic method now called diathermy. Other ideas were simply written down with no attempt to patent or even publicize them.

We now know that Tesla was interested and experimented in such "wild" ideas as free energy, antigravity, invisibility and even time travel. Its no surprise that Tesla in his day was loathe to speak of these kinds of interests – after all, even today these areas of study still come under fire by some "mainstream" scientists, who refuse to use their imaginations and intellect, and scorn such interests with terms such as "bad science" and quackery.

## TESLA THOUGHT "OUTSIDE THE BOX"

In my years as a military intelligence operative I came into contact with a number of top-secret programs that were either investigating, or, shockingly enough, actively using technology based on some of Tesla's "wild" ideas. Both the United States and Russia have active Particle Beam and RF (radio frequency) weaponry that has been in operation since the early 1970's – all as a result of Tesla's early 19th and 20th Century experiments. To say that there are other black budget projects involving Tesla-based research would wildly underestimate the total amount of research and development being conducted right now by many countries worldwide. And these are the projects that we know about.

Who knows how many deep, dark, secret projects are being conducted right now with science that could be decades, even hundreds of years beyond what civilian science knows today.

## SMALL DISCOVERIES LEAD TO GREAT THINGS

In 1895, while conducting research with his step-up transformer, Nikola Tesla had his first indications that time and space could be influenced by using highly charged, rotating magnetic fields. Part of this revelation came about from Tesla's experimentation with radio frequencies and the transmission of electrical energy through the atmosphere.

Tesla's simple discovery would, years later, lead to the infamous Philadelphia Experiment and the Montauk time travel projects. But even before these highly top-secret military programs came about, Tesla made some fascinating discoveries on the nature of time and the real possibilities of time travel. With these experiments in high-voltage electricity and magnetic fields, Tesla discovered that time and space could be breached, or warped, creating a "doorway" that could lead to other time frames. But with this monumental discovery, Tesla also discovered, through personal experience, the very real dangers inherent with time travel.

Tesla's first brush with time travel came in March 1895. A reporter for the New York Herald wrote on March 13 that he came across the inventor in a small café, looking shaken after being hit by 3.5 million volts.

"I am afraid," said Tesla, "that you won't find me a pleasant companion tonight. The fact is I was almost killed today. The spark jumped three feet through the air and struck me here on the right shoulder. If my assistant had not turned off the current instantly in might have been the end of me."

Tesla, on contact with the resonating electromagnetic charge, found himself outside his time-frame reference. He reported that he could see the immediate past - present and future, all at once.

But he was paralyzed within the electromagnetic field, unable to help himself. His assistant, by turning off the current, released Tesla before any permanent damage was done. A repeat of this very incident would occur years later during the Philadelphia Experiment. Unfortunately, the sailors involved were left outside their time-frame reference for too long with disastrous results. I have made some incredible discoveries concerning the pioneering efforts by Tesla in the science of time travel. This will be revealed with the publication of my forthcoming book: Nikola Tesla Time Travel Chronicles.

# CONSPIRACY JOURNAL READER: THE DEEPEST, DAARKEST SECRETS

## MOON MADNESS AND HOLOGRAPHIC MIND CONTROL

### Project Blue Beam Unleashed Upon The World

By Sean Casteel

Among the almost countless number of schemes and subterfuges employed by the New World Order, there is one that stands out as being both ingenious and awe inspiring in its simplicity: the use of holographic images to deceive, terrify and subdue the masses and place the leash around the necks of the blind and uninformed.

One possible clue to what will probably prove to be the inevitable deployment of holographic technology as a mass deception turned up on the pages of the online Rumor Mill News. In a lively exchange of emails, the following discussion on the strange movements of the Moon took place.

"A considerate reader from Southern California," the first email began, "has taken the time to put her thoughts on paper concerning the 'Much Ado' about the Moon. She offers a real possibility as a reason for the seemingly unexplainable activities of the Moon as have been recently witnessed by widely separated groups of individuals."

Perhaps at this point the question becomes, "What unexplainable activities of the Moon?" Whatever those odd patterns were, they were never publicized in the media, so we are forced to trust in the "widely separated group of individuals" referred to above.

Those odd patterns include reported distortions in the moon's appearance, such as shining with odd colors like green or red, as well as appearing in positions and portions of the sky that were out of synch with its usual passage across the heavens. There were even accounts of the moon failing to work through its phases in the proper order.

Another contributor to the Rumor Mill News wrote, "Somewhere, and I'm not sure where, I read something about a PSYOP that would project visions in the sky. And then I got to thinking, 'Why would some see the Moon doing strange things?' What if, and this is a big what if, what do you think about a holographic projection? What if 'they' are testing this, and what if 'they' don't want this 'test' questioned yet? Seems as if there would be a big deal made to discredit anyone getting too close. What if 'they' have figured out a way to refract the Moon or distort what we might or might not naturally be able to see above?"

Another contributor flatly declared that physical tricks are indeed being employed to make things like the odd patterns of the moon perceptible to the general population and called it "the greatest PSYOPS campaign ever carried out in the history of the world." Holograms are being used to make objects appear to the naked eye that are not really there. The false reality that is created will eventually be used to create panic in the masses.

### Project Blue Beam

What are all those people making such a fuss about? It all has to do with a covert NASA program called "Project Blue Beam." The Rumor Mill News emails explained it thusly:

"According to a comprehensive report by Canadian investigative journalist Serge Monast, entitled 'Project Blue Beam,' this holographic technology, used in conjunction with high-tech, mind-control weapons utilizing the effects of radio-frequency waves on the brain, is capable of projecting an image in the sky and causing collective thought to convince people they are seeing an alien invasion or the Second Coming of Christ."

As reported through several sources on the Internet, the Project Blue Beam program involves four separate stages before it is completed. Not surprisingly, the overall plan is one of a worldwide religious deception that would enslave the entire population of the Earth in a few swift, broad strokes.

"The infamous NASA Project Blue Beam has four different steps in order to implement the New Age religion with the Antichrist at its head. We must remember that the New Age religion is the very foundation for the New World Government, without which religion the dictatorship of the New World Order is completely impossible."

Having established a motive, the report goes on to explain the method.

"The first step concerns the breakdown of all archeological knowledge. It deals with the setup of artificially created earthquakes at certain precise locations on the planet where supposedly new discoveries will finally explain to all people the error of all fundamental religious doctrines. The falsification of this information will be used to make all nations believe that their religious doctrines have been misinterpreted and misunderstood for centuries. What is important to understand in the first step is that those earthquakes will hit at different parts of the world where scientific and archeological teachings have indicated that arcane mysteries have been buried. By those types of earthquakes, it will be possible for scientists to 'rediscover' those arcane mysteries, which will be used to discredit all fundamental religious doctrines.

"The second step involves a gigantic 'space show' with three dimensional optical holograms and sounds, laser projection of multiple holographic images to different parts of the world, each receiving a different image according to the predominating regional national religious faith. This new 'voice of God' will be speaking in all languages."

That last effect is created by a Soviet-developed computer system that is encoded with the languages of all cultures and their localized religious symbolism.

"With computer animation and sounds appearing to emanate from the very depths of space, astonished ardent followers of the various creeds will witness their own returned Messiahs in convincing lifelike reality. Naturally, this superbly staged falsification will result in social and religious disorder on a grand scale, each nation blaming the other for the deception, setting loose millions of programmed religious fanatics."

The third step in NASA's Project Blue Beam is called "Telepathic Electronic Two-Way Communication." The report quotes Lt. Col. John Alexander, an early researcher of "non-lethal weapons," who went public with claims of the development of a technology by which unsuspecting people are force fed thoughts that are not their own.

"If it is possible to feed artificial thought," Alexander said, "into the multi-genic field via satellite, the mind control of the whole planet is now possible. Other mind-to-mind induction techniques are now being considered. If perfected, this capability could allow the direct transference of thought via telepathy from one mind or group of minds to a select target audience. The unique factor is that the recipient will not be aware that thoughts had been implanted from an external source. He or she will believe the thoughts are original."

The fourth step is a three-pronged attack that includes aspects of the first three steps. Throughout the world, supernatural manifestations will be achieved by electronic means in order to carry out a false alien invasion, a false rapture, and a false unleashing of Satanic ghosts and goblins, intended to "push all populations to the edge of hysteria and madness, to drown them in a wave of suicide, murder and permanent psychological disorders."

### Household Holograms

After that rather unnerving overview of the use of holograms to deceive the entire population of the planet, it may also be helpful to look at the use of holograms on a smaller, more personal scale. The case of Steve Lee, a resident of the exclusive Black Forest area near Colorado Springs, is instructive in those terms.

In 1998, I spoke with Colorado resident Steve Lee, who does a daily battle with extremely strange happenings around his house. Everything from laser-like shafts of light that shine through the walls and then tie themselves in knots to ghostly faces that peer back at him from his mirrors are part of everyday life for Steve and his family.

In article I wrote at the time, Lee described a couple of strange encounters with holograms experienced by he and his family and friends. One of the encounters began when Lee went out on his front porch to have a cigarette.

"I saw these three guys in snow-camouflage about fifty yards out in front of the house with rifles pointing at me. I went, 'What the hell?' So I went inside and got my rifle and got my wife and she got the camera. I said, 'You see those guys?' She said, 'Yeah.' So I started walking towards them, looking through my scope, and I'm ready to shoot. I get fifteen feet from them and one of them says, 'Easy does it buddy.' And bam, they just vanished. There was fresh snow on the ground, but there were no tracks or anything."

Another similar incident involving twelve disappearing soldiers happened a short time later, when Lee was being visited by some friends who worked at Martin-Marietta as space engineers. Lee's friends were very interested in the strange activities around his home.

"So we're looking with infrared binoculars over towards a nearby house," Lee said, "and we started seeing these twelve guys in camouflage go into my neighbors damn doghouse! After about the third one, one guy said, 'Hey, that many people can't fit in a doghouse!' So we walked right over to the fence. And these guys continued to walk in there, and there's a guy on the outside guarding it. They're acting like we're not even there. We're talking to them, and they don't even look at us. So afterward I was wondering, did we really see that stuff or was it a hologram?"

Lee's theory about it being a hologram is not that farfetched. The soldiers seemed to disappear into a space much too small to contain them and to be completely oblivious to the presence of Lee and his friends, as one might expect from a holographic projection that "wasn't really there."

Lee told the story of still another confrontation with a hologram, this time involving a neighbor who was a Viet Nam veteran. The neighbor was diagnosed as being mentally ill after   talking to someone about intruders he had repeatedly sighted near his home.

"This guy kept seeing these two men in military fatigues on his property," Lee said. "I've seen these same two guys on my property as well. I've shot at them, and the bullets go right through them, so I know they're holograms. Anyway, this guy served in Viet Nam, so they said, 'Oh, well, there you go. He's having flashbacks.' And they put him away, too. Whoever is behind that one, I think that's pretty low."

Lee puts the blame firmly on the covert mind control programs of the   government.

"Every bit of technology that's being used here," he said, "is used in mind control. There is nobody else that could get away with this for this amount of time without getting caught. Whoever is doing this has no fear of law enforcement in any shape or form. So who else could it be?"

### The Cuban Virgin Mary Crisis

World-renowned Hispanic UFO investigator and journalist Scott Corrales wrote an article on holograms that appeared in the March 2003 issue of "FATE Magazine" in which he dealt with a bizarre incident that took place in Cuba in 1982.

"Hundreds of Cubans, taking their nightly walk along the seaside promenade known as the Malecon, witnessed a sudden flash over Havana Bay which immediately made them suspect that they were under attack. But bombs did not rain out of the sky; instead, there was an overwhelming brightness that gradually coalesced into an image of the Blessed Virgin—more specifically Cuba's patroness, la Caridad del Cobre—extending her arms toward the startled masses on the promenade, as she remained suspended in the night sky. Unlike traditional images of the Blessed Virgin, this one did not bear the Christ-child in her arms, nor were there any other religious items such as crosses associated with it. The divine protector appeared to be wearing a snow-white mantle that contrasted brightly against the prevailing darkness."

According to Corrales' sources, Cuban authorities stepped in to try to suppress and debunk the story, but radio stations based in Miami broadcast news of the event anyway. A second sighting of the Virgin Mary image was reported only days later in a port city called Mariel, and this time soldiers opened fire on the image, one of whom subsequently required psychiatric treatment. During another appearance, local militiamen "opened automatic gunfire against the unknown entity in a show of force. Bullets, according to eyewitnesses, splashed harmlessly in the water around the phenomenon. At times, the machine-gun blasts could be seen to pass right through the phenomenon."

Corrales also writes that it was later suggested that a U.S. Navy submarine had projected an advanced holographic image as part of psychological warfare operations against the Cuban government. The U.S. intelligence community is also believed to have planned a follow-up to its successful 1982 demonstration: to spread the belief among Cubans that Fidel Castro was the Antichrist foretold in the Book of Revelation, projecting a holographic image of Christ over the skies. It was believed that this "miraculous" event would unleash a rebellion that would overthrow the government.

The 40-year political battle to unseat Cuba's revolutionary government from power seems to have resulted in the use of experimental holography, among many other tactics employed over the years. But this is surely the most mind-blowing of them all!

### Are Holograms A Factor In Alien Abduction?

Budd Hopkins, generally considered to be the world's foremost expert on alien abduction, along with his wife Carol Rainey, a futurist and nonfiction filmmaker, co-wrote a book together called "Sight Unseen, Science, UFO Invisibility And Transgenic Beings" (Atria Books, 2003). Among the many aspects of the abduction phenomenon covered in the book, the subject of holograms is given some interesting play.

In a section called "Clues From The Hologram," the authors explain a little about just how a hologram actually functions.

"You might recall that in the first 'Star Wars' movie, Luke Skywalker's journey begins when a beam of light shoots out from a robot and projects a small, three-dimensional image of Princess Leia. Mesmerized by the ghostly figure pleading for help, Luke is hooked forever. The Princess Leia that Luke sees is a hologram, a 3-D image made with the aid of laser lights and a phenomenon known as interference patterns.

Luke would be able to walk around the hologram and see the entire princess from every angle. She would turn, speak, and actually seem to 'be there.' But if Luke reached out to touch her, his hand would pass right through the lovely lady.

"Technically, what makes a hologram possible is the phenomenon of 'interference.' This refers to the rippling pattern that occurs when two waves cross paths. If, for example, you dropped two rocks into a pond, each one would send off a series of concentric waves expanding outward. When the two sets of expanding waves cross each other, it's in the crests and troughs of these waves that the interference pattern occurs. Waves of water, waves of sound—any wavelike phenomena—can create interference patterns. In creating a visual image, scientists have found that laser light, being pure and coherent, is especially good at recording interference patterns on film.

"But all you see by looking directly at the film is a jumble of crisscrossing wavelike images. It's only when the film is illuminated later with another laser that a 3-D image of the original object reappears in front of your eyes."

Having established some of the technical background, the authors go on to discuss the possible use by the aliens of holographic projections during an abduction encounter.

"One of the most bizarre—if not downright comic—incidents of alien attempts to ingratiate themselves with an abductee was told to Budd by Karla Turner, a writer, abduction researcher and abductee. In one of her first conscious memories, she was outside alone in the middle of the night. She was five-years-old, and looking up at a six-to-seven-foot tall praying mantis towering over her. When she cried out that she wanted her mother, the creature said to the child, 'I AM your mother.'

"Very few children, I suspect, would find that a comforting remark to hear. We have to speculate about what is happening in instances like these: Perhaps the aliens are testing the human limits of tolerance at seeing them in their actual physical form. Or perhaps the mantis was a screen memory, an image generated in the child's mind to soften an even more disconcerting sight. Another possibility that increasingly strikes me as credible is that the alien beings may have no set form at all. If they are, instead, HOLOGRAPHIC or thought projections from either another dimension or another planet, they could literally take material form of any kind, any species, even as discrete beings that we don't recognize as living beings and therefore might not even see."

The idea being that close encounter witnesses may never have seen the aliens' true form at all, but rather only holographic images that appear in their place instead. To take the idea a little further, the aliens may ultimately have no physical forms as we perceive the word "physical," so holograms will have to suffice for the present.

### The Religious Implications

It should be pointed out that many abductees report seeing holographic images of the world on fire while they are onboard UFOs and undergoing the parts of the experience in which information about the future is imparted to them. Perhaps the simple image is intended to tell the story of the apocalypse in a compact, easy to understand form.

But there is also speculation in regard to the notorious "image of the Beast" prophesied in Revelations Chapter 13: verses 14-15. Those verses are as follows: "And by the signs it was allowed to work in the presence of the beast, it deceives those who dwell on earth, bidding them make an image for the beast which was wounded by the sword and yet lived; and it was allowed to give breath to the image of the beast so that the image of the beast should even speak, and to cause those who would not worship the image of the beast to be slain."

Could the prophet have been referring to a hologram when he described the image of the beast as having a living, breathing force within it, such that it could miraculously speak to its captive audience and seem to be completely, palpably alive? There are many who feel that such could be the case, and that an abominable, hologram-driven deception is somewhere in our near future.

## DO THE MYSTERIOUS LIGHTS OF BROWN MOUNTAIN

## HOLD THE KEY TO TESLA'S DEATH RAY?

### By Sean Casteel

· The spirits of Cherokee and Catawba Indians who died in battle around the year 1200 have often been blamed for the mysterious lights in the Brown Mountains of North Carolina. But does this eerie phenomenon have an even more unorthodox explanation, one rooted in hard science? The research of one acclaimed parapsychologist is ample proof that the lights are open to several interpretations.

· Why does the local tourism board refuse to promote the Brown Mountain Lights? Why are they "suspiciously silent" on the subject? Are they perhaps covering up a region of intense natural energy anomalies at the behest of the U.S. military?

· Read how understanding the energies at play on Brown Mountain could one day be used to create "Star Trek" phaser-type weapons, and even serve as the source of what talk show host and knowledgeable researcher Joshua Warren calls "the ultimate weapon," the Tesla Death Ray.

The Brown Mountain Lights are an excellent example of what have been termed "spook lights" or earthlights that have plagued specific areas around the globe for hundreds of years and seem to be associated with paranormal phenomena in these regions. Nestled squarely in the Tar Heel State of North Carolina, the lights that rise and fall and swirl around the forest-lined mountain ridges have both fascinated and terrified locals and tourists alike who have confronted them—some at very close range.

Joshua Warren, a researcher and author with a long history as an investigator of the Brown Mountain Lights, has been hiking in the haunted trails in the area since he was a child. Warren's interest in the paranormal began at age thirteen, when his first book, a collection of scary short stories and poems was published. Already a literary prodigy, the North Carolina native next began working with the local newspaper, The Asheville Citizen-Times.

"Since I'd written a book of spooky stories," Warren said, "my first article was coming out around Halloween. I decided to go and investigate places in the area that were supposedly haunted. After this piece was published, I got literally hundreds of phone calls and letters from people all over the region who said, 'Hey, this is great that you're investigating these places, and if you want to see a really active site, come spend the night at my house.'"

Warren began to follow up on the leads he received, which included invitations from police chiefs, doctors and judges who had strange tales of their own to tell.

By the early 1990s, Warren decided that there was so much data out there to be collected that the only way to do an efficient, comprehensive job was to gather a group of people who were experts in various areas of data collection to help him out. The idea was to look for patterns and correlations and to use the scientific method to understand more of what was happening. The organization Warren assembled came to be called LEMUR, an acronym for League of Energy Materialization and Unexplained Phenomena Research.

"Basically, all we're really doing," Warren said, "is looking at the possible connections between energy and the various ways it manifests and what people describe as unexplainable or paranormal activity. Even though we specialize in ghost research, we're open-minded about addressing reports of UFOs or crypto-zoology or psychic phenomena."

While Warren is an expert on a great many paranormal phenomena, it his expertise in the study of the Brown Mountain Lights that recently attracted our attention. In collaboration with Conspiracy Journal publisher Tim Beckley, we had picked Joshua Warren's brain as part of our own research into the strange, earthbound occurrences often associated with such ghostly activities. We were working full steam on the just-published book, Our Alien Planet: This Eerie Earth and found Warren to be a tremendous source for anecdotes on Brown Mountain as well as for sorting out some of the far-flung theories that had been offered up as our research continued.

Warren has lived near the mountain his entire life, and has many childhood memories of the folklore that has grown up around the strange lights. He even recalled a popular bluegrass song about the lights that was a local hit.

The area is also popular as a hangout for local teenagers and should have an automatic appeal to tourists.

"You'd think that the tourism department here," Warren said, "would try to do more in order to promote the lights. But actually, as it turns out, throughout the years they've always been sort of secretive about them. It's like they don't want people to know that much about the phenomenon. I've always found that intriguing."

Warren said he had approached the Travel and Tourism Commission himself, asking for support for his research—money, access, or even just an official blessing for LEMUR's work, and found to his surprise that the commission had no interest in the group's efforts at all.

"It was almost, some might say, 'suspicious,'" Warren said. "It's like they know something about the lights that other people do not know. I wouldn't quite go so far as to say that there's an organized cover-up, but I don't understand why something so spectacular down the road would not be embraced and celebrated more than it is. I don't even know of a single sign in the county with the phrase 'Brown Mountain' or 'Brown Mountain Lights' on it."

Along with the tourism commission's suspicious lack of interest in the area, there are strange stories told by some of the locals that also imply a covert interest in the area on the part of the more shadowy realms of the government. Warren said he had spoken to hunters who had journeyed into the nearby Pisgah National Forest to look for game and come out shaken by what they had seen.

"There was one fellow," Warren said, "who said that he knew for a fact that the government, particularly the army, had been doing training exercises on Brown Mountain. He referred me to another fellow who I met in person at the overlook one night."

The second informant told Warren that his family owned a restaurant in Morganton, right down the road from the mountain. At one point, the restaurant had gotten a contract to feed hundreds of people on the mountain for a period of a couple of weeks. Every day, the man's family would meet a couple of military policemen who would collect the food, pay for it, and then depart the scene. The family never saw where the food was going, but they knew there was clearly a large group of people up on the mountain.

A local hunter told Warren another strange story.

"He told me about being up there one day," Warren recalled, "and looking over at a valley close to Brown Mountain and seeing what appeared to him to be something very shiny, silvery and shiny, gleaming in the middle of the field there. He made his way over to the shiny object, and when he got there, he couldn't find it. But when he got to the location where he thought it was, he saw there was a small hole drilled in the ground that didn't seem to be more than a few inches deep."

A few days after sighting the disappearing shiny object, the same hunter was in back in the same area. It was towards evening. He saw a large group of military vehicles circling the exact spot where he had previously seen the small hole. The vehicles had their headlights on, illuminating the area. The hunter stared in fascination at the eerie scene.

"All of a sudden," Warren went on, "he said that dozens and dozens of guns just let loose, firing, one after the other. He said it was the most god-awful racket he'd ever heard. He just turned and hightailed it out of there."

Warren said that after hearing these strange kinds of stories that people relate about the government's interest in the region, and having himself made what he feels are scientific advances in understanding the anomalous energies at play in the Brown Mountain Lights phenomenon, that perhaps there is a logical reason for the government's covert presence there.

"I think there is a form of energy being produced there naturally," Warren explained, "that if harnessed and produced artificially and controlled, could have enormous implications for weaponry both lethal, and perhaps more importantly, non-lethal, as well as wireless communication, transportation and propulsion. So I would think that maybe if there is some kind of a cover-up, it has a connection to national security."

Warren further feels that the technological implications of what he and LEMUR are finding on Brown Mountain and in their own laboratory experiments are amazing.

"What we're talking about here," he said, "is the ability to take a form of electricity that can be focused and controlled on a particular subject, target, or destination, and to contain within that electrical form information. We could take the same type of signal that you might need in order to get the radio signal that you're listening to and instead of having to worry about getting reception, because you live in the mountains, you could actually have a variety of different transmitters that would each broadcast a tiny little bit of the signal. And if they all intersected at your antenna, you're going to get a signal that can pass through mountains. Because it's more than one individual signal."

Which makes possible, for one thing, a "Star Trek" type phaser weapon, which would stun a subject without actually hurting him.

"Say you want to be able to shoot somebody who is standing on the other side of a hostage," Warren said, "and you don't want to hit the hostage. Well, if you have a gun that has numerous different points, on something like a satellite dish or a concave dish, and each of these points is broadcasting one little part of the signal, and they all converge on the target, then anything that's between the weapon and the target is not going to be damaged. But at that one point where they converge on the target, you can shock somebody into unconsciousness, and they should have no permanent damage afterwards, except maybe a burn or something at the most. Or you could kill somebody."

Following from there, the weapons potential sounds even more like science fiction.

"You could use it on a much wider scale," Warren said, "for weapons potential, in creating these huge balls—I mean city-sized balls—of electricity that can go through and basically render a whole city unconscious at one point in time, for a temporary period, if need be. That might even be part of what the HAARP Project is working on up there in Alaska, because in order to get that type of energy, you'd really want to tap into the ionosphere.

"It would be a lot easier as well, because if you have some type of a short circuit, essentially a short circuit taking place between the earth and the ionosphere, and you're able to get that short circuit coming from various points to intersect on a target, then that's probably the most powerful weapon you can imagine.

"I would think it would very much qualify," he said, "as something like Nikola Tesla's Death Ray. So the implications for understanding how our world works, understanding a lot of the paranormal reports, understanding ways of improving our technology for the better or the worse, are all wrapped up in this. That's why I think Brown Mountain is sort of the ultimate place for me to investigate, especially considering that I live about an hour and a half down the road."

Warren says he stays intrigued by the Brown Mountain lights because of their multi-faceted nature and because an investigation of the phenomenon offers so many different dimensions and dynamics in just one location. What amazes him the most may be how the lights represent themselves to different individuals. The phenomenon is truly in the eye of the beholder.

"You can appreciate it aesthetically," he said, "if you just want to go look at the pretty lights on the mountain. You can appreciate it creatively, if you want to write a song about the lights having some kind of meaning, or being omens or something more mystical. Or you can go there if you want to see something that is probably a glimpse of our future technology."

Warren explains all this in more elaborate detail in Our Alien Planet: This Eerie Earth in which Tim Beckley and I focused our attention on all sorts of unexplainable events that would seem to be on the cutting edge of today's rapidly expanding view of the universe. Does that glimpse of our future technology Warren alludes to also foretell the creation of an actual working weapon—the longtime rumored Nikola Tesla Death Ray actually brought to life? Can the strange lights and energy visible on Brown Mountain someday be harnessed for military purposes that at present seem like so much science fiction? Joshua Warren and his LEMUR group of fellow researchers may be able to answer those questions sooner than we think.

[Visit Sean Casteel's UFO Journalist website at: www.seancasteel.com Casteel is also the author of UFOs, Prophecy and the End of Time and Signs and Symbols of the Second Coming. He is most recently the coauthor with Timothy Green Beckley of Our Alien Planet: This Eerie Earth.]

## RUSSIA'S PRAVDA --

## AN HISTORICAL LOOK:

## FROM WORKERS DAILY TO WORLD WIDE WEIRD

### By Tim Swartz

Pravda is Russian for "truth," it is also the name of a succession of famous newspapers of the former Soviet Union. An official publication of the Communist Party between 1918 and 1991, the paper is still in operation in Russia, but it has taken some interesting journalistic avenues since its heyday as a Soviet government mouthpiece.

What has made Pravda stand out recently is its inclusion of articles dealing with UFO, the paranormal and strange events. Some Western journalists have even gone as far as declaring Pravda has become the "World Weekly News" of Russia.

Origins

Pravda was founded as a newspaper for workers in 1912; the Bolsheviks started legal publication of the newspaper in St. Petersburg on April 22, 1913. It was a time of unrest, with 400,000 workers striking on May Day 1913, and letters from common workers were encouraged and published in the papers, showing and stirring the workers' anger. The communists regarded Pravda as a successor to the socialist newspaper Iskra.

The Russian government attempted to suppress publication of the newspaper, but the Bolsheviks built up a loyal readership of over 40,000 and a network of distributors. Pravda was dependent on financial support from workers. When the paper was shut down, the Bolsheviks continued to distribute newspapers illegally.

At the end of the Russian revolution in 1917, Pravda was allowed to reopen and was selling nearly 100,000 copies daily. The offices of the newspaper were transferred to Moscow in 1918, and Pravda became an official publication, or "organ", of the Soviet Communist Party. The newspaper became the conduit for announcing official policy and policy changes. It would remain so until 1991.

On August 22, 1991, a decree by Russian President Boris Yeltsin shut down the

Communist Party and seized all of its property, including Pravda. A few weeks later, Pravda's team of journalists registered a new paper with the same name.

A few months later, the then-editor Gennady Seleznyov sold Pravda to a family of Greek entrepreneurs, the Yannikoses. The next editor-in-chief, Alexander Ilyin, handed Pravda's trademark - the Order of Lenin medals - and the new registration certificate over to the new owners.

By that time, a serious split occurred in the editorial office. Over 90% of the journalists who had been working for Pravda until 1991 quit their jobs. They established their own version of the newspaper, which was later shut under government pressure. These same journalists, in January 1999, launched Pravda Online, or Pravda.ru, the first web-based newspaper in the Russian language; English and Portuguese versions are also available.

The new Pravda newspaper and Pravda.ru are not related in any way, although the journalists of both publications are still in touch with each other. The paper Pravda tends to analyse events from a leftist point of view, while the web-based newspaper often takes a Nationalist approach. What makes Pravda.ru so interesting is that it also publishes stories concerning UFOs, psychic powers and other paranormal topics.

To show just how far Pravda.ru has grown from its original roots, back in 1968 Pravda stated tersely that: "no UFO was ever recorded over the USSR." Actually, at that time, there had just been a major wave of UFO sightings in the skies over Russia. Indeed, according to Marina Popovich, a distinguished Soviet test pilot and scientist, at least 14,000 recorded UFO sightings in the Soviet Union from the mid-1960s until that country fell in 1991.

### The World Wide Weird

In the 21st century Pravda.ru has become an international source for paranormal investigators and for those just interested in the types of stories that other major news outlets are loathe to cover. Pravda.ru cooperates with dozens of Russian and foreign mass media, both electronic and press media, and their correspondents work in many countries of the world, for example in the United States, Great Britain, Brazil, Portugal, and China.

One recent story carried in Pravda.ru is an article detailing a Russian scientist that claims to have deciphered a message from aliens. Extraterrestrial beings visited planet Earth and left their calendar and a message to the human civilization, Russian mathematician Vladimir Pakhomov believes. "I did not find the message from aliens by accident. I was searching for it, because I was sure that they had visited our planet," the scientist said.

The article continues by suggesting that a lot of specialists have paid attention to several coincidences, which are found in many different legends and tales, particularly with those that tell of extraterrestrial beings visiting Earth in ancient times.

Explorer and traveler, Erich von Daeniken, wrote that it was extremely difficult for humans to find aliens' traces on Earth. The global ocean takes two-thirds of the planet's surface, ice covers the planet on its poles, and vast deserts and immense woods occupy the rest of the planet's territory. The explorer supposed that aliens, if they had ever landed on Earth, would of course have to think, what kind of a message they could leave on the planet so that it could be saved through thousands of ages.

Scientist Vladimir Pakhomov believes that aliens probably decided to leave their calendar on the planet. Egyptian pharaohs, for example, were taking a rather strange oath when they were acceding to the throne: they promised not to make even slightest changes in the calendar.

A lot of ancient manuscripts tell of the god of wisdom that was known under two names - Thoth and Hermes. Legends say that the god wrote and hid certain "books" before he returned to heaven. Legends say that the god did not want humans to find and read the books, for the human race did not deserve such an honor.

Pakhomov said that he was shocked with the matrix of the eternal calendar, which was found on the walls of the Sophia Cathedral in Kiev, Ukraine. The matrix makes it possible to determine the calendar structure of any year. For example, you can easily find out the day of your birthday in a hundred years with the help of this eternal calendar. The scientist used the calendar of the Sophia Cathedral as the starting point to decipher ancient cryptograms.

## A Real Interest in the Paranormal

Critics of Pravda.ru often site its inclusion of paranormal and UFO articles to show just how far the paper has fallen from their halcyon days as the official mouthpiece of the Soviet Union. This of course was to be expected as the communists took a dim view of anything dealing with UFOs, the paranormal, religion, and everything else they regarded as dangerous superstitions.

However, the Russians, like many others across the globe, are fascinated by these bizarre stories, and many now publicly admit to believing in UFOs, ghosts, and a wide range of other paranormal phenomena. It was not that long ago that such admission in the Soviet Union would have led to an official investigation and probable internment in a government mental institution.

In fact, Pravda.ru is fairly restrained in the types of unusual stories that they do publish. Other papers and magazines that have emerged in Russia since the fall of the Soviet Union are more akin to the sensationalistic supermarket tabloids found in Western countries. Headlines such as: "UFOs Brought AIDs to Earth", and, "Boy Claims to be

From Mars", can now be found in magazine stands and shops all over Eastern Europe.

Recently, Pravda.ru Editor-In-Chief, Vadim Gorshenin, defended his decision to include news reports about unusual phenomenon, saying that it was a disservice to the readers to leave out such stories just because a few skeptics voice their disapproval.

"At one time," Gorshenin said, "people did not believe that stones could fall from the sky. We now know that this is a scientific fact. So just because something like UFOs and ESP does not fit current scientific beliefs, does not mean that they are not real. We have a duty to report the news as it happens, not to censor it just because it seems too fantastic."

Other international websites are now taking Pravda.ru's example by including stories of UFOs, ghosts, and other paranormal activities. Indiadaily.com is a good example of a news website devoted mostly to politics and current events in India. However, the editors have also made room for such stories as, "UFOs May Have Secret Base on Border with China", and "UFOs Use Electromagnetic Stealth to Remain Invisible".

With the development of the Internet, news now flows almost freely around the world. Despite some countries attempts to stifle the distribution of free news, information is getting to people in ways never before seen in the civilized world. This also means that news reports about strange and unusual phenomena is also being carried far and wide as more news outlets realize that their readers are interested in such stories. Hopefully, this will lead to more in-depth investigations and a wider acceptance of just how little we really know about the world we live in. That is why it is the duty of the media to accurately report on unusual events and phenomena, and not try to cover them up just because they seem a little too weird from the current accepted norm.

### INNER EARTH TALES: THE SHAVER MYSTERY

### A Probing Interview With Inner Earth Expert Tim Swartz

**QUESTION:** Many of our readers I would suspect may know a bit about the Shaver Mystery — that the overriding theme has to do with Richard Shaver's contact with two groups of beings who live beneath the Earth's surface. The dero being the "bad guys" who are out to cause chaos on the surface through their ancient mind controlling rays, and the tero who are a smaller group of "good guys" who attempt as much as they can to keep the demented dero in check. Can you bring those uninformed readers up to speed as to how Shaver first learned of the existence of the subterranean realm, and how his findings were first made public?

**SWARTZ:** Richard Sharpe Shaver first came to the public's attention in 1943 when Ray Palmer, editor of Amazing Stories, a popular pulp science fiction magazine, rescued a letter from the wastebasket. The letter was from Shaver, and in it he wrote about his discovery of an ancient language that was the roots of all modern languages.

Shaver wrote: "Sirs, Am sending this in hope you will insert it in an issue to keep from dying with me. It would arouse a lot of discussion. Am sending you the language so that some time you can have it looked at by some one in the college or a friend who is a student of antique times. The language seems to me to be definite proof of the Atlantean legend. A great number of our English words have come down intact as romantic -ro man tic-'science of man patterning by control,' Trocadero - t ro see a dero- 'good one see a bad one'- applied now together. It is an immensely important find, suggesting the god legends have a base in some wiser race than modern man; but to understand it takes a good head as it contains multi-thoughts like many puns on the same subject. It is too deep for ordinary man - who thinks it is a mistake. A little study reveals ancient words in English occurring many times. It should be saved and placed in wise hands. I can't, will you? It really has an immense significance, and will perhaps put me right in your thoughts again if you will really understand this. I need a little encouragement."

Along with the letter was a document called ***"The Mantong Alphabet."*** Palmer, who was always looking for a good story, ran Shaver's letter in the December 1943 issue of Amazing Stories.

The results were amazing, readers sent Palmer hundreds of letters asking for more information about Richard Shaver and the source for his incredible alphabet. Palmer wrote back to Shaver asking if he had anything else and Shaver responded with a 10,000-word letter entitled ***"A Warning For Man."*** Palmer rewrote it into a 31,000 word story and renamed it ***"I Remember Lemuria!"***

This was the beginning of what was to be called ***"The Shaver Mystery."*** In a nutshell, Shaver said that the Earth was populated in ancient times by a race of beings he called the Elder Race. These beings came from the stars and inhabited our prehistoric planet, building great cities and enjoying fantastic scientific feats.

However, due to natural events, the sun became active, producing for the first time sunspots and solar flares. In turn this sent streams of radioactive particles shooting throughout the solar system and making the Earth uninhabitable. The Elder Race left the planet in search of a new home, but some remained behind, deciding to live underwater, or in natural caves and constructed caverns. They took with them the amazing machines and technologies in order to help repair the physical damage caused by the suns radiations.

Unfortunately, as the years went by, this once mighty race slowly mutated into creatures that Shaver called the "Abandondero" or dero for short. Due to the effects of radiation, and the abuse of the healing and stimulation rays of their machines, the dero were deformed and by our terms, insane. They delight in using their technology to harass and torture people who live on the surface. Shaver believed that the old tales of underground demons and devils were race memories of encounters with the deros.

Shaver also claimed that along with the deros were men, also descendants of the Elder race, he called the teros. This group had managed to prevent the damaging effects of mutation and remain human. The teros, even though smaller in number than the dero, were dedicated to fighting the dero and assisting those on the surface who had the unfortunate luck to come under the attentions of the dero.

**QUESTION:** What is there that is so fascinating with the Shaver Mystery that it has endured since the 1940s...I mean that is a long time for a supernatural yarn, for lack of a better term, to stay entrenched in the minds of readers?

**SWARTZ:** The Shaver Mystery resonates with people for some reason. It strikes right at the heart of our deepest childhood fears of the dark and the unspeakable things that could be waiting within. As well, the idea is appealing that the bad things that happen to us, the accidents, crime, madness, could be from an outside malevolent force. It is an answer to the age-old question "why do bad things happen to good people?" Shaver says it is all the fault of the dero with their ray machines hidden deep within the Earth.

I think the Shaver Mystery is also attractive because it takes some responsibility away from us. After all if the bad things that happen are all caused by the dero, well then, possibly we are not quite the evil sinners that we had been brought up to believe. Maybe our world would not be so bad off if it weren't for the dero. This new book hopefully will find a new following of people, who, like Shaver, suspect that there is more going on behind the scenes then we are privileged to know. Sort of an underworld conspiracy.

**QUESTION:** I know that you have been working on editing a collection of material based on Shaver's writings — some of which has never been published before. What's it called and what's new in it that would interest our readers? And furthermore how does Shavers interest in what he called the "rock books" come into play?

**SWARTZ:** The book is called ***"Richard Shaver-Reality of the Inner Earth."*** In the early 1970's Timothy Green Beckley published a small newsletter called SEARCHLIGHT. In it, Shaver wrote a small column answering questions submitted by readers. By this time, Shaver was obsessed with what he called Rock Books. These were rocks that when thinly sliced and polished, apparently showed what Shaver believed were pictures of a race of beings that once lived on Earth in pre-deluge times. Shaver sent Beckley boxes of these rocks, much to the chagrin of his mother who consigned them to their back yard. But with these rocks, Shaver also sent Beckley several long article/stories detailing an experience Shaver had with the rock books and the dero who desperately wanted one.

Beckley, unfortunately, didn't have the space in his newsletter to run long articles, and he filed them away for possible future use. It was not until last year, when a burst water pipe in his apartment forced him to move files he hadn't looked at for years. There he rediscovered Shavers articles and approached me with the opportunity to read through and edit them into a book. One article titled: "The Rock Books Reveal Their Secrets" is an amazing piece that harks back to Shavers golden days of writing in the 1940's. He reveals that he was able to communicate with a stored memory hidden within a rock book and was shown how the rock books actually were to be used and the amazing history of the Elder race and what happened to the Earth, and us, after the old ones left.

He continues in another chapter that his rock book was desired by a dero, who, with the help of his machines, was able to zero in on Shaver and kidnap him to the nearby caves. Shavers writing in these articles is amazing and at times, highly erotic. Much of his earlier, published stories were censored with the erotic elements cut out. However, I felt that the eroticism was an important part of the story and it would have been a disservice to remove it. This is an aspect of Shavers writings that has never been published before and I think that many people will be surprised on how good a writer Shaver really was.

**QUESTION:** I think a lot of people are confused when they hear about the Shaver Mystery for the first time — they tend to lump it in with the so-called Hollow Earth Mystery...that there are openings at the North and South Pole that Admiral Byrd was supposed to have entered. Is it possible to separate the two ideas?

**SWARTZ:** The Hollow Earth Mystery involves the theory that our planet is completely hollow inside and that a small internal sun warms the interior allowing for abundant life. This interior world is supposed to be accessible by two huge opening at the North and South Poles. Over the years stories of great civilizations with highly developed and spiritual inhabitants have been written by those who claim to have actually entered the inside world, either physically or in the astral body.

Shaver, on the other hand, said that the planets crust was full of natural and manmade caves and caverns, but there was no completely hollow center with its own sun. And instead of spiritual gurus who were just a step away from God, Shavers inner world was filled with monsters and maniacs. It is interesting to note that a majority of the myths and legends that have been handed down to us state that the underworld is a terrible place to be feared and avoided. Most ancient societies believed that the underworld was the abode of the dead, a misty, twilight world where everyone, good and evil, ended up upon death.

**QUESTION:** In support of Shaver aren't there all sorts of accounts from miners and cave explorers that detail encounters with strange and terrifying beings?

**SWARTZ:** One reason that readers found Shavers works so fascinating were the strange experiences that miners and cave explorers had when they were underground.

# CONSPIRACY JOURNAL READER: THE DEEPEST, DAARKEST SECRETS

Many people had family members who were underground miners, and stories of weird noises, unexplained lights, and awful creatures seen deep within the mines were whispered about and widely believed.

Readers also mailed in letters detailing their own personal experiences with the caves. One such letter, which I have included in the book, was from Margaret Rogers. Ms. Rogers letter was published in the January 1947 issue of Amazing Stories under the title: ***"I Have Been to the Caves."***

Rogers account details her visit to a subterranean kingdom beneath the region near Itaccihuatl, Mexico.

"As in a dream, I saw the whole mass of greenery slide to one side, to reveal a large opening. By now, it seemed that anything could happen, but for some reason, I had no fear. He might have been leading me to my death in some sadistic rite, yet I followed him boldly in.

"The door closed. For a split second darkness reigned, then the cave was filled with a strange bluish light. I walked as through I were ordered to do so, to a large block of black marble along one wall of the cave, and lay down upon it.

"I dreamed (or did I?), that many giant figures were all about me. That a soft lavender light was shining down on me, but I felt such heavenly relief from pain that I had had for so long, that I floated away again. I seemed to realize that I was on a table and that I was entirely unclothed, and one of those giant figures was bending over me. When at last I really and truly awakened, I looked around me in wonder, unable to understand where I was and how I came there. For a moment I was sure I had died; that room was so large and all the furniture in it had been made for a giant to use."

These letters, I believe, is one of the main reasons that the Shaver Mystery has endured. People are more inclined to share their own strange experiences when they read of others who have been through the same thing.

This is something that readers will not want to miss with this book. If Shaver had been alone with his theories and stories, then he probably would have sank into oblivion a long time ago. But, what makes Shavers stories so compelling is the fact that a lot of people have said: "Hey, the same thing has happened to me!" So I hope that Richard Shaver-Reality of the Inner Earth will help bring new sheep into the fold, so to speak, people who have never heard of Shaver, yet have had experiences just like what is written in this incredible book.

**QUESTION:** It has been written that Shaver and his publisher, Ray Palmer, were responsible for starting the flying saucer mystery. What was Shaver's take on UFOs and interplanetary craft?

**SWARTZ:** Palmer was often called the guy who invented flying saucers...something that he enjoyed repeating whenever the opportunity arose.

Shaver wrote about disc-shaped spacecraft years before the modern UFO era began in 1949. He speculated that the flying saucers could be 3D illusions beamed by the dero to distract and confound people. He also acknowledged that the Elder race flew in spacecraft that resembled modern UFOs. Shaver considered that some of these ancient spaceships were still operational and used by the tero, or even the dero. Moreover, he said that there could be alien races visiting the planet and conducting trade of some kind with the underground races.

Shaver worried that the extraterrestrials dealing with the dero were either under the control of the dero, or inclined to exploiting us surface people for their own end. Either way, Shaver did not think that the UFOs were here to benefit mankind.

A large section in Richard Shaver-Reality of the Inner Earth details the incredible space arks that the Elder race built in order to leave Earth. It is interesting to note how similar these ships are too modern day reports of UFOs and flying saucers.

**QUESTION:** Some say Shaver's experiences were astral - that they took place during out of body travel. He always maintained it was the real McCoy; that his trips to the caves were in the physical body. What evidence do we have for either theory?

**SWARTZ:** Shaver hated that theory. All along he insisted that the dero were real, physical creatures, not spirits on a lower astral plane. Shaver was very much a realist and did not give much credence to ghosts, spirits, or even God. Shaver didn't believe in a spirit world or astral planes of existence. He felt that the universe was big enough without other levels of spiritual realities.

Shaver always maintained that his experiences with the dero and other underground races were real, not a dream or vision. He said that if the deros kidnapped you, tortured and killed you, you would be dead, that's it.

Others have speculated that Shaver had mistaken his psychic visions for reality; that the dero do exist, but on a different plane of reality. For centuries, mystics have said that there are lower planes of existence that are populated by evil beings and bizarre creatures that bear a striking resemblance to Shavers deros.

If you were to be in these other realities, it would be as real and seemingly physical as our own world. Shaver may have mentally, or with his astral self, visited one of these spirit worlds and thought that it was our own reality.

However, to the end, Shaver said that the dero and the caves in which they dwelt, were real. I suppose it will be up to the readers to decide for themselves about the Shaver Mystery. It has been a long time since anyone has had the opportunity to read some of Shavers old stories. Some were definitely works of fiction that used his central thesis of an underground world and ancient races from the stars. But the fact remains that Shaver truly believed in his experiences and that many, many others were also convinced in its reality.

Richard Shaver-Reality of the Inner Earth really adds a new chapter to the strange life of Richard S. Shaver, and I highly recommend that everyone buy's a copy for themselves in order to better understand the beginnings of the Shaver Mystery, and the final revelations that were made shortly before he passed away. It will give you a completely new insight on this world and the strange, unknown world buried beneath our feet.


## WHAT THE BLEEP IS IT ALL ABOUT ANYWAY?

### The Bizarre World Of Synchronicity And Coincidence

### By Sean Casteel

·        Two Little Birdies: A golfer watched his perfect drive collide with a ball hit by another player from the opposite direction. Astounded by the coincidence, both players met and introduced themselves—they were both called Kevin O'Brien.

·        Sisters' Grave Error: Sisters Doris Jean Hall and Sheila Wentworth both decided to drop in on each other for a surprise visit. As they were traveling in opposite directions on the rural American highway, Alabama 25, their identical jeeps collided and both were killed.

·        Where There's Muck: Barbara Hutton accidentally flushed her antique bracelet down the toilet. Months later, Barbara was in a jeweler's when a man brought in her bracelet to be valued. He had found it while working in a sewer.

The above capsule descriptions of amazing synchronistic experiences come from a book called "Beyond Coincidence" by Martin Plimmer and Brian King.

Meanwhile, Timothy Green Beckley, Mr. UFO and publisher of "The Bizarre Bazaar" and "The Conspiracy Journal," has wrangled with synchronicity more then once himself.

"Synchronicities come in all kinds of shapes and sizes," Beckley said. "Some are more impressive than others."

Beckley began the tale of one his experiences this way: He had been invited to speak at a UFO conference in Bordentown, New Jersey, hosted by Pat Marcattilio, but Beckley was unable to attend because of prior commitments. He knew that an old friend of his, well-known UFO researcher and author Antonio Huneeus, was going to the conference as a backup speaker in case some of the other presenters didn't show up.

Huneeus had recently moved from his New York apartment to somewhere in Virginia, but Beckley didn't know at that point how to reach him. Beckley remained anxious to hear how the New Jersey conference had gone.

"Anyway, I'm coming back from out of state," Beckley said, "and I arrived in Manhattan at Penn Station. I get off the train and I'm headed towards the escalator onto Seventh Avenue. And here right behind me is Antonio, wheeling a cart full of his slide projector and some of his books that he was selling at the conference. So I say, 'Antonio, how have you been?' And he said, 'Oh, I'm just coming back from Pat Marcattilio's.'

"So here we are in Manhattan, in Penn Station," Beckley continued. "There are probably 5000 people walking through Penn Station at any one time. What are your chances of running into Antonio Huneeus? It's impossible to calculate. It certainly is beyond chance. But it doesn't have any particular, specific meaning, except that Antonio knows this happens to me an awful lot. We had a nice little chat for fifteen minutes, and then we ended our conversation and we both went on our merry way."

A more recent experience of Beckley's also involved a train, this time the express train to Trenton, New Jersey. Beckley was on his way to his offices in New Brunswick, which was his custom. This time however, he was informed by the ticket taker that he had boarded the train at the one time of day that it didn't stop in New Brunswick. So he disembarked and was waiting on the platform to catch the right train to get him to his destination.

"And lo and behold," Beckley said, "I see somebody pointing at me and shouting my name. 'Tim, Tim, is that you?' I looked at this person and I didn't immediately recognize him. And he says, 'Oh, you don't recognize me? I'm your friend Damian from Colorado.'

"Well, now, Damian I see maybe twice a year when I go out to the slopes. He's one of the local characters there. He's a bartender and a very good chef. Every year when I go out there I run into him, but that's not so unusual because Aspen is a relatively small community."

Damian told Beckley that he had recently moved back to the East Coast and was on his way to visit his parents in New Jersey. Damian was staying at the New Yorker Hotel in Manhattan, where—"coincidentally"—Beckley had promoted weekly seminars over a decade ago.

"So we had both gotten off at the same stop and had a chance encounter there on the platform," Beckley said, "and then we got back on the train and chatted for the next hour on the way to our destination. So, again, this isn't shocking, but what are the chances of meeting somebody on the train platform like that, 3000 miles away from where you would normally run into him? I asked the question, but I don't have a particular answer."

Twenty-five years ago, Beckley made his first trip to San Francisco to lecture at a conference. After delivering his talk on Saturday night, he was on his way to the airport the next morning when he and the event's organizers decided to stop for brunch since they had a couple of hours to kill.

"We just picked a place at random. It looked like a nice little café of sorts in a quaint area near Cobble Hill. We went in and I had a Bloody Mary and we sat down to chat. During the course of the conversation I happened to mention that I wish I had had a little more time or a little bit more foresight because I would have liked to track down an old friend of mine, Allan Vaughn."

Vaughn, who had moved from New York to the City By The Bay, was at the time the publisher of a prestigious periodical called "Psychic Magazine," long since out of business. Vaughn and Beckley had shared a few laughs together in New York over the years and Vaughn had even taught some classes at Beckley's School of Occult Arts and Sciences.

"But I didn't have his phone number in San Francisco," Beckley lamented. "Anyway, the conference organizers nodded and said they knew who he was. Two minutes later, as we carried on our conversation, who walks through the door but Alan Vaughn. Now, what is the chance of somebody in a city where you've never been before, and you haven't spoken to this person in maybe about three years, walking into a place? So of course, 'Alan, is that you?'"

Vaughn sat down with Beckley and ordered a beer. Beckley asked Vaughn what he was working on currently.

"And he said, 'Well, just by coincidence, I happen to be doing a book on coincidence. I'm going to use this incident in the book.' So if you happen to find a copy of the book, *'Incredible Coincidences: The Baffling World of Synchronicity'* (Ballantine Books), this particular episode of my running into Allan is one of the case studies in the book. He devotes a couple of paragraphs to it. So to me that is a little bit beyond just coincidence."

There is still another story of synchronicity in Beckley's grab bag of experiences.

"This one has played on my mind for many, many years," he said, "because the person involved became a friend of mine."

The story begins in the mid-1970s when Beckley was a frequent guest on the Long John Nebel all-night talk show, heard in fifteen states from midnight to five a.m.

"Long before Art Bell," Beckley said, "there was Long John. I was on the program one night discussing haunted houses in and around the metropolitan area. The next day I get a call from a young lady who tells me that she'd heard the program and was very impressed."

The young woman was a columnist for "New York Magazine," and her interest in the paranormal had prompted her to call Beckley for more information for a future column on local haunted houses.

"Finally, after fifteen or twenty minutes," Beckley recalled, "I said, Terry—her name was Terry—I said, 'Why don't I send you some literature in the mail instead of discussing this further. It might be easier to proceed that way.'"

Beckley asked for Terry's address.

"And she gives me the address," he went on, "and I said to her, 'That can't possibly be, because that's my address.'"

It turns out that Terry and Beckley lived in the same building! Terry had an office two floors above Beckley's, and after that first conversation, they would often meet one another coming and going. Terry was a good friend of the Dali Lama, and had written a book about him, long before the Tibetan exile received the kind of publicity he currently enjoys. But tragically, Terry suffered a brain tumor and died while in her late thirties.

Still, the story of the synchronicities linked to Terry was not over.

"One night recently," Beckley said, "I'm downtown at my favorite watering hole in Greenwich Village and I'm having a few drinks with a lady friend. There's a gentleman next to us who, after a bit of chitchat, offers to buy us a round of drinks. He seemed to be very jubilant about something. I asked him why he seemed to be having such a really good time, and he remarked, 'Oh, this afternoon I just signed a four figure deal with a major publisher to put out my book on human relationships.'"

Beckley told the man that he was a publisher himself, though he would never have been able to offer him anything like four figures. The man asked Beckley what type of books he published. Beckley answered that he specialized in New Age subject matter, like Nostradamus and the Eastern mystic T. Lobsang Rampa, who wrote extensively about Tibet. The man responded by saying that he had visited Tibet and India in the 1970s, and had even met the Dali Lama. At which point, Beckley mentioned his friendship with Terry.

"He just turned absolutely white," Beckley remembered. "He said, 'You won't believe this, but she was the love of my life. I had a terrible crush on her, and I was very sad when I heard that she had passed away.'

"Now there's a bit of synchronicity with a double-edged blade, I would say. This one has continued over thirty years. What it proves, I have absolutely no idea. My thought about it at the time, of course after having a couple of shots of Absolut, was that maybe it was an attempt by Terry to communicate with him through me. I have had some mediumistic experiences over the years."

Beckley said he gets a real kick out of yet another story, one that took place in an after hours bar in New York.

"They were quite popular at the time," he said, "and kind of quasi-illegal. There were certain places you could go if the guy at the door knew you and you could get in and have a couple of drinks until six or seven a.m. Some of them even had illegal gambling going on, which I wasn't too interested in, because even though I have a lot of coincidences and synchronicities, I couldn't win a dollar or a dime gambling. So it was something that I always stayed away from. If anything, just the opposite happens to me if I try to play cards or roulette."

Unlucky at cards, lucky in a synchronistic pickup. The after hours bar was indeed raided that night. Beckley happened to be standing next to a cute blonde as the lights went on and the customers were ordered to leave. The two struck up a conversation, and the woman asked Beckley what he did for a living. He answered that he was a publisher of New Age and metaphysical books.

"And she says, 'Oh, I'm very interested in that.' And I said to myself, 'Yeah, yeah, maybe it's just a subtle come-on or everybody always just says something like that just to be saying it.' But I said, 'Oh, really, who are your favorite authors?' I figured maybe she would say Edgar Cayce or something like that."

The woman completely astonished Beckley by saying her favorite authors were Brad and Sherry Steiger.

"Brad and Sherry Steiger!" Beckley exclaimed to the petit gal. "What a coincidence! It turns out that I publish books by Brad and Sherry, and I'm having dinner with them tomorrow. Would you like to come have dinner with us?"

The attractive blonde happily obliged, and she and Beckley had what he called "a minor fling" for a while. He still sees her occasionally at New Age conferences in the area.

"So that's certainly another synchronicity," he said. "That might have been one with a little bit of a positive touch to it."

In spite of so many bewildering incidents of synchronicity and coincidence, Beckely refuses to draw any conclusions about what it all means.

"People have different ideas," he said. "People say to me, 'Oh, it proves that there's a Creator.' Well, I don't necessarily see how it proves that there's a Creator. Now [veteran paranormal researcher and author] John Keel has speculated that there might be some kind of giant computer in the sky that's responsible for all the synchronicity, like someone is shuffling the deck and things just happen at random. In his book, 'Disneyland of the Gods,' Keel talks about how this giant computer is kind of playful, almost like a cosmic trickster of sorts.

"I guess one of the most baffling cases in this regard is the similarities between the Lincoln and Kennedy assassinations," Beckley said. "For example, Lincoln was shot in Ford's Theater, and Kennedy was killed while riding in a convertible manufactured by Ford. Both men were succeeded by Vice-Presidents called Johnson, who were Southern Democrats and former senators. You can speculate on this as much as you want, but I don't know what the answer is."

Beckley continued in that vein.

"Maybe we don't even know what coincidence is," he said. "Coincidence seems to be something that's farfetched and beyond random, but when it happens, it takes it out of that category. How do you really gauge what coincidence is or what your chances are of meeting somebody say on a train platform or in a bar whose favorite authors are Brad and Sherry Steiger and you're having dinner with them tomorrow? It seems millions to one, but if it happens, it narrows it down.

"Yet other people, when you mention this to them, they look at you like you're nuts. They've never had anything like that happen to them, and they think you've done too much LSD. On the other hand, I've had people sit here and tell me their synchronicities and I say to myself, 'Jeez, these people think they're the center of the universe or something, that the world revolves around them and that it's so important.' To me, it's only important in most cases to the person it happens to.

So what the bleep is the meaning of all this anyway?

"I don't see where you have any final, definitive proof of anything in the universe, to be honest with you. Even the speed of light may be subject to change. If nothing else, at least synchronicity is a topic for intriguing conversation and something to make you think. In today's age of computers and things that are mathematically and politically correct, that isn't easy to do anymore."

[Visit Sean Casteel's UFO Journalist Website at www.seancasteel.com]


## THE LOST JOURNALS

## NIKOLA TESLA – HIS UNPUBLICIZED, TOP-SECRET, PROJECTS

by

Timothy Green Beckley

Unlike in years past, the public has a hunger and a fascination with Nikola Tesla. They eat up anything they can find on his life and his work. It was not always that way believe me friend.

Up until maybe ten years ago you would be hard pressed to find material dealing with this genius who invented everything from the X ray to alternating current. Tesla was a man possessed, determined to make the world a better place to live. He was convinced that the earth and the universe could – and would – provide us with an abundance of power to make our lives less stressful.

Tesla summed it up best when in 1891 he stated: "We are whirling through endless space, with an inconceivable speed, all around us everything is spinning, everything is moving, everywhere there is energy. There must be some way of availing ourselves of this energy more directly.

"Then, with the light from the medium, with the power derived from it, with every form of energy obtained without effort, from the store forever inexhaustible, humanity will advance with giant strides. The mere contemplation of these magnificent possibilities expands our minds, strengthens our hopes and fills our hearts with supreme delight."

About a decade ago, the publisher of this little zine began corresponding with Emmy Award winner and journalist Tim Swartz about putting together some obscure papers we had come across dealing with the "lost works" of Tesla, material that had never been put into the public arena, and for a good part had actually been kept under sealed wraps by our own government, and which seemingly might have even fallen into the hands of an elitist cabal made up of millionaire industrialists and their wall street henchmen who were hell bent in keeping these little known ideas of Tesla to themselves so they could not be marketed by those who saw options outside of big oil and greedy corporations.

The end result of this preliminary research was the first edition of what quickly became a hot selling book. ***THE LOST JOURNALS OF NIKOLA TESLA*** has gone into six printings and has remained as a high ranking item on Amazon.com since it was first released. In fact, since its initial release date it has been the number one book on Tesla available for purchase on the web.

## TIME TRAVEL, ALTERNATIVE ENERGY AND NAZI FLYING DISCS

But that was nearly ten years ago, and we have come a bit further in our thinking here at the Conspiracy Journal, so much so that we have decided to pull the first edition of Lost Journals from the shelves and replace it with an updated version that includes approximately fifty more pages, that are presented in a larger (easier to read) format.

The new edition pulls no punches. It gets deeply into Tesla's involvement with time travel, alternative energy and the likelihood that the Nazi's appropriated some of Nikola's work to build craft that look a lot like, and could be responsible, for at least some of the reports of circular "flying saucer" style craft.

Tim Swartz discovered, for example, that Tesla had come across the secrets of time travel the hard way:

Tesla's brush with time travel came in March 1895. A reporter for the New York Herald wrote on March 13 that he came across the inventor in a small café, looking shaken after being hit by 3.5 million volts, "I am afraid," said Tesla, "that you won't find me a pleasant companion tonight. The fact is I was almost killed today. The spark jumped three feet through the air and struck me here on the right shoulder. If my assistant had not turned off the current instantly I might have been the end of me."

Tesla, on contact with the resonating electromagnetic charge, found himself outside his time-frame reference.

He reported that he could see the immediate past - present and future, all at once. But he was paralyzed within the electromagnetic field, unable to help himself. His assistant, by turning off the current, released Tesla before any permanent damage was done.

Because of this accident, Tesla began to theorize about electricity and magnetism's power to warp, or rather change, space and time and the procedure by which man could

forcibly control this power. Near the end of his life, Tesla was fascinated with the idea of light as both a particle and a wave, a fundamental proposition already incorporated into quantum physics.

This field of inquiry led to the idea of creating a "wall of light" by manipulating electromagnetic waves in a certain pattern. This mysterious wall of light would enable time, space, gravity and matter to be altered at will, and engendered an array of Tesla proposals that seem to leap straight out of science fiction, including anti-gravity airships, tele-portation, and time travel.

## TESLA'S DYNAMIC THEORY OF "ANTI-GRAVITY"

Swartz contends that there might have been at least one individual inside Tesla's inner sanctum that was taking Nikola's secret projects back to the SS who were long fascinated with Tesla and a possible "occult connection."

One person started up a restaurant to filter out information from the customers; another spy worked at an airline to report Allied ships crossing the ocean; others worked as delivery people so they could communicate secret messages. Without a doubt there were other undetected Nazi spy rings that were firmly entrenched, especially in large cities such as New York and Philadelphia.

The purpose of these espionage outfits was to seek out new and innovative technologies that could be sent back to benefit the Nazi war machine. There have even been some allegations that a longtime business associate of Tesla, George H. Scherff, Sr., was actually stealing Tesla's research papers to sell to the German government.

In the new edition of Lost Journals Tim Swartz presents his theory that Tesla's secret work might have been behind the Nazi's developing the Bell Craft. A device used in the experiments was known as the "Nazi Bell" device, and modern speculation by John Deering, a U.S. scientist and engineer working on current advanced projects, indicates that the German WWII research was intended to create a powerful propulsion effect by engineering applications of Tesla's equations.

Within Tesla's and Einstein's theories, there is a link between the 'vector magnetic potential' and torsion. Put simply, the effects of curved space-time (resulting from a massive body, like the Earth) can be locally offset by creating 'Torsion'.

Thus, using Tesla's gravitational theory, electromagnetic interactions are harnessed to induce torsion, which in turn can then null out gravitation. The result is a sort of counteraction to gravity or 'antigravity' field.

Another Conspiracy Journal favorite by Commander X in a still-available work titled, *NIKOLA TESLA, FREE ENERGY AND THE WHITE DOVE,* rolls out impressive evidence that a lot of Tesla's ideas were "appropriated" by the secret government working in collaboration with former Nazi engineers bought to the U.S. under Project Paper Clip, ending up as part of the top secret research undertaken inside Area 51's underground laboratories (see *UNDERGROUND ALIEN BASES* for more supportive evidence of this claim).

### MORE REVELATIONS

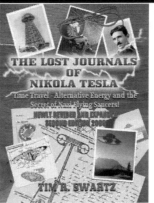
There are many more revelations to be found in the updated version of *LOST JOURNALS* that we do not have room to elaborate on within these meager pages. Sufficient to say that we want to keep the high lights to ourselves in hopes that your appetite

will be sufficient to cast a coin for this updated work that hopefully will fry the brains of at least a few dastardly corporate bigwigs and their NWO fear-mongering allies.

## THE MADNESS OF SHERLOCK HOLMES:

## FIRST GHOST BUSTER AND PSYCHIC DETECTIVE

by

Timothy Green Beckley

It's been approximately 80 years since the passing of Sir Arthur Conan Doyle, creator of the Sherlock Holmes series, and yet his works are as well known now as they were when he was sitting behind his desk at the fictional 221B Baker Street in London. There are dozens of literary collections available to an ever present legion of literary fans and movie goers who never get tired of seeing the detective's presence on the big screen accompanied by the bumbling Dr Watson.

I probably read my first Sherlock Holmes excerpt at around the age of twelve in a magazine called *Boys Life* which was a popular monthly aimed at an early teen audience. What young man wouldn't thrill at the saga of a detective who used "modern" science to unravel the most puzzling crimes. Basil Rathbone starred in the first Holmes motion picture. Hound of the Baskervilles was a perfect Conan Doyle endeavor to usher in a continual flow of movies starting in 1939 and continuing right up to last year's Hollywood blockbuster starring Robert Downey Jr. Even more recent is the straight to DVD Sherlock Holmes film distributed by Asylum which features monsters and robots attacking London.

To "celebrate" this renewed interest in the master sleuth Inner Light/Global Communications is pleased to announce a trilogy of Doyle's works dealing with his fanatical interest in psychic phenomenon, life after death, clairvoyance and spiritualism in particular.

These three books (plus a DVD from Reality Entertainment called *The Madness Of Sherlock Holmes*) are advertised herein for the first time and are: *The Charismatic Martyred Life Of Joan of Arc* (received through Leon Denis a French medium and translated by Doyle), *Revealing The Psychic Secrets Of Houdini*, and *The Paranormal World Of Sherlock Holmes* in which prolific author Tim Swartz opens Doyle's confidential paranormal files for the first time in more than half a century.

As a prelude to the release of these three titles — all of which should be available at the time this issue arrives in your mail box— we interviewed Tim Swartz on Doyle. Swartz is the editor of the on line version of www.ConspiracyJournal.com and author of such works as *Admiral Byrds Journey Beyond The Poles, Tele-portation From Star Trek To Tesla, Lost Journals of Nikola Tesla*. He can also be heard on numerous talk shows such as Coast To Coast AM, The ParaCast, and Captain Jack's Badlands.

BECKLEY: Wouldn't you say that the character of Sherlock Holmes is known around the world by almost everyone? It must be amazing how many millions of copies Sir Arthur Conan Doyle's books have sold internationally. Yet his belief in the supernatural and in the possibility of life after death probably is not known by most readers. How did Doyle become so fixated on such matters?

SWARTZ: I would say that Sherlock Holmes is probably the most recognized detective in the world. You would have to have been living in a cave all of your life to never have heard of the exploits of Holmes and Dr. Watson.

However, as famous as Sherlock Holmes is, the name of the man who conceived the fictional detective of Baker Street is not so widely known. During his lifetime (he was born in 1859 and died in 1930), Arthur Conan Doyle was undoubtedly one of the most celebrated writers of his time. Yet, Doyle often felt that the popularity of Sherlock Holmes prevented him from finding an audience for his other interests, especially his fascination with Spiritualism and the possibilities of life after death.

Most biographers place Doyle's interests in the esoteric sometime shortly after the end of World War One. However, Doyle had been schooled at home during his childhood where his mother regaled him with the traditional myths and legends of fairies, banshees, ghosts and other creatures of the night. This later developed into a fascination with the mystical aspects of Catholicism. Later, as with a lot of teenagers, Doyle began to doubt his faith during his years at the Jesuit schools.

BECKLEY: What was some of the paranormal phenomenon he investigated?

SWARTZ: Doyle first looked into the phenomenon called table tipping which had become popular in the late 1880s. Table tipping had been widely used during séances as an alleged means of communicating with the spirits, but it had also become fashionable to hold parties where the guests would table tip for the fun of it. After participating with several groups where tables were made to move around the room and tap out messages, Doyle came to the conclusion that the phenomenon involved the involuntary movements of the participants and was not connected to spirits.

Another case that involved Doyle was in 1894 after Doyle had joined the British Society for Psychical Research. In 1894 Colonel Elmore asked the organization to investigate strangesounds coming from his home in Dorset. At night Elmore, his wife and adult daughter could hear chains being dragged across a wooden floor and moaning that sounded like a soul in torment. The family dog refused to enter certain parts of the home and most of Elmore's staff had left.

Conan Doyle, Dr. Sydney Scott and Frank Podmore were sent to investigate the possible haunting. They spent several evenings in the home and one night the investigators were disturbed by a "fearsome uproar." Upon investigating, they found nothing out of place or any cause for the noise. Doyle left the Dorset home unsure if it was actually haunted. Later, the body of a child was discovered buried in the garden and Doyle became convinced that he really had wit-

nessed ghostly phenomena. You could say that Sir Conan Doyle was one of the first ghost hunters.

QUESTION: Do you think there has been an attempt by his family and estate to sweep such an interest under the rug so to speak?

SWARTZ: While Doyle was alive his family had no problems with his interest in the paranormal. Some of his friends and acquaintances, however, thought that he had succumbed to dementia. Many modern biographies about Sir Conan Doyle refer to his fascination with the paranormal as if it were some type of moral failure. But say for instance that his investigations had been more along the lines of the mystical, sacramental, or Eucharistic aspects of Catholicism; I doubt that there would have been any controversy or questioning of his intellectual capabilities.

BECKLEY: Are there any references to the occult in any of his Sherlock Holmes books? You know sort of hidden away?

SWARTZ: It's funny, but Sir Conan Doyle kept Sherlock Holmes very down to earth and dismissive about anything that had to do with the occult. When presented with a case involving possible vampirism in his 1924 story, The Adventure of the Sussex Vampire, the detective jokes: "This agency stands flat-footed upon the ground, and there it must remain. The world is big enough for us. No ghosts need apply."

Doyle, while very much a believer in the supernatural, took a very scientific and analytical attitude towards his ghostly investigations. He was intellectually honest, if he suspected a medium was fraudulent, he took the necessary steps to scientifically ascertain how trickery was involved and to publicly reveal his findings when his investigation was complete.

QUESTION: I know you investigated the fairy photos that captivated Doyle so much. What is the story behind these pictures and didn't one of the young women involved later recant her story; but the second witness still held fast to her belief that she really did see and photograph these wee beings?

SWARTZ: The December 1920 issue of *Strand* magazine ran an article by Sir Conan Doyle about several allegedly authentic photographs of fairies that had been taken by two young girls, Elsie Wright and her cousin Frances Griffiths, near the village of Cottingley. One plate taken by Elsie in the summer of 1917, when she was 16, captured her 10-year-old cousin seated on the grass surrounded by four dancing fairies. Another, taken a few months later, showed Elsie coaxing a tiny gnome onto her lap.

After consulting with some photographic experts, Doyle became convinced that the photos were real. With the help of Theosophist Edward Gardner, Doyle provided Elsie and Frances with another camera and twenty fresh photographic plates. The girls produced three more fairy photographs and the story was later included in Doyle's 1922 book *The Coming of the Fairies*.

Many years later, both Frances and Elsie admitted that they had faked the photos using paper cut-outs and hatpins. However, Frances continued to insist that they had indeed seen fairies in the woods but they had been unable to photograph them. The very last photograph they took, which Conan Doyle called "The Fairy Bower," was real Frances said.

BECKLEY: A contemporary of Doyle's was Harry Houdini the famed magician and escape artist. I am putting together a book on their personal conflict over spiritualism and medium-ship. Why do you think Houdini was so opposed to the subject and don't we see magicians today like James Randi following in Houdini's footsteps? What causes such a negative reaction among magicians?

SWARTZ: Sir Conan Doyle and Harry Houdini actually became good friends after Doyle and his wife met Houdini in 1920 after one of his performances at the Hippodrome in Brighton, England. It has been said that Houdini was not a disbeliever in life after death, but unlike Doyle who was a steadfast believer, he was convinced that a majority of spirit mediums were using magician stage tricks in all their séances.

I think that people such as Houdini become skeptics of spirit communication and mediums because they can see how these types of demonstrations can be easily done using well known magician techniques. It is one thing to put on a magic show and awe the audience with a performance that everyone knows are tricks performed by a very talented artist. It is another thing all together for someone to use the very same tricks and claim that they are real and being done by your dead Grandma Sue. I think that Houdini was morally outraged that innocent people were being duped out of their money and given what he considered false hope that they were in contact with their deceased loved ones.

On the other hand, I think that other magicians have jumped onto this bandwagon as the arch-skeptic not for any moral reason, but instead to bolster their otherwise non-existent careers and to make a few bucks.

I believe, as did Sir Conan Doyle, that just because you can replicate a strange phenomenon using magician tricks that does not necessarily mean that every instance of that phenomenon is produced through fakery.

We can credit Sir Conan Doyle for being one of the first men to use science and deductive thinking to try and better understand those mysteries that seem to defy rational understanding.

No doubt that Sherlock Holmes would have been proud.


## MIDNIGHT MADNESS IN THE DESERT

### EASY RIDERS, SPACEMEN AND CHARLES MANSON'S FAMILY

by Timothy Green Beckley

Let's be blunt. I'll never forget the scene with Peter Fonda and Jack Nicholson in Easy Rider as they hunker down around a crackling camp fire and begin to speak of things extraterrestrial.

"'That was a UFO beamin' back at ya! Me and Eric Heisman was down in Mexico about two weeks ago and we'd seen 40 of 'em flying in formation. They… they… they've got bases all over the world now, you know. They've been coming here ever since 1946 when the scientists first started bouncing radar beams off of the moon. And they have been living and working among us in vast quantities ever since. The government knows all about 'em'"

On the other hand, I'm the kind of person who likes to coast into a nice motel or resort and partake of the grandeur the way God and my American Express card intended.  It's easy to spend a bundle being a paranormal researcher in the desert in search of some of the strangest and most peculiar sites and experiences you are likely ever to partake of. It is awfully tempting to say the hell with it and set up base camp in Palm Springs and do day trips from there. But if you're serious and want to really get down with nature and hobnob with the unseen it's possible to be brave and tempt the elements.

The first time I ventured into the Mojave I was awestruck. The stars were like a brilliant prism and appeared so close that they reminded me of dazzling strings of golf balls. To my eyes the universe looked as if it had just exploded. It was like someone had taken body paint and smeared it around and around over the intense blackness of space. The result being that when I peered heavenward I felt like I was surrounded – almost smothered – by a multitude of splashing colors that were both mesmerizing and awe-inspiring.

As a youngster, I listened to the all night broadcasts of radio talk show host Long John Nebel as he described the incredible tales of the men and women known as UFO Contactees who claimed to have met beings from outer space. There was George Adamski, who had a telepathic conversation with Orthon, and George Van Tassel, who was told to build a "time machine" of sorts, as well as Orfeo Angelucci and Truman Bethrum.

And while their contacts varied somewhat they all had one thing in common. They transpired in a very sacred place – the California desert.

But there are more than UFOs and Spacemen that we can talk about.

There are many visionaries to confront. There are many mysteries to deal with. Above all else there is the strange and unknown to meet head on and even the most terrifying elements of humanity to avoid.

I've journeyed to and spent considerable time in Death Valley and driven across the great Mojave and have always been amazed by the stories I have heard along the way. After years of gathering anecdotes and amassing both a library of rare books and yellowing newspaper clippings and corresponding with others who were willing to add to my reminiscences, I decided to put together a work that would serve as the ultimate road trip across this most mysterious and haunted part of America.

In her introduction to the desert Diane Tessman offers starry visions of unidenti-fied starships over-head and alien encounters under the watchful eyes of monster rock formations. She reminds us there are many stories of Coyote Man and the dreaded Chupacabra, and  that that mysticism is expressed even in songs like The Eagles' "Ho-tel California," where you can check out anytime you want but you can never leave.

Then we have reprinted for the first time the entire text of George Van Tassel's I Rode In A Flying Saucer, the vintage 1950s classic by the late inventor and contactee whose "time machine" still stands in the desert as a memorial to times past when the

Space Brothers willingly passed on incredible technologies to those willing to listen and believe.

There are unsettling tales of abandoned mines, strange creatures, eerie spook lights, phantom stagecoaches, a haunted opera house in the middle of Death Valley and the petrifying story of a 12 foot levitating clown as related by one of the members of our Shaver Mystery group.

Perhaps most chilling of all are the revelations made about Charles Manson's belief that an entrance to the inner or hollow earth exists in the desert. Adam Gorightly contributes an entire chapter about Manson's thoughts on what has become known as the Devil's Hole, located in the northwest corner of Death Valley. Says Gorightly, the famous alternative writer, "The Devil's Hole, which is fenced off, is a forbidding pit of water, murky and ominous. In 1965, two young men went scuba diving at night into The Devil's Hole and were never seen again. Afterwards, rescue divers recovered only a flashlight, which suggested to many that The Devil's Hole led to a huge underground cavern.

"On one occasion, Charlie Manson sat crossed-legged before Devil's Hole for three straight days, meditating with all his metaphysical might, contemplating the ultimate meaning of this bottomless well. After the third day, it dawned on Charlie that the water in the Devil's Hole was the door – or blocking mechanism – preventing entrance into the Underworld.

"All Charlie had to do was find a way to suck the water out, and – lo and behold! – the secret passageway would be revealed."

### A FASCINATING MINI INTERVIEW WITH REGAN LEE

Regan Lee is a UFO witness who writes on her own UFO related sightings and experiences in several internet blogs including www.orangeorb.net  She also writes about the paranormal in general, including cryptozoological and esoteric subjects. One of her specialties is the contactee movement and the Golden Age of Flying Saucers. In her writing, she has continually expressed a deep spiritual sensitivity about the desert. Recently, we hooked up with her for a brief, but fascinating, interview.

. . . . .

QUESTION: The latest book of ours that you've contributed to is Secrets of Death Valley: Mysteries and Haunts Of The Mojave Desert. You've also done introductions to the two books by one of the few female contactees from the metaphysical-New Age movement of the 1950s that was centered in Southern California. We've recently re-printed Dana Howard's Up Rainbow Hill and Over The Threshold. In fact, we only just heard from Dana Howard's grand niece.

Most of Dana's experiences took place in the barren regions of California. Why the mystical attraction of the desert as far as the contactees go? Why do we hear so much about Southern California and Joshua Tree in particular where Van Tassel had his UFO contacts?

REGAN LEE: The desert acts as a stage for mystical experiences on all kinds of levels: the esoteric, the existentialist, the spiritual. It's vast, open, empty, away from crowds, exposed to sand and sky. Open to whatever may come. And if UFOs and enti-ties from elsewhere want to do their thing covertly, or only show themselves to a few people, what better place than the desert? The desert is both scary and beautiful, full of contrasts. I'm guessing that a mystical pull was felt by some of these contactees, like Howard and Van Tassel. The desert was out of the way. Some of us are loners and just like to be elsewhere. Many find it beautiful; it allows for introspection.

Not all of the contactees did their thing in the desert, but the desert is a common motif for UFO/contactee experiences. Also, the military presence in the desert can't be ignored; many of the contactees were in the military and stationed in the deserts in California or other parts of the Southwest.

BECKLEY: Can you summarize what Howard's grandniece told us?

REGAN LEE: Her grandniece, in a couple of e-mails, shared with me that she had fond memories of her great aunt Dana. Many in the family apparently considered her kind of a kook, or eccentric, but her grandniece and mom thought Dana, or "Aunt Tillie" as they called her, was pretty neat and interesting. She described how Dana, who, as her grandniece put it, was considered a "nut case" by many, would come to visit in a black sedan. Howard had an interesting life; she was a ghost writer for Walter Winchell, married to a film producer, was in a movie or two – this according to her grandniece. Dana Howard loved the desert and lived in a commune. Dana died of Parkinson's in the early 1970s in California.

BECKLEY: So what's your thinking – are we really being visited from space or is it all a spiritual, mystical experience?

REGAN LEE: I think we really are being visited by aliens from space in a very literal, nuts and bolts way. I also think there are all kinds of spiritual mystical experi-ences that are often a part of the alien experience. Not to mistake advanced technology for advanced spirituality, however. I don't believe that simply because a species of alien is more advanced than we are technology-wise, that it means they're also nicer, more ethical or moral than us, and more together spiritually. Some of them may be, some of them may not be.

There are also a lot of other things, including what we'd call "alien," going on around us that aren't literal ETs from outer space, but something else, and that includes a mysti-

cal or spiritual aspect. I think we have to be careful of deciding all this is just one thing: one kind of alien, from one kind of place, and with one kind of intent. It's a lot of different things happening at once, and some are playing us – for example, tweaking our mystical bent and making us believe that's what it's about – and some aren't, and everything in between.

Among the many UFO experiences I've had, I wouldn't say they were anything mystical or spiritual, and yet I've also had a whole lifetime of spiritual experiences. And I'd say, yeah, I'm a spiritual New Agey kind of dame. For example, there is something about crop circles that has moved me very profoundly – and that's just being on the edges of the phenomena. I've never seen a crop circle in person. I've had lots of out-of-body, telepathic experiences, some involving entities and a Sasquatch once, but I don't know if that's exactly spiritual, more like communicating on another channel.

BECKLEY: Where are we – and you! – headed?

REGAN LEE: I have no idea. It'd be outrageously arrogant for me to say where "we're" headed, and I barely know where I'm headed. I'll give it a go however. If you mean "where are we headed" in UFO and related research, I think we're becoming more integrated as to accepting all kinds of theories to help understand UFOs, which is a very good thing. Things are not only changing in the "real" world, all the physical, global changes as well as systems and infrastruc-tures, but in the esoteric realm as well. Look at the shameful David Jacobs mess, and the MUFON disruptions . . . things are really churning. I think these two worlds – the veils between them – are even now becoming thinner, and they're going to, I wouldn't say "collide," but meet, or merge, in some ways.

As for me personally, I'm on the journey. It's the process itself which is the answer, not any one big final answer to a single UFO question. I'm not sure what the question is, and anyway, I'm just paranoid enough to believe that any answer given is sure to be partially intentionally deceitful and laden with disinformation. Not in any fundamental religious satanic way, but in a Trickster, psy ops "who the hell knows?" kind of way.

---

## UFOS IN THE LAKE OF FIRE

by Timothy Green Beckley

It's UFOlogy's dirty little secret. It's something that is better left swept under the rug. Stanton Friedman doesn't talk about it. Stephen Bassett most assuredly would keep the subject at arm's length. The late Richard Hall would have deleted you from his address book. And Steven Greer would never consider it part of his ongoing Disclosure program.

To coin ourselves a catch-all phrase that brings together all the negative aspects of the subject, I prefer to call it the *DARK SIDE OF UFOLOGY!*

It would appear – at least at first glance – that only those who consider themselves Christian fundamentalists have a rigorous drum to beat on behalf of the subject matter we are considering – that at least some UFOs can rightfully be tied in with Demonic phenomenon. It would seem to be almost an exclusive element of their zealous faith based belief system that contends anything remotely occult or supernatural—and that would definitely include UFOs — has a staunch ally in the devil and his minions. Christian apologist, Dave Hunt has stated, "the same people that run UFOs are the same people that run haunted houses."

Indeed, it has become more apparent even by those who for decades held dearly to a deep belief that UFOs must be interplanetary in nature, that there is a paranormal nature to this enigma that cannot easily be set aside. Several top notch researchers — such as the late Dr J. Allen Hynek's former associates Ted Phillips and Philip Imbrogno — have come to realize that we are NOT dealing solely with physical craft from outer space occupied by off-world astronauts coming to warn us that we might possibly annihilate ourselves either ecologically or in the course of our warlike nature.

More and more emphasis needs to be placed on the spiritual, occult and paranormal nature of the phenomenon seen in our skies and invading our homes and personal boundaries. It's not all "sweetness and light," kiddies. The truth is that there are a host of negative elements associated with UFO encounters. Some of the entities involved could very well be leading us down the primrose path. You can believe, and the evidence clearly is undisputable, that there are cosmic criminals in our midst who have successfully managed to possess and control the minds of utterly frightened participants who had no warning that they were to be caught up inside a nightmarish web of confusion and chaos.

There are numerous aspects of this dark side of UFOs that we examine closely in our just published book *Round Trip To Hell In A Flying Saucer: UFO Parasites, Alien Soul Suckers, Invaders From Demonic Realms.*

+ The connection between UFOs, demons, and possibly Satan himself.

+ The fascination for and the link between Nazism, occultism and post World War Two German-made flying saucers.

+ The ghastly exercise of blood draining and human sacrifice throughout antiquity and their relationship to animal and human mutilations and blood letting in modern times, which align closely to the appearance of UFOs in specific theaters of operation on our planet.

+ The weird claims of John Lear that aliens are coming here to kidnap humans and not return them. That people are being used for food, and how "they" are performing sadistic experimentations upon us, and are attempting to suck out our souls and place them in "containers" for their own perverted use.

+ The Islamic belief in the normally invisible elementals identified in the Koran as the Jinn and how these malevolent spirits are able to misrepresent themselves by camouflaging their true identity and traveling around at fantastic speeds.

+ Shape shifters who can turn into human looking beings, animals, orbs, fireballs or manifest themselves even as physical "hardware" to fool us into believing they are mechanical devices.

+ The casting of magical spells, occult rituals and the ability to conjure up spirits and beings often mistaken for UFOnauts but more closely aligned with the elemental kingdom.

## UFO REPORTS ARE STRIKINGLY SIMILAR TO

## DEMONIC POSSESSION AND PSYCHIC PHENOMENON

I don't think a week went by when my mail box (not the one that is part of your Windows or Mac, but the one that stands, or used to stand, at the curb) wasn't jammed with a couple of large manila envelopes from William C. Lamb.

To be honest, our "correspondence" was mostly one sided. To me, Lamb was a bit of a nutter (British for crackpot). He claimed to have images of heaven and even God's throne that astronomers had photographed through high powered telescopes that exist on the edge of the galaxy. To him the ole man in the clouds was as real as you or I and the Lord's Kingdom was a place you could actually see if you had a powerful enough telescope. Kind of crazy, right? Well, the story doesn't end there.

According to Lamb, he knew all about God and Satan firsthand because he had seen Beelzebub with his own eyes. No! It wasn't part of a near-death or out-of-body experience, but a component of a UFO landing.

Lamb had been out hunting in a snowstorm around four or five AM in February 1922, as he explained, when he heard a buzzing sound and saw this huge spherical craft hovering over a nearby field. It was so large and brilliant to his eyes that it blocked out the stars and he found himself mesmerized by its sudden appearance. He watched in awe as a partition opened on the side of the craft and a gigantic creature with wings flew to the ground and landed in the snow. The being was somewhere between seven and eight feet tall and appeared demonic in its facial features and physical form. Lamb said he hid behind a tree and watched as it tracked through the snow, its hooves – yes, I said hooves – melting down to the tundra as it went along. Eventually it came to a sturdy wire fence and managed to just walk through it, burning through the mesh and leaving it looking red hot.

At the time I had every reason to believe Lamb was totally delusional. It was obvious that he saw everything through the eyes of orthodox religion. So much so that when he was approached by this ghoulish figure he managed to get it to fly off, using the name of Jesus and commanding it to depart.

The case is known to others besides me. Apparently a letter or two from W.C. was also preserved in the Air Force's Project Blue Book files because astute researcher Jacques Vallee mentions it in his book Passport to Magonia. Vallee has long expressed his opinions that, "UFOs are real but they are not physical. They are messengers of deception," and that, ". . .the UFOs beings of today belong to the same class of manifestation as the (occult) entities that were described in centuries past."

As far back as the 1960s – perhaps earlier! — certain fractions in the U.S. government and military acknowledged the occult nature of what were still referred to in many circles as flying saucers. In 1969 the U.S. Printing Office issued a 400-page publication entitled UFOs And Related Subjects, a huge compendium of over 1000 books, literature and testimonies of UFO contactees. The document was compiled for the Air Force and the Library of Congress by Lynn Catoe who in its Introduction matter-of-factly states: "A large part of the available UFO literature is closely linked with mysticism and the metaphysical. It deals with subjects like mental telepathy, automatic writing and invisible entities as well as phenomenon like poltergeist manifestations and possession. Many of the UFO reports now being published in the popular press recount alleged incidents that are strikingly similar to demonic possession and psychic phenomenon that have long been known to theologians and parapsychologists." Others with a decisively Christian bent have expressed concern that "the aliens often encourage illicit sex, and other ungodly things." One abductee Calvin Parker told me that aliens had caused the AIDS virus and that, "I think they are demons. I feel like it's evil. It could come from another world, but I think it's kind of interdimensional in this one," Parker explained to a reporter.

Ann Druffel has been active in investigating UFOs since 1957 when she joined the National Investigations Committee on Unidentified Flying Objects. The affable author of *Tujunga Canyon Contacts* (co-authored by D. Scott Rogo) and *How To Defend Yourself Against Alien Abduction* is a no nonsense type of individual. She has paid her dues and everyone respects her opinions, even when she unhesitantly states : "The entities who pose as 'extraterrestrials' are not what they say they are. Rather, they are apparently unwholesome entities who have deceived and interacted with humans since the dawn of history. Be they mythic, 'real,' 'spiritual,' interdimensional or from a 'hidden world' which somehow exists in or alongside our own earth plane, I cannot say, since proof still eludes us. I do know for certain, however, that interfering, shape shifting, 'otherworldly' entities have been described by every major culture (and many smaller cultures) on the face of the earth down through the millennia, and that these older cultures developed means to fend them off or, at the very least, recognized them for what they were."

## UNCLE SAM'S DEMONIC THINK TANK

Nick Redfern is one of the few investigative journalists who is almost universally respected in a field where disagreements and lingering grudges between UFOlogists are fairly common. Recently, Redfern authored a book, *Final Events: And The Secret Government Group on UFOs and the Afterlife* which just about ruined his near perfect reputation. The work details the history of a hidden think tank within the U.S. Government that believes rather than having alien origins, UFOs are really a tool of the Devil.

We sat down for a lengthy interview with Redfern to be found in *Round Trip To Hell In A Flying Saucer*. Redfern explained to me that the think tank was begun to try and exploit the mental powers of what they called "Non-Human Entities," commonly known as the Grays. "There were people in the official world," Nick says, "that wanted to see if the mind-power of the Grays could be utilized as a form of mind-weaponry by the Pentagon, and the Department of Defense; something along the lines of a next generation Remote Viewing type program." The more the Pentagon group got into the project, "the more they came to believe that the Grays were highly deceptive, and they also came to believe the Grays were actually – and quite literally – deceptive demons from Hell, who were here to deceive us about their true agenda – which was to bring people over to the dark side and prepare things for Armageddon, but to do it under the guise of a faked alien appearance," or so Redfern reveals.

"As for abductions, the think tank believes the whole alien scenario is a scam – a series of brain-induced hallucinations provoked by these entities as a means to reinforce the idea that they are aliens here to experiment on us." Furthermore, the they can seemingly, "provoke hallucinatory imagery in the mind: aliens, goblins, Bigfoot, etc. to make us believe we're seeing something physical and external."

The group came to conclude, says Redfern, "That Earth is a farm, and that we are the cattle. . .that these entities essentially are here to harvest and feed upon the energy of our soul at death because these demonic creatures are basically energy-based, and our energy feeds and fuels them." This task is further expanded upon in our book by retired CIA "jockey" and ace pilot John Leer who has long maintained such a "peculiar" theory.

For our book *Round Trip To Hell In A Flying Saucer*, we have gathered together our own "think tank" of prominent individuals to express their opinions and to collectively publish their own findings. Included in this roster are Brad Steiger, Adam Gorightly, Kenn Thomas, Brent Raynes as well as the posthumous John Keel, author of *Trojan Horse* and *Mothman Prophecies*.

Incorporated in this large sized work is also a little known tome published in 1955 from which we adapted the overall title of our own work. Not only did Cecil Michael claim to rub shoulders with Mr Scratch, but he says he went with him straight to hell. Proclaims the flyleaf on a very rare copy: "Here is one of the most startling stories ever written! The narrator, calmly working in his auto repair shop, suddenly finds himself playing host to a pair of visitors from outer space. From that moment his entire life is changed.

"For weeks the Spacemen practice all types of weird experiments upon their bewildered friend, who is too terrified to protest. Finally, wearying of their ingenious super-games, they decide to take the poor auto mechanic on a trip to Hell. . .And, as you descend with the narrator into a modern Inferno, you will pray, with the auto mechanic who tells the story, that his visit will be a short one."

The British publication Magonia encapsulates Cecil Michael's bizarre *Round Trip To Hell In A Flying Saucer* in this manner:

"The craft went off into space, eventually arriving at a bleak red planet with a lake of fire into which coffins were cast, the dead bodies inside them then coming to life and burning in agony. He was afraid that he would be trapped there permanently, but apparently he was saved by a vision of Christ that appeared in a beam of white light, and returned to Earth. The trip seemed to have taken four days, but only four hours had passed."

Without a doubt this can be said to be our oddest contribution to the overall body of UFO and paranormal literature we have published over the last five decades. It discusses a theory that is straight out of the movie The Exorcist.

## CONSPIRACY JOURNAL READER: THE DEEPEST, DAARKEST SECRETS

To many it will be a difficult to accept concept. To others it is something that they already recognize as part of their on going faith. It is none the less a premise that needs to be explored.

ROUND TRIP TO HELL IN A FLYING SAUCER – 300 PAGE BOOK AND BONUS DVD SPECIAL – Order now and our readers will get the book 20% less than on Amazon PLUS we will include a BONUS DVD at no additional cost. This DVD contains two full length discourses on Satan's Serpents and UFOs and The Mysteries of the Pyramids. Send $22.00 + $5.00 S/H to: Timothy Beckley · Box 753 · New Brunswick, NJ 08903

## ARE ANGELS REAL? ARE THEY OUR PERSONAL "PROTECTORS?"

## WHAT IS THEIR ASSOCIATION WITH UFOS?

## NOW IT IS POSSIBLE TO LEARN HOW TO

## COMMAND ANGELS TO DO YOUR BIDDING

By Timothy Green Beckley

They are known as The Watchers. The Protectors. Heavenly Benefactors. Or simply God's Angels. And each one of us is said to have one or more personal "Guardian Angels" sent to observe, guide, and remove us from harm's way. They are invisible, but yet we are led to believe they are never far from our side. In fact, if we are to accept as factual the Scriptures, the Creator has given us the power to command Angels to do our bidding. . .and they CANNOT refuse!

Ok let me say first off – and anyone who knows me can verify this – I am not a religious person in any way, means or form. Seldom go to church. Don't watch televangelists, and haven't picked up a Bible unless it's to check out some reference to what might have been an ancient UFO sighting described in the Holy Book. I did visit the Vatican and you can find an ad for my DVD/CD set elsewhere in this issue.

Let me explain that I am not an atheist, but I am prone to wanting to examine the evidence and demand proof from scholars, not religious rhetoric. To me, some of the Good Book is just absurd. But I am interested in the supernatural and in miracles, and in visions, and the Bible is a great reference, a fabulous study of a great deal of paranormal activity. And Angels, of course, are as supernatural as you can get.

To prove that we practice "individuality" here at the Conspiracy Journal/Bizarre Bazaar, not everyone on our staff is of the same mind. Associate and the author/co-author of numerous books for Inner Light/Global Communications, California-based Sean Casteel expresses his Christianity openly. While he does not have any actual degrees in Biblical studies, he is about as well-versed on the Bible as a layman is likely to get. In addition, he has cultivated friendships with several Christian clergy and even fundamentalists. He is one of the few researchers to have a close Christian connection that he manages to relate to UFOs, though most of his writings are of a secular nature, not being one to proselytize.

Recently, Sean and I worked on a book together that has caused a certain degree of controversy, it being a topic that is a bit out of the scope of what I normally would tackle to either research or write on. Round Trip To Hell In A Flying Saucer pertains to what I call "the dark side of UFOlogy," i.e. demonic influences, blood rituals, animal and human mutilations, the Nazi tie-in, the shape shifting powers of aliens as well as the morphing of their craft, the Jinn, and a host of other horrifying, shadowy aspects that seem to go hand in hand with the sightings, encounters and abductions. Some UFO witnesses, it turns out, are literally pulled down to hell after what they have experienced. UFOlogists, for the most part not wishing to deal with the possible "Satanic influences," have avoided this area of investigation like the plague. Its UFOlogy's "dirty little secret," but one Sean and I were not willing to sweep under the rug. So, with the help of a number of other luminaries in the field such as Nick Redfern, Chris O'Brien, Allen Greenfield, Adam Gorightly, Tim Swartz, and Scott Corrales, among others, we tackled the subject head on, offering up some pretty startling and frightening conclusions as to what sinister force might be behind this phenomenon.

From the outset of our laboring to edit this material together in a comprehensive manner, Sean was concerned that we might be giving only one side of the story – that we hadn't told the entire tale. He felt that if some of the UFOs are occupied by "demons," there have to be others coming here of good will that are of a highly evolved spiritual nature. These beings, whether of a flesh and blood consistency or of a pure etheric serenity in form, are what apparently are referred to in the Bible as Angels that would be part of God's Heavenly forces.

## WAS MY LIFE SAVED BY A GUARDIAN ANGEL?

During the time I have been involved in UFO research and in publishing books on what I like to term "alternative studies," several people have asked me if I have ever had an abduction experience or feel that I am being guided to do this work since hardly anyone else can claim they have made a career since the age of 14 out of publishing such diverse, almost inspired, books and magazines, resulting in printing hundreds of titles which would probably otherwise never have seen the light of day. Well, the only missing time I can recall was in first grade when I tripped over my own two feet while playing a game of kickball in the school playground and ended up in the hospital with a loss of memory and my late sister looking down over me when I came to. I could have been lifted out of my body in some astral way then, but let's not go that far. Early on, at the age of three or four, I did have a "near death" experience of sorts which I haven't related previously and which may have involved a guardian angel or some other corporal being.

My father was raised in Kentucky, in the small town of Shelbyville, located about 30 or 35 miles from Louisville. It's the home of the king of fried chicken, Colonel Sanders .My parents met and married in Kentucky, but soon relocated back to my mom's home state of New Jersey. My mother had asthma and other allergies, which were relieved by a yearly trip to Kentucky in the family Oldsmobile. Naturally, I went along on the trip, which lasted three or four days, nestled in the back seat with my blanket and toys. One time, as the family "legend" goes, it was getting really late and there were still a few hours of driving to do. My father was at the wheel and wanted to continue right through to their destination. But it was getting increasingly foggy and my mother insisted he pull over to the side of the road right away so as not to meet any unseen traffic.

The next morning, when the sun came up and cut through the fog, it turns out the vehicle we were in was on the cusp of going over the side of a mountain cliff. If they had driven another two feet, I would not be here today to tell you this story or to be the publisher of so many works on spiritual and paranormal subjects. Of course, I can't prove it, but with all the other things that have happened in my life, there is a good possibility that angels and UFOs are related. I do believe that they are inter-dimensional beings and come from another realm. So it's quite possible that my life was actually saved by an "angelic being" of some type so that I could carry out my life's work, which might in turn benefit their overall mission. I guess it wasn't my turn to go. Someone is sort of sitting "up there," to see that we don't end up dying before our appointed time.

## GOD CREATED ANGELS TO DO OUR BIDDING

Of course it's all well and good that Angels are assisting us in our personal lives, as well as protecting the planet from Satan's ravages. Sometimes they come in the whispering of the wind, wielding their fiery swords (i.e. Sodom and Gomorrah). At other times they may enter our world using craft known to us as UFOs or flying saucers. Many of the old religious paintings show beings surrounded in light, thus the concept of Angels having halos. Adding wings was a good indication that they flew about one way or another. They were said to look just like you and me, but were always bathed in a golden aura.

One of the things most people don't fully realize is that God created Angels to do our bidding. It's not a sin to push them to help you out. But one of the primary things is that you know HOW to contact them and WHEN it is the best time.

My late friend, William Alexander Oribello, was one of the most advanced spiritists to have ever served the planet. His works, such as Candle Burning With The Psalms, God Spells and Master Book Of Spiritual Power, have provided a great deal of enlightenment and satisfaction to those who have diligently studied his study guides. Because of the continued demand for his work, we have updated and considerably expanded a previous edition of *ANGELS OF THE LORD – CALLING UPON YOUR GUARDIAN ANGEL FOR GUIDANCE AND PROTECTION.* In this rejuvenated edition, Oribello discusses not only his own ongoing relationship with Angels that started visiting him, materializing on the street and in his bedroom at an early age, but how with a few simple rituals which include burning different colored candles and knowing what is the best time of day to attempt to communicate, makes them highly receptive to our demands. Your Guardian Angel MUST assist you – he has been created by God to do so and nothing else!

***ANGELS OF THE LORD*** tells you how to make use of your own angels and so much more.

## SEAN CASTEEL SPEAKS OUT ABOUT ANGELS

But I defer to Sean Casteel to assist in putting together this edition as he is the "expert" on matters of this nature. In fact, I was inquisitive myself, so I recently conducted a mini interview with Sean on the subject of Angels to expand on my own knowledge and am hereby sharing his responses with you.

BECKLEY: When we were putting together Round Trip To Hell In A Flying Saucer you mentioned how you felt that we should provide evidence for the "other side of the coin," to tell people that not all UFOs are operated by negative beings, but that some of them harbor positive forces and angelic beings. Do you think we have completed our task with Angels Of The Lord? And why do you feel this was so essential when there have been hordes of books about angels before this one?

CASTEEL: I guess I felt that we needed to make a personal statement about angelic, righteous UFOs to sort of shine a little light into all the darkness involved in our work on Round Trip To Hell In A Flying Saucer. I freely admit that there are hordes of books that argue for angelic UFOs, but I also wanted to reaffirm my own angel karma, so to speak, so that the benevolent Watchers would know for sure where I stood on the issue.

BECKLEY: You are one of the few fulltime UFOlogists who seem to allow for bringing religious concepts into their writing. It's a subject that most researchers shy away from, with the exception of the Reverend Barry Downing and Professor G.C. Schellhorn. Why do you think this is? And what are your general feelings about UFOs that lead you to conclude that we should venture down this path, a path which is certainly outside of the boundaries of a normal scientific investigation?

CASTEEL: To answer that question is sort of a complicated undertaking. Let's just say that I had a profound conversion to Christianity shortly after I suffered a near fatal industrial accident over 30 years ago, and I've perceived the world in religious terms ever since. And even though I didn't begin studying UFOlogy until many years after that, I was always open to things like Erich Von Daniken's "Chariots of the Gods" approach to human history, that aliens were the gods of our more technological age, what the ancient Jews used to call Elohim or God in a kind of collective sense. It took a while to put everything together, but reading Whitley Strieber's "Communion" back in 1989 sort of put the last brick in place. As to why this is such a minority opinion, that's a question I don't really know how to answer. It seems to be the obvious one to me and maybe it will appear to be obvious to everyone eventually.

BECKLEY: What personal experiences have you had in the UFO arena?

CASTEEL: I sighted a pair of ships over my apartment house in 1982. They were a shiny, metallic kind of green and gold and totally silent except for a faint sound of wind as they moved through the air. But no kind of engine or propulsion sound at all. I've also got some "screen memories" of very strange moments in my life, where I do think there was a kind of telepathic contact happening. But I don't have any memories of seeing grays or Nordics face to face or anything like that.

BECKLEY: Have you had any negative experiences that would draw you closer to a Christian path in life?

CASTEEL: Yeah, like I said, I had a near fatal industrial accident and was actually baptized while I was in the hospital recuperating. I had a lot of the typical teenage angst and depression as well around that same time, so converting to Christianity was kind of a response to all that, a lifeline to another way of seeing the world.

BECKLEY: Have you had any angelic experiences? Why are you so convinced these Messengers of God really exist?

CASTEEL: I think I have angelic experiences every day. I definitely believe someone angelic is there helping me cope with day to day existence, keeping me from going around the bend with anxiety or depression or whatever. I think I can feel them sometimes correcting my thinking and keeping me straight. I can also literally feel a sense of peace and love, a truly physical sense of well-being that I believe is spiritually separate from my consciousness and is not just something my mind is conjuring up.

BECKLEY: What exactly are angels? Are they flesh and blood? What do they look like? Can we touch them? In the Bible they are said to enter homes and eat alongside of humans. Don't their wings get in the way?

CASTEEL: I think those questions are impossible to answer really. I don't think anyone truly knows whether angels are flesh and blood and can be touched like any physical creature or what they look like. I do think it's good to be hospitable, however. As the Bible says, some have entertained angels unaware.

BECKLEY: Have there been incidents where angels might have changed the course of history or at least influenced it?

CASTEEL: In Angels Of The Lord, there's a section that deals with a prophetic vision that was experienced by George Washington. Washington would pray often, with tears running down his face, asking for God to help him cope with the poor condition of his soldiers and for victory in battle. At one point, he saw a beautiful female as he sat at his table preparing a dispatch. He asked her who she was then found himself unable to speak. The figure addressed him as "Son of the Republic," then showed him a series of visions of America being settled from one coast to the other with beautiful towns and cities and defeating a vast array of enemies from throughout the world. It's a fascinating part of the book.

There's also the story of the Angels of Mons told in the book, which took place in France in August of 1914, in a famous battle of World War I. The British forces were greatly outnumbered by the Germans, and it was a terrible time of retreat and utter weariness on the part of the British. A British soldier later reported seeing a strange light over the battlefield with a shape in the center that looked like spread wings. The soldier said that all those present with him also saw the light, which they watched for forty-five minutes. A yellowish mist was seen rising up before the Germans, which revealed a tall man with yellow hair and golden armor on a white horse brandishing a sword. Instantly the Germans turned and retreated in panic and confusion. The intervention of the Angel of Mons turned the tide of battle and gave new strength to the British war effort.

BECKLEY: How are people able to communicate with their personal angel?

CASTEEL: That's a question that everyone must answer for themselves. I think the kind of communication you're talking about is different for everybody. Contact with angels comes in all kinds of forms and through all kinds of methods of communication. One simply has to be open to the possibility, to show enough faith that contact with angels can really happen in the real world. An angel will manifest in many different ways, depending on what the given situation calls for. Often an angel is there helping you before you even realize you need help at all.

**BONUS DVD WITH ORDER**

**ANGELS OF THE LORD**

**—EXPANDED EDITION—**

**FOR OUR READERS ONLY!**

Send **$24.00 + $5.00 S/H** for *ANGELS OF THE LORD – EXPANDED EDITION* and receive a Bonus DVD on Angels. Book is fully illustrated large format. Easy to read. Many rituals you can perform to call out to your own Guardian Angel for help and support.

**Order From: Timothy Beckley · Box 753 · New Brunswick, NJ 08903**

## RESEARCHER PREDICTS RETURN OF THE ANCIENT WARRIORS

By Sean Casteel

· W. Raymond Drake is little known these days, but his research into the ancient astronauts theory knows few equals. Read how the late British historian broke new ground in understanding the mysterious origins and development of humankind.

· Do you think ancient astronauts are only relevant to our past? Learn some of the connections between the gods of old and our present day UFO phenomenon.

· Prophecies from the Hopis and Incas are being fulfilled right before our eyes. How did the indigenous natives know the future?

· W. Raymond Drake's work preceded that of Erich von Daniken and Zechariah Sitchin. Own the new reprints of two of Drake's classic works and see how it all began!

One of the most popular shows on cable television these days is a weekly program on the History Channel. *"Ancient Aliens"* is partially the brainchild of the man with the wild hair: the editor of the publication *"Legendary Times,"* Giorgio Tsoukalos. He is also the U.S. representative for the writer and researcher who started it all in terms of public awareness, Erich von Daniken.

Indeed, when one hears the words "ancient astronauts" or "ancient aliens," most people think immediately of von Daniken and his breakthrough bestseller *"Chariots of the Gods?"* first published in the U.S. in 1968. While we do not seek to undervalue von Daniken's work, it is still important for the student of the ancient astronauts theory to also factor in the work of W. Raymond Drake, the late British historian who was researching and publishing on the notion that the gods of old were visitors from outer space many years before von Daniken began to make his name for work along very similar lines.

So who was W. R. Drake? For one thing, he was a disciple of Charles Fort and followed in that famed researcher's footsteps by studying in exquisite detail the writings of ancient chroniclers of the times when man had no technology of his own to speak of and so greeted the UFOs and their occupants as gods come down from heaven. In his book about the ancient Mediterranean's strange relationship with the sky people, Drake utilized over fifty writers of antiquity and scrutinized their works through a UFO "lens."

He spent many years digging through huge archives of material, looking for anomalies that could support his theories of space aliens impacting human history. As Drake himself said, "I aspired to collect as many facts as possible from ancient literature to chronicle for the past what Charles Fort has so brilliantly done for the present century."

Drake wrote a dozen books on the Space Gods phenomenon, and Global Communications has recently reprinted and re-titled two of them, adding a good deal of updated material . The new books are ***Alien Space Gods of Ancient Greece and Rome – Revelations of the Oracle of Delphi*** and ***Ancient Secrets of Mysterious America***. The contact between man and the visitors from space has left evidence of itself behind throughout the world and influenced every race and tribe on Earth, but these two new books being offered here deal specifically with, as the titles imply, the ancient civilizations of the Mediterranean region and the Americas.

But the new offerings from Global Communications provide more than just a re-printing of Drake's classic works. Publisher Timothy Green Beckley has also gathered a roster of writers to input new and updated material on the stories of the ancients as well as research that has taken place in the years since Drake's death in 1989.

In ***Alien Space Gods of Ancient Greece and Rome – Revelations of the Oracle of Delphi***, Beckley tells the story of his personal journey to see the Oracle's ancient domicile in modern day Greece. With his good friend Penny Melis, a gifted psychic, Beckley, winded but determined, climbs the treacherous path to be right there on the scene of where the Oracle inhaled her magical vapors and babbled stories of the future for her priestly attendants to translate. The question becomes, was the Oracle an instrument of the aliens in her time? Was she something we might call a *"trance channeler"* today? Is there a genuine relationship between ancient methods of prophecy and the prophets of the New Age movement? A single source of information that bridges all time and space?

In any case, that's the wide-ranging idea. We must look not only to the past to see the contact between the aliens and earlier, more primitive cultures. We must also see how that same alien contact extends into our own present times and will affect our future as well.

Which brings us to my contribution to ***Alien Space Gods of Ancient Greece and Rome***. I began my chapter by talking about W. R. Drake and his contention that the gods of antiquity were not just illusionary but were instead real flesh and blood beings who emerged from the skies and made themselves right at home, as if they owned the place, which perhaps they did. The chapter also deals with UFO cases in the Greece and Rome of the present era, the point being to illustrate the parallel relationship between the gods of antiquity and the UFO phenomena of today.

This is the primary idea that the author feels it is so urgent to bring forth, that we are not simply adrift in a sea of chaos and uncertainty but are instead standing on the cusp of a great deliverance. The ancient gods have not deserted us, but are as present and ubiquitous as ever, simply waiting their time to reveal themselves and offer us salvation.

### A GREAT TRIBULATION?

But that salvation will not come without a price. As the **Ancient Secrets Of America** book so clearly states, the indigenous peoples of the Americas knew full well that the times they are a'changing. I wrote a chapter for the book on the Americas in which I discuss the Incan word *"pachacuti"* in an interview with author Judith Bluestone Polich.

"They called the time preceding a world age shift *'pachacuti,'*" she told me. "Now, *'pacha'* means all of the physical manifestations, and *'cuti'* means to turn upside down. So a really tumultuous time, a time of overturning of time/space reality, always preceded a world shift. Sometimes that would take the form of catastrophic physical events in which the threads to the past were broken and so a new understanding of reality emerged. Other times it might be more of a psychic event, something that happened at a deeper, structural level, that caused reality to shift. So certainly we're in a time of pachacuti right now, a time of very rapid change, a change of our understanding of reality."

### AN ANCIENT SKULL

My chapter also tells the story of the *"Star Child,"* a misshapen, child-sized skull found in Mexico in the late 20th century. The skull is structured to hold more cubic centimeters of brain than a normal human skull, and has other anomalous features as well. Its current caretaker is an expert on hominoids named Lloyd Pye, and he believes the skull may be evidence of the interbreeding between aliens and human females, a phenomenon mentioned in the Bible and also in the myths of Greece and Rome and other civilizations. Pye's story is a fascinating one and dovetails neatly with the idea of the gods returning to claim what is theirs.

Another researcher, Angela Sangster, contributed a chapter on the Kachina masks worn by some Native Americans in many of their ceremonial dances. The masks are intended to pay tribute to the gods from the sky that have intervened on their people's behalf down through the ages, rescuing the hapless natives from floods, drought and famine and keeping a watchful eye over their civilization even now.

Joshua Shapiro, known as the Crystal Skull Explorer, explains how the centuries old crystal skulls found throughout Mexico and other locales south of the border are crucially important to our understanding of the ancient people and their interaction with the aliens. The skulls could not have been "carved" using the primitive tools and skills of the people there and were most likely, at least at first, given as a gift to the people by the aliens. Today, the skulls continue to emit a palpable psychic energy that is felt by "sensitives" and even, at times, the uninitiated.

# CONSPIRACY JOURNAL READER: THE DEEPEST, DAARKEST SECRETS

Publisher Beckley comments on a recent UFO sightings flap in New York City that got considerable press coverage, but the media did not mention a possible link between the sightings and the appearance of several Mayan elders who were in Manhattan visiting representative countries of the United Nations. They had journeyed from their homelands with 13 crystal skulls to focus on the phenomenon known as "2012." They declared that, while the world would not end as many doomsday seers predicted, a wave of renewed spiritual values could help move our planet into a Golden Age of Enlightenment.

These elders came with their skulls to energize the populace. Some 500 truth seekers from the local Edgar Cayce society attended a seminar the day before the mass UFO sightings and within two blocks – something the public and press remain unaware of.

And then there is contributor Brent Raynes, who talks about a personal mystical encounter he had after participating in a Native American "Sweat Lodge" ceremony. He feels he had a vision of the interconnectedness of the gods of old and our modern-era UFOs, among other things.

So that sums up the new material contained in the two W. R. Drake reprints. The thrust of the additional work is to help establish for the reader a continuum that links the ancient gods to our times in a joyful yet sober way. We are not alone, meaning we have help out there. The same gods who taught the ways of civilization to primitive man will also deliver that civilization from our inept misuse of it and our self-destructive ways. We as a race are not without hope, and whether we are rescued by a modern incarnation of the Greek god Zeus or a wrathful Jesus Christ, the end result of salvation will be the same.

In short, if you enjoy the television show *"Ancient Aliens"* and the works of von Daniken, you will want to explore these two books by W. Raymond Drake and fellow ancient astronaut authorities. Drake is a skillful writer and researcher and his exhaustively detailed examination of the alien presence in the world of ancient man knows few equals. Nothing escapes his scrutinizing eyes as he fixes his gaze upon the evidence left to our era to examine. Read Drake for the sweep of history he moves over, and read him also to find your own place in the cosmic dance of mankind through the veils of time and space.

---

Published to sell at $27 we are offering either volume for $22.00 or both for **$39.95 plus $5.00 S/H.**

**Order From: Timothy Beckley · Box 753**

**New Brunswick, NJ 08903**

**Or through Pay Pal or our 24 hour order hot line at 732 602-3407**

## A TRILOGY OF TERROR

## — WHAT BECAME OF THE MYSTERIOUS

## "NEW AGE" FIGURE KNOWN AS "MICHAEL X"?

If you have been following what is roughly known as the UFO, New Age communities you would probably have heard of the mysterious figure known as "Michael X" as he was known as one of the great avatars of the early Flying Saucer-Contactee movement of the 1950s. He spoke with great articulation and sincerity at many of the well attended outdoor conventions held annually at Giant Rock, a private landing strip just out of Joshua Tree in the hot Mojave Desert of Southern Calif. He spoke calmly and collectively about the arrival of the silvery spaceships, dubbed flying saucers, explaining how they were piloted by friendly space beings from this solar system and way beyond.

On a mission of peace and harmony, Michael hailed the arrival of the Space Brotherhood whom he believed were materializing here to offer assistance in any way possible to elevate our consciousness to a more harmonious one. Their goal? Allowing us to join the cosmic league of nations, a federation of spiritually advanced worlds who exist all around us in this and other dimensions, whether we believe it or not!

I guess you could call Michael X a guru of sorts, though he didn't head a religious cult nor was he looking to attract a fanatical following in the manner of other more self absorbent "masters" of universal wisdom. No! Michael X was an avatar in the true sense of the word – an advocate for all of humanity. So that he didn't become part of a cult of personality, Michael refused to reveal his last name but added the X after his first name as sort of a symbol that represented all of the mysteries of our world and the space and time we inhabit, even if we had not officially acknowledged the legitimacy of others hobnobbing among the stars.

If one owned a complete collection of Michael X's monographs, which I estimate number around 25 and were self published by his Futura Press from roughly 1956 through the late 60s or early 70s, one might be able to put together some incomplete biographical notes.

We know that Michael Barton was residing in Los Angeles when he found his life changed when his best friend Jim became very ill with a condition that baffled the best doctors. While meditating over his buddy's deteriorating circumstance, Michael found he was able to receive telepathic communications beamed to him from more advanced cosmic souls.

Not wanting to alienate his business clients, but desperate to get the information he had collected out to a growing number of adherents in UFO and New Age philosophy, he began to self-publish courses and monographs under the pseudonym of Michael X. His work was read and distributed widely as believers and skeptics alike instinctively took to what he had to say and recognized the importance of its content.

You see, Michael X didn't just write about lights in the sky —or about close encounters for that matter. No, Michael X got his information first hand via telepathy from his extraterrestrial "guides." And they taught him much; everything from health secrets to how the Space Brother's understanding of science, philosophy and religion, could possibly propel us forward into a New Age of reason and enlightenment.

Above all else Michael X shared what he learned from the "Venusians" — whom he said were his closest acquaintances – in a series of very concise study guides which he sold mainly at UFO and metaphysical meetings, but also advertised in publications like Fate and Ray Palmer's Flying Saucers From Outer Space magazine. In fact, truth be told, I was selling Michael X's books when I was 15. We would advertise them in our little mimeographed publications and Michael would drop ship them to our readers. He had books on cosmic telepathy, how to initiate contact with the UFOnauts, health secrets, visions at Fatima, Nazi UFO secrets and so forth. Before he vanished from the scene he sold most of his books to Gray Barker of Saucerian Press. When Barker passed I purchased all the remaining copies and had them lying around in various cubbyholes for years but now feel it is important for these monographs to be brought back into circulation.

I do not know if Michael X is still with us or not. If he is I know he will not be resentful of the fact that we have decided to compile and reissue some of his most vital writings for an entirely new generation to consume and gain knowledge from. We have already reprinted his work Flying Saucer Revelations as a bonus section in the book Vi Venus: Starchild, now obtainable directly through us, or on Amazon.com, of course.

## INSIDE INFORMATION

But, as it turns out, Michael X's career was not only involved with the sweetness and light aspects of the New Age movement, but he had stumbled upon the darker side of UFOlogy which frightened him so much that he eventually left behind the work he loved so much. This is a little known "secret" about Michael X that I don't believe has ever been presented before.

I got this information from a buddy, Dr. Frank E. Stranges author of Stranger at the Pentagon and a fairly good friend of Michael's. For years they crossed paths speaking at the same venues, mainly California-based metaphysical centers and Spiritualist churches, who were open to ideas involving extraterrestrials, doubtlessly because of their highly evolved secular appeal.

As you can see from reviewing the presentation of the material published in this compilation of Michael X's varied work, he did not rule out the negative aspects of what he was involved in; though I don't believe he ever felt his life would be placed in great jeopardy as it eventually turned out to be.

In this Trilogy Of Terror we present what might be considered to be information on the seamier side of the subjects at hand.

Here is information on Nazi UFOs, which Michael spoke about years before anyone else dared touch the theory that German scientists had stumbled upon a revolutionary form of propulsion and had constructed disc-shaped devices that they had hoped would help them win the war. There is also a warning from the space people to get our tail off the moon and never return – OR ELSE! And if you think David Icke was the first to write about reptilians roaming the earth, guess again for Michael told about the existence of a race of serpents running around inside Rainbow City as part of an inner earth contingent.

Apparently, he went TOO FAR somewhere along the line in releasing this information and "they" went out of their way to get him!

Call it the Psychic Mafia if you want, whatever, it doesn't make much difference. The threat turned out to be real and VERY DEADLY.

During one of his meditations a "voice" came to Michael and gave a specific place and time to meet for a face to face encounter with his supposed alien friends. They promised to reveal some information that had not been disclosed before that would be helpful in the dissemination of his work.

Michael was sent to an out of the way place in the Mojave Desert where they could be secluded from others who might see their landed ship and "turn them in."

At first when Michael got to the desolate spot he saw nothing so he sat in his car and waited. Suddenly he saw the glint of something in the sunlight. Thinking it was their glittering craft, Barton got out of his vehicle and began to walk in the direction of where he had seen the reflection.

All of a sudden, he felt something was just not right. He heard an inner voice telling him to get out of there RIGHT AWAY or he would be in big trouble. At the point of sliding back into his automobile he looked back over his shoulder and saw the men he was going to meet, putting down their rifle which they had been pointing in his direction. The rifle was the object that he had actually seen glittering in the sunlight.

Michael quickly realized he had every reason to be concerned – frightened might be a better term. He had his family to think of. He had second thoughts about continuing with this work, if it was going to put his and his loved ones lives in danger. And so Michael X quickly retreated from the field, never to be heard from again. A great loss for everyone – especially for humanity who could certainly gain from his teachings (be they from extraterrestrials or not).

I did manage to get Michael on the phone by using a contact number Dr. Stranges had given me. He refused to talk about what had happened, feeling it was better to leave well enough alone. But he did confirm the basic facts of the account I have just revealed, and so we should take him at his word and leave him alone and be content with reading the work he left behind for all of us to learn from.

So here are three of the most controversial works penned by Michael X during his illustrious writing and research careers. Contemplate upon this material and decide for yourself the true nature and validity of these highly controversial claims, for the outcome of our lives may very well depend upon material such as this in the end.

\* \* \* \* \*

*To order your copy of the "over sized" edition of TRILOGY OF TERROR use the order form on the back cover of this issue and include payment of 20.00 + $5.00 shipping and handling. You can of course order using our credit card hotline at 732 602-3407, or place an order through PayPal at MRUFO8@hotmail.com or on our website www.ConspiracyJournal.Com*

## UNMASKING THE "ALIENS" IN

## THE EVIL EMPIRE OF THE ETs AND ULTRA-TERRESTRIALS

By Sean Casteel

· Are the extraterrestrials here implementing plans to take control of the planet?

· Are the aliens offering solutions to mankind's problems as a kind of Trojan horse in order to get their foot in the door so they can lead us to a totalitarian form of world government?

· Do the ultra-terrestrials utilize religion – and fundamentalism in particular – to influence and even control the current program of terrorism?

· Will mankind one day be ruled over by hybrid humans/aliens whose superior mental powers will completely subjugate us?

· Have we secretly achieved a new military technology that may one day provide us with effective weapons to use against an alien invasion?

\* \* \* \* \*

Is the human race at the so-called "mercy" of hostile, even monstrous aliens? For the late Dr. Karla Turner, it was always impossible to turn her alien abduction experiences into a "blissful" New Age blessing. Unlike the many who took the experience to be a form of contact with angels or benevolent entities of some kind, Turner always adamantly hammered home her belief that alien contact was a negative, frightening, even heartbreaking burden that was to be resisted and fought with every ounce of a person's strength. When she died of breast cancer in 1996, it was openly speculated that she had been "silenced" by her abductors for her outspoken beliefs in their fundamental evil, though we cannot know if that is true.

As part of an innovative "Conspiracy Reader" series, Tim Beckley has just packaged the rather shocking, "*Evil Empire of the ETs and the Ultra-Terrestrials*" that offers not only a reprint of Turner's seminal work "Into The Fringe," a manuscript based on the private journals she kept in 1988 and 1989, but also presents the more recent efforts of other researchers that make the case for interpreting alien abduction as a fiendishly painful trip through an alien-controlled hell. Overall, it is an easy-to- comprehend 284 page — large size — volume that is divided into several sections, each one being authored by a different "celebrity" UFO researcher.

In the overture to her contribution, Turner gives us a short synopsis of the cluster of people she will be writing about, which includes her husband, her son, her son's girlfriend and her son's male roommate, as well as other friends and researchers she would come to know along the way.

"We discovered that we were victims," Turner writes, "of abductions by some alien force. We learned that this force, this alien presence had, in fact, been part of our lives for many years. And through sharing our experiences, and seeking answers and help from others who had also encountered these beings, we learned to survive with our sanity intact and our perspective on life immeasurably expanded."

Many of the experiences Turner writes about are common among abductees. But one aspect of abduction that even the hardiest believer in alien benevolence has trouble dealing with is the sexual procedures frequently performed during an alien encounter.

For instance, Turner writes about a man named "Fred" (a pseudonym) who recalls under hypnosis a horrifying sexual experience involving a half human/half animal creature.

"I feel like they are doing something to me with the animal," Fred begins. "They are doing something with me, my blood, my sperm, and my genes. They are injecting my fluids into this animal. I think it's stupid, and I don't like it. Why are they doing this?"

His facial expression becomes disturbed.

"Seems like the animal is part human, part animal," Fred continues. "Like a small child around two years old. The one animal that appears to be part human seems to be real hairy."

Fred begins to feel angry, watching as the aliens inject fluids into the apparently female animal. He next starts to shake all over, in "wrenching spasms" that continued for several minutes, which are then followed by his sobbing and moaning in distress.

After a while, he recovers his composure and returns to telling his story. He now remembers seeing gray aliens levitating the small human/animal, who is spread-eagled on her back.

"There is one now," Fred goes on, "that is sticking a needle device up her groin or vaginal area. It has hooves, like a cow."

Fred realizes that he is naked and strapped down, unable to move.

"Seems like there is a nude woman," he says. "She's been opened up and has a vertical incision from the top of her chest to straight down to her groin area. They have moved her close to me. The one that had my stuff in the tube is going over to her. He's putting his hand inside her. His hand entered through the chest opening and was directed down towards the reproductive area. It looks like he's got a long, tube-like instrument going in through her vagina."

Next, a gray alien takes a lighted object and pulls the woman's skin together, sealing it up as if there was never a cut there at all. Fred restates his belief that his sperm, blood, etc. had been inserted into the both the half animal/half human creature and the human female. After some frightening moments in which the aliens insert a long, thin rod into both his eyeball and his navel, Fred is brought out of hypnosis, still upset and affirming his statements that he had seen the typical gray aliens throughout the experience.

The aforementioned roommate of Turner's son, called by the pseudonym "James," also had a harrowing sexual encounter.

"I saw a beautiful blond woman facing me," James said. "She was really pretty and looked totally human. And she was acting sort of sexy and alluring to me. She held out her arms like she wanted to hug me, so I went to her. I thought she was going to kiss me, but when we got really close together, it all changed. She wasn't pretty anymore, and she damn sure didn't look human. It was ugly, whatever it was."

The female figure looked "terrible, real dark and bumpy, like there were warts all over the body. And slimy."

Seeing the creature's transformation into something so ugly frightened James. The creature shoved something down his throat, after which his memory cuts off. He awakened the next morning to a sore throat and a bitter taste in his mouth, "like bile." He also discovered three parallel scratches on his neck, which served to indicate the experience hadn't been a dream.

Turner's son, called by the pseudonym "David," told her that he awoke one night in his bed feeling "as if he were oscillating violently, as if his body were about to explode or disintegrate into its atomic particles.

"It felt really scary," David said, "like if that sensation went on much longer, I was literally going to come apart. I was just getting ready to scream, I was so scared, and then the sensation suddenly stopped."

Along with Turner's *"Into The Fringe,"* the new book *"Evil Empire of the ETs and the Ultra-Terrestrials"* also includes an opening chapter by Timothy Green Beckley called "Strange Brew." Beckley tells the nightmarish stories of several couples who encountered ships and aliens while driving the freeway that doggedly pursued the hapless motorists for many miles. In one case, husband and wife Bob and Jackie Blair told their story to a newspaper reporter in Sauk Centre, Minnesota.

"They had been experiencing unexplainable phenomena for three days," the newspaper report said, "for 900 miles across three states, and when they stopped in Sauk Centre, Minnesota, hardly anyone believed them."

The pursuit had begun in Montana when what the Blairs at first took to be stars in the night sky turned out to be nine small ships and one large one. Things turned hostile quickly when the couple's car was shot with needle-like shavings of silver metal that penetrated the couple's windshield. The shavings ruined the truck's new paint job and when Jackie touched them they caused her fingers to break out in blisters; Bob had a similar blister on his wrist. The reporter says that their fingers glowed from the unknown substance they had touched and Bob exclaimed, "We might be dying right now! We don't know what it is. We have to get to a doctor!"

Beckley's chapter also deals with a terrifying highway encounter that happened to a young woman named Mickie and her girlfriend, an experience so blatantly bizarre that Beckley compared the story to an LSD trip. At one point in the women's drive across the country, with the UFOs in hot pursuit, a monster "dog" appeared in their backseat complete with glowing red eyes. Beckley believes this adds considerable weight to the ultra-terrestrial concept, meaning that other realities are merging with our own in many close encounter cases, placing the abnormalities outside the realm of wandering spaceships and alien occupants into a totally different conceptual dimension.

My contribution, "The Shadowy Universe of Alien Thought Control," deals with such unsettling possibilities as the mental co-opting of world leaders in government, religion and economics and the open hostility of the alien presence. In an interview I did with researcher and political activist Michael Brownlee, he argues quite convincingly that if anyone else were to abduct members of our citizenry by the millions or over-fly and disable our nuclear missile sites, we would regard it as an act of war and respond accordingly.

Why is it we give the aliens a free pass in those terms? One answer may be that we are humiliatingly outgunned and outmanned, and the authorities simply can't go public with a situation they can neither control nor influence. However, efforts like the Star Wars Space Defense program, begun under President Ronald Reagan, seem to be a step in the right direction, Brownlee said, and he knows personally people in the defense industry who are continuing to work to develop adequate technology to fight back against the aliens' superior weaponry.

Writer, editor and Emmy Award-winning producer Tim Swartz also contributes a chapter to "*Evil Empire of the ETs and the Ultra-Terrestrials.*" Swartz points out that the meetings between beautiful-looking Nordic blondes and the early contactees cut against the grain of the alien-related popular culture and Cold War paranoia of the 1950s. With potential atomic warfare between the USA and the USSR casting a dark cloud over the era, combined with science fiction movies about hostile aliens such as "War of the Worlds" and "Invasion of the Body Snatchers," the benevolent Nordics seem out of place and too good to be true.

Which they were, according to Swartz, who provides several case histories of negative UFO contact from that same timeframe. In one case, which took place in Caracas, Venezuela, in 1954, two truck drivers found their way blocked by a glowing disc-shaped object about ten feet in diameter and hovering about six feet above the street. They next encountered a hairy dwarf whose yellow, catlike eyes glowed in the headlights of their truck. The creature began to claw at one of the truck drivers with webbed hands, and when the driver fought back with a knife, the blade glanced off the being's shoulder as if the creature were made of steel. After the encounter, a doctor determined that both men were in a state of shock and that neither of them had been drinking. Swartz also writes about similar stories from throughout the world that bolster the arguments for declaring the UFO presence to be a hostile one.

"*Evil Empire of the ETs and the Ultra-Terrestrials*" concludes with a chapter by Brad and Sherry Steiger, distinguished authors and longtime veterans of UFO and paranormal research, who open their files to relate some further bizarre contact episodes with a wicked ET force that does literal and irreparable harm to its human victims.

In one story, which took place in 1970, a 40-year-old, healthy farmer near Sao Paulo, Brazil, was stunned and knocked to the ground by a mysterious beam of light from the sky. In tremendous pain, he managed to make his way to the home of his sister.

While the farmer showed no evidence of burns, within a matter of hours the once robust man began to deteriorate right before the eyes of his startled friends and family. Although the man did not complain of pain at any point, his "insides began to show, and

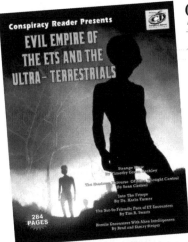
the flesh started to look as though it had been cooked for many hours in boiling water. The flesh began to come away from the bones, falling in lumps from his jaws, his chest, his arms, his hands, his fingers. Soon every part of him had reached a state of deterioration beyond imagination. His teeth and his bones stood revealed, utterly bare of flesh. His nose and ears fell off."

Six hours after being struck by the terrible beam of light, the farmer died. He was unable to reach a hospital before he was reduced to a grotesque skeleton, and he passed away attempting to communicate details of his awful experience.

This has been a brief overview of the many frightening stories and episodes of contact provided in *"Evil Empire of the ETs and the Ultra-Terrestrials."* As the reader can see, a lot of the material included here is not for the squeamish, yet one should face the ET threat as bravely as possible and hope that the courage of mere mortals is enough to sustain us in this strange warping of reality as we know it.

[If you enjoyed this article, visit Sean Casteel's "UFO Journalist" website at www.seancasteel.com to read more of his work and to purchase his books.]

**LEGACY OF THE SKY PEOPLE:**

**WAS NOAH'S ARK A**

**STRANGE VEHICLE FROM MARS?**

By Sean Casteel

Timothy Green Beckley just keeps those hits coming! Like a favorite Golden Oldies radio station, the old days are never really gone, and new shades of meaning continue to accrue.

Beckley's latest blast from the past is a greatly expanded update of Brinsley Le Poer Trench's "The Sky People," one of the earliest books to emerge on what is now the familiar concept of Ancient Astronauts. Most people nowadays consider Erich von Daniken and the late Zechariah Stichen to be the headliners for this ancient aliens show, but Trench, an Englishman who was also the 8th Earl of Clancarty and thus a member of the House of Lords in the British Parliament, was there ahead of both those distinguished gentlemen with his groundbreaking "The Sky People" from the early 1960s.

The story of Brinsley Le Poer Trench is close to Beckley's heart. Beckley began to correspond with Trench in the 1960s when Beckley was just starting out as a UFO journalist and publisher. The two flying saucer enthusiasts exchanged their respective publications (*Flying Saucer Review* published in the UK and Beckley's *Interplanetary News Service Report* in the U.S.) and shared a warm correspondence for many years. In the 1970s, Trench invited Beckley to speak before a special committee on UFOs at the House of Lords, and Beckley made the trip to London without hesitation. Over forty years later, Beckley still speaks fondly of the late Earl of Clancarty, who died in 1995.

It should be noted that Beckley's *Bizarre Bazaar/Conspiracy Journal* publishing "empire" has not shied away from publishing works of great historical value on the arrival of interstellar beings throughout antiquity. He has previously published works of the great Sir Walter R. Drake (i.e. *Alien Space Gods of Ancient Greece and Rome/ Ancient Secrets of Mysterious America*) as well as the controversial George Hunt Williamson (*Other Tongues Other Flesh/Ancient Secrets of the Andes and the Golden Sun Disc*).

But Beckley hasn't merely repackaged Trench's book. He has also added new material from some of the best writers in Ufology with their personal studies of ancient astronauts theory. For example, Nick Redfern, one of the top researchers in the paranormal today, contributes a longish chapter to the new book in which he discusses the Biblical story of Noah's Ark.

Everyone is familiar with the story, taken from the Book of Genesis. But are you aware that the story – a great, world-destroying flood from which God spared only a handful of righteous mortals and two of every kind of beast – is also an integral part of other religious traditions, such as the Sumerian, the Babylonian, and the ancient Hindus? Redfern explains how the story of a human being instructed to build a ship to shelter a remnant of mankind from a looming world cataclysm is one of the most universal of religious myths, spanning the globe with its timeless tale of good triumphing over evil.

But Redfern's examination of the Ark story doesn't end there. Legend has it that Noah's Ark came to rest on Turkey's Mount Ararat. Redfern tells the intriguing story of how in 1949, a U.S. Air Force flight crew photographed an anomalous structure protruding from the ice and snow of Mount Ararat and started a decades-long effort by the military and intelligence communities to understand what the mysterious object actually is.

Working from declassified files obtained through the Freedom of Information Act, Redfern recounts how the anomalous object was thought to be something metallic, not the gopher-wood of Noah's construction, and therefore possibly a crashed alien ship. The chain of documents uncovered by Redfern makes for fascinating reading.

When 1950s-era alien contactees like George Van Tassel also took an interest in the mystery atop Mount Ararat, they came under the watchful eye of the CIA and FBI. Information on the structure was at one point leaking like a sieve, according to Redfern, and the government was determined to plug those leaks. What was the government so determined to hide? Was the discovery of Noah's Ark a national security issue? Or was it a case of another crashed UFO? Turkey's own version of the Roswell Incident?

My own contributions to the new edition of *"The Sky People"* are a couple of chapters in which I speak to Brad Steiger, one of the most prolific writers on the strange and supernatural in the world, and Giorgio Tsoukalos, the official spokesman for Erich von Daniken in the English-speaking world, and the personality with that wild and crazy styled hair on **Ancient Aliens** broadcast over the History Channel II.

Steiger recalls attending an Ancient Astronauts conference in the early 1980s at which the main speakers were Erich von Daniken, Josef Blumrich (author of *"The Spaceships of Ezekiel,"* written when he worked at NASA) and Steiger himself. Not in attendance was our man of the hour, Brinsley Le Poer Trench.

"He was probably generally neglected," Steiger said, "because Erich von Daniken was the fair-haired boy at that time and was given a great deal of credit for coming up with the whole ancient astronauts concept. It was easier to do then. We didn't have the media that we do now. And a book such as 'The Sky People' was read by a few individuals, but the great masses of people then were not interested. Then something comes out and gets a lot of attention, like 'Chariots of the Gods?' As people said, von Daniken just happened to be standing in front of the cosmic slot machine when it paid off."

Stieger also praised Trench for his theories concerning the Planet Mars, specifically the idea that instead of Noah being an ancient Israelite, he was a great leader on Mars and the Ark was a giant spaceship intended to carry a surviving remnant to Earth.

"At the time Trench said it," Stieger continued, "people weren't prepared. But it's been interesting to see that in most polls the idea of life existing on other planets or in other solar systems is now generally accepted by young people. Whereas back in the 1950s and 1960s, it was rejected by nearly everyone. More and more, the idea that life could have existed elsewhere in our solar system doesn't get a door slammed immediately."

Steiger said he has come to feel that, "We have met the Martians and they are us," meaning we may have been genetically engineered by a superior race who originated on Mars and brought life to Earth for whatever unknown cosmic reason.

"I think, the more I study," Steiger said, "that we are definitely hardwired to perceive advanced beings as godlike, and I think we are hardwired just to perceive and understand a concept of God. Now, whether that has been hardwired by our progenitors from outer space, or it is just hardwired in terms of our evolution and our DNA, for how we perceive entities greater than we, is a question we could discuss endlessly. But I think it's just hardwired into us to perceive that we are part of a greater cosmic entity."

I also discussed the God angle with Giorgio Tsoukalos, who, along with his mentor Erich von Daniken, draws a definite line in the sand when it comes to calling the ancient astronauts the literal Creator God.

"Let's say you and I create an intelligent species in the lab," Tsoukalos said. "That does not make you and me God. The whole 'God question' transcends the extraterrestrial presence. The extraterrestrials that Erich von Daniken and I talk about are not ethereal beings. They were flesh and blood, physical people consisting of the same atoms and molecules and particles that every single human being and every single thing has here on Planet Earth.

"That is also why the extraterrestrials look like us," he continued. "The whole idea that extraterrestrials look like something out of the movie 'Aliens' or 'Independence Day,' that's a Hollywood stereotype. But both Erich and I think that there is an all-encompassing force in the universe. But you can't really put your finger on it. You can't really touch it. Even the extraterrestrials have the same exact questions about life, death, God and religion and all those different things that we are struggling with today. To suggest that the extraterrestrials have all the mysteries solved – I think it's not that easy."

Tim Swartz, another major writer for Global Communications and the editor of the online "Conspiracy Journal," also contributes a chapter to this updated edition of "The Sky People." Swartz gives the kind of broad overview of the ancient astronauts theory that will be very helpful for those new to the subject as well as for those more familiar with this strange territory. He begins by talking about paintings found in caves around the world.

"Cave paintings from Tanzania," Swartz writes, "estimated to be up to 29,000 years old, depict several disc-shaped objects that appear to be hovering over the landscape. Another painting shows four humanoid entities surrounding a woman while another entity looks down from the sky inside some sort of box.

"Inside the French cave of Pech Merle," Swartz continues, "near Le Cabrerets, are paintings from around 17,000 to 15,000 BCE that show landscapes full of wildlife with a number of saucer-shaped objects. One painting actually shows the figure of a man looking up at one of the overhead saucers. In northern Australia, there are a number of cave paintings, possibly more than 5,000 years old, that show strange beings with large heads and eyes, wearing spacesuit-like garments. The Aborigines call these creatures Wandjina, and according to legend, the Wandjina came down from the stars in the Milky Way during the Dreamtime and created the Earth and all its inhabitants."

The phenomenon of the cave paintings Swartz describes is the sort of thing that inspired Brinsley Le Poer Trench and the other researchers of the ancient astronauts theory to begin with, although Trench's ideas also depended a great deal on his groundbreaking interpretation of the Book of Genesis.

Trench was among the first to recognize that Genesis actually contains two different versions of the Creation Story and the Great Flood account. This has puzzled Biblical scholars for many years, who believe that the differing versions were probably inexpertly grafted together from earlier oral and written traditions. This fact is not taught in Sunday school or preached from the pulpits, but it is there for anyone to read.

What was Trench's take on the two different Creation Stories? For him, it was simple: two different races of man were created by two separate Creator Gods, one called the Elohim (which is actually a plural term) and the other called Jehovah, which Trench says is also a plural term, though not generally thought of as such.

The Elohim created a form of man who is telepathic, intelligent and sensitive. The Jehovah created a more primitive form of man, designed to till the gods' gardens on the Earth and otherwise be servile and docile. According to Trench, both races have survived into modern times, but it is the superior form of mankind created by the Elohim who will eventually win out. Some of us are rapidly reacquiring the telepathy we were meant to have from our very earliest beginnings and mankind will eventually become a sensitive, caring race living again in a virtual paradise. Meanwhile, the strain of mankind created by the Jehovah will eventually flounder in its paranoia and delusions of grandeur and gradually cease to exist.

This all sounds a little like the coming of a Biblically-inspired Super Man, and one wonders if the entire race being telepathic might not be a little uncomfortable at times. Alien abduction researcher David Jacobs also believes in a future telepathic world, but he questions how a person might function without the privacy of his thoughts? Like many issues raised by Trench, this one is not so easily resolved.

Trench also has a prescient moment or two when he writes about global warming and the threat posed by radical religious fundamentalism. Writing over 50 years ago, he seems to have his finger on the pulse of our own times. Was he a prophet himself?

The ancient aliens are still with us today, according to Trench. Some of them live among us unseen, working and raising families and going about the same everyday activities we all do. This also has been touched upon by more current UFO researchers, like the late Budd Hopkins, who claimed that alien/human hybrid creatures – who appear utterly human physically – walk among us equipped with telepathic and other "supernatural" capabilities. These same aliens, Trench believed, will prevent us from perishing by our own hand, with nuclear weapons or ecological suicide, which is a welcome departure from the more vocal prophets of doom. For Trench, our survival was guaranteed, not our demise.

So whether you're Bible-believing or a staunch agnostic, Brinsley Le Poer Trench and the other contributors to this updated version of "The Sky People" will give you new and different perspectives on many truths you may have long taken for granted about God and the evolution of mankind. Be prepared for a fascinating and complex dive into the unknown that will surely be worth more than the cover price.

**LEGACY OF THE SKY PEOPLE** can be ordered directly from the publisher for the special Conspiracy Journal reader's price of just **$20.00 + $5 S/H.** Address all orders to:**TIMOTHY G. BECKLEY · BOX 753 · NEW BRUNSWICK, NJ 08903**

## WANT TO KNOW MORE ABOUT ANCIENT ASTRONAUTS? - THE FOLLOWING ARE RECOMMENDED.

*ALIEN SPACE GODS OF ANCIENT GREECE AND ROME – REVELATIONS OF THE ORACLE OF DELPHI* – W.R. Drake , Tim Beckley and Sean Casteel ask:

Was the Mediterranean region of our planet visited by a race of "super beings" in Ancient Times? And was the Oracle of Delphi a conduit for prophetic messages from outer space – perhaps the first telepathic channeler? Fully illustrated. Approx 300 pages. - **$24.00**

*ANCIENT SECRETS OF MYSTERIOUS AMERICA – REVEALING OUR TRUE COSMIC DESTINY* – W.R. Drake, Joshua Shapiro and Brent Raynes want to know if WE ARE READY FOR THE RETURN OF THE ANCIENT WARRIORS? Do strange alien artifacts discovered throughout the Americas prove ancient astronauts once winged to Earth and shared their wisdom with early humans? - **$21.95**

**MYSTERIES OF MOUNT SHASTA — HOME OF THE UNDERGROUND DWELLERS AND ANCIENT GODS**—One of the most magical sites in America, this mystical mountain plays a significant part in inner earth and outer space connections and has existed as a doorway to another dimension since the beginning of time. It is an entry point on the Light Grid and has been headquarters for the Lemurians (one of the original races upon the earth).

—**$21.95**

**LONG LOST WORLDS AND UNDERGROUND MYSTERIES OF THE FAR EAST** — Here are first hand accounts of lost cities and civilizations. A 150 year old Saint who flies. The dreaded serpent race. Shape Shifters of the jungle. Underground Realms. Forbidden and eerie rites and rituals.— **$20.00**

**SUPER SPECIAL – All five critically acclaimed books titles listed above (including LEGACY OF THE SKY PEOPLE) for just $82.00 + $8 S/H**

## CAN HUMANS "FLY" OR WALK THROUGH WALLS?

### Unleashing The Super Powers Of Invisibility and Levitation

By Tim R. Swartz

OUT of all the magical secrets that mankind has sought over the ages, probably the two most universal desires would be the ability to become invisible and to fly, or levitate at will. Countless spells, incantations, potions and talismans have been created, all with the purpose to achieve the goals of invisibility and unaided flight. Now thanks to researcher Tim R. Swartz and retired military intelligence operative Commander X, working in tandem with others, we are happily prepared to proclaim the secrets to fulfilling these mystical "dreams" are at hand. A new book by the publisher of this newsletter reveals the most astounding information on these mind blowing concepts.

\* \* \* \* \*

Many people today would scoff at the notion that one can become invisible, or fly with the help of magical or occult powers. However, ancient wisdom passed down from antiquity indicates that such "powers" are available if one only knows the true secrets of the lost wisdom of the ages.

These secrets, some which have been lost for centuries, have now been gathered together from the four corners of the Earth. It is now the 21st century, and the time is right for these lost teachings to be revealed to those willing to take on the great responsibility that such incredible powers can endow on an individual.

For those who would use these abilities on a quest for knowledge, or to help their fellow man, then they will find their path is readily before them, with guides and assistance to help them along their spiritual journey.

Throughout history there have been those individuals who claim that they can make their flesh and bones "fade" from view. These master adepts use mystical, metaphysical or occult powers. They are advanced humans who have discovered various techniques that give them supernatural powers. Some of them have used magick, others have superior mental abilities.

A serious student of raja yoga was once taught that certain supernormal powers, called Siddhas, were a natural outcome of gaining mastery over one's mind and environment, and were used as valuable indications of the student's spiritual progress. One of these yogic Siddhas was human invisibility.

Patanjali, author of the *Yoga-sutra*, one of the earliest documents among the early Indian writings, described the process to produce human invisibility. He said that concentration and meditation can make the body imperceptible to other men, and "a direct contact with the light of the eyes no longer existing, the body disappears." The light engendered in the eye of the observer no longer comes into contact with the body that has become invisible, and the observer sees nothing at all. The mystery is how this could possibly occur, the explanation of the process of invisibility was most likely left up to the teacher to impart to the student directly.

The infamous – or famous, depending upon your perception – magi Aleister Crowley wrote: "The real secret of invisibility is not concerned with the laws of optics at all. The trick is to prevent people noticing you when they would normally do so. Said another expert: "When the mind inhabits emanation of its radioactivity it ceases to be the source of mental stimuli to others, so that they become unconscious of the presence of an Adept of the Art, just as they are unconscious of invisible beings living in a rate of vibration unlike their own."

## THE PECULIAR TALENT TO LEVITATE

Newton's law of gravity does not always work. There are some humans who defy the law without meaning to. They apparently have no control over themselves and will float skyward without expending any effort. Madame Alexandra David-Neal, the French explorer who spent 14 years in Tibet, relates a strange case in her book, *Mystere et magique en Tibet*.

She wrote that she had once seen a naked man weighed down with heavy chains. A friend of his told the author that because of intense mystical training, his body had become so light that if he didn't drape himself in chains he would float away.

Stories about human levitation are not rare. It is perhaps the most commonly mentioned miracle in yogic and Tibetan Buddhist Literature and in the lore of the Roman Catholic Saints.

Unknown to most people is the fact that just about anyone can levitate. You don't have to be a psychic. You don't have to have some kind of magical formula. All you have to know is the rules of levitation, and be willing to obey them.

Those who have truly accomplished the art of levitation say that with few exceptions the phenomenon requires training and discipline for a long period of time. There is a mysterious law at work, a law that says the body will be given permission to defy the law of gravity.

Spontaneous or random levitations may also work on this principle. The levitator may accidentally stumble upon the natural ability that permits them to rise into the air. Investigator Charles Fort, who wrote huge volumes of strange events during the early part of this century came across a case of a 12-year old boy named Henry Jones from

Shepton Mallet in England who rose to the ceiling on several occasions. The year was 1657. At one time the boy was observed sailing over a garden wall. The distance was 30 yards. If he knew the secret formula, it didn't last long for him. After one year he lost his ability to levitate. Afterwards he was shunned by the townspeople who believed him bewitched.

## SCIENCE OR MYSTICISM?

One way to find useful clues as to how human levitation might work is to analyze what the various groups that occasionally produce such reports have in common. Several connections are obvious. A belief in spirits and/or a spiritual realm is integral to shamanism, mysticism, spiritualism, spirit possession and poltergeist activity. Although such beliefs do not actually amount to proof that spirits and a spirit realm actually exist, they do suggest that something is going on; but what?

The people who belong to these groups often enter trances or altered states of consciousness—either voluntarily or involuntarily—and many of them develop paranormal abilities other than levitation. This introduces the closely related and often controversial subjects of parapsychology and consciousness research, which will be discussed later. Alien abductions also have several interesting similarities with these groups.

Many abduction experiences closely resemble shamanic initiation experiences. Like shamans, abductees often develop an animistic perspective in which they see aliens as a type of spiritual being from another realm or dimension. They may also develop various paranormal abilities, including healing. Like some shamans this may involve the ability to look into a person's body and diagnose illness, almost as if they had x-ray vision.

Do these "powers" come from supernatural entities, extraterrestrials or are they the product of our own subconscious? It doesn't really matter if the powers that are transmitted are useful to us in a positive way!

Historical accounts suggest that some mystics were most reluctant to reveal instances of spontaneous levitation in case they were thought to be possessed. The Catholic researcher Olivier Leroy in his book Levitation: An Examination of the Evidence and Explanations (1928) makes it quite plain that he believes that saints that levitate are divinely blessed, while spirit mediums are just being duped by demonic entities. Leroy is clearly biased, but one wonders what he would have thought about alien abductions if he were still alive.

The Catholic church's apparent ambivalence about miraculous phenomena makes human levitation harder to investigate because it reduces the number of witnesses and subsequent documentation of such events. For example, the Croatian stigmatist Father Zlatko Sudac, who visited America early in 2002, claims to have "the gifts of levitation, bilocation, illumination, and the knowledge of upcoming events." However, when asked about them during a recent interview, he declined to elaborate until the Catholic hierarchy had made a pronouncement about the matter.

A variation on religious ambivalence is the poor documentation of miraculous events in cultures where paranormal abilities are taken for granted. Such a blasé attitude is illustrated by a story about the Tibetan yogi Milarepa (1052-1135) who is reported to have once levitated over the heads of some distant relatives who were plowing a field.

The man's son spotted the levitating monk and called to his father to stop work and observe the miracle. Milarepa's relative looked up, saw the levitating holy man, and firmly instructed his son to ignore that "good-for-nothing" and get back to work.

## THE WEIRD WORLD OF CRYSTAL SKULLS AND THEIR UFO CONNECTIONS

By Sean Casteel

The name Joshua Shapiro has become synonymous with crystal skulls and he is one of the leading experts on what they may ultimately mean. For more than 30 years, he has investigated the mystery surrounding these crystalline carvings, which are human-shaped skulls made out of different types of quartz crystals and other gemstones. Many of the early crystal skulls were initially found in the 1800s in Mexico within or near ancient tombs. Today, however, skulls have been discovered worldwide, including in China, Mongolia, Peru, Australia and throughout Europe.

Shapiro has concentrated a great deal of his efforts on one particular crystal skull which he calls the Blue Skull. In a new book, published by Timothy Green Beckley of Global Communications and titled *"Journeys of the Crystal Skull Explorers, Travelogue Number Two, Search for the Blue Skull in Peru,"* Shapiro tells a fascinating story of how some unseen force seemed to be guiding him to find the Blue Skull, a search that led him to northern Peru and included physical and emotional hardships along the way. Shapiro never actually found the Blue Skull, but his story aptly illustrates that sometimes the journey itself is the real point, not the destination and what one hoped to find there.

Along the path to writing the new book, Shapiro became a huge fan of the flying saucer contactee George Hunt Williamson. While reading one of Williamson's books, *"Other Tongues, Other Flesh,"* Shapiro started to cry when he read about Williamson's "Cosmic Wanderers," who are cosmic "chimney-sweeps" who go from planet to planet, lifting them into the light. Shapiro recognized himself in *"Other Tongues, Other Flesh,"* even though it was written in the 1950s and he was reading it in the 1980s.

"It was like this was an explanation about the essence of my soul," Shapiro said.

Shapiro subsequently corresponded by letter with Williamson, who counseled the younger man to be patient and not to push things too fast.

Shapiro also shares the same birthday as the hugely influential contactee George Adamski, April 17th, and thus believes he has a spiritual connection with the elder statesman of the Space Brother interpretation of UFOs.

After his many journeys to South America, Shapiro has come to feel the people of Peru, at least the non-urban ones, are very down to earth.

159

"If there's a sighting in Peru," Shapiro said, "they don't think anything about it. They just say, 'Wow, that's great. I'm excited to hear that happened.' If they didn't see it, they feel like they missed it. A lot of people in Peru just accept living in nature and paranormal phenomena that go on. If UFOs show up, if a dimensional door opens and something happens, this is just a part of their ancient traditions and culture. It's really natural for them, versus some more modern countries."

Shapiro has had some near misses with UFO contact himself. While traveling by car to Chicago with a friend, around the time Shapiro was beginning his first book, called "Journeys of an Aquarian Age Networker," he and his friend started to notice that the clouds in the sky were doing strange things and were oddly shaped.

"We were thinking that we were having some contact with UFOs," Shapiro said. "They weren't necessarily following us, but there was some kind of UFO activity going on."

On that same trip, Shapiro and his friend met contactee Daniel Fry in the vicinity of Alamogordo, New Mexico, where the first atomic bomb was tested in 1945. As well as being a UFO contactee, Fry had also been a military officer.

"He told us that one night when he was on duty," Shapiro said, "a UFO landed and he went onboard. It flew him around and took him to different places."

The UFO-related incidents on the trip changed Shapiro's perspective, he said.

"I became very aware of clouds and stars in the sky that are NOT clouds or stars in the sky. They're hiding extraterrestrial craft. The 'clouds' would be the electromagnetic frequency of the craft ionizing the air molecules, which creates the cloud. Then the 'stars' are obviously just the ship shining multicolored lights and moving around in the sky."

Shapiro also heard a story from a friend who had worked for the government who claimed to have seen reptilian aliens change form.

"They looked like humans," Shapiro recounted, "but there for a brief moment he surprised them and they lost their ability to keep their form

and he saw them change into reptilians. There's no doubt that we're being visited, and that we have been visited for thousands of years."

Shapiro predicts the day will come when there is open contact between humankind and the extraterrestrials.

"I know this is our destiny," he declared, "and I know that the UFOs are coming here to the Earth to assist in this process because Planet Earth has to evolve into a higher state along with every other planet in this solar system. As far as some of the negative aliens, I think they've already lost. There's nothing they can do to stop humanity from going forward into this higher state. It's ordained by the highest sources that exist, whatever you want to call it, possibly the Highest Creative Soul."

And how does all this talk of UFOs relate to the crystal skulls that are the main focus of Shapiro's work?

"It's hard to imagine," he answered, "that a primitive people could have made some of the skulls that we've found. Modern carvers right now are able to do a very good job. But they use these diamond-tipped tools which didn't exist until the 1970s or 80s. Crystal skulls were being found of a superior form long before that. So one of the possibilities we talk about is that perhaps some of the very old crystal skulls have a connection with extraterrestrials. The question is: could 'gods' have been responsible for bringing the original crystal skulls here as tools to awaken consciousness in humanity?"

Some of the crystal skulls, according to Shapiro, will change internally and display holographic images of spacecraft and extraterrestrials. Unfortunately, no scientists have been willing to work with Shapiro on definitively proving the images are real. A handful of crystal skulls made to appear not exactly human are perhaps another link to ET life.

"Every time you turn around," Shapiro said, "and try to figure out where the crystal skulls are coming from, there's always some kind of lead to UFOs that comes up."

Whether or not the source of the crystal skulls is something extraterrestrial, Shapiro remains optimistic about the future.

"There is definitely a strong desire," Shapiro said, "by these other intelligences, whether they're spirits or extraterrestrials, to make a more direct contact with us. They've been doing it gradually because a lot of people may be afraid of this. It's something that's invisible, that our physical senses can't detect. Something of a miraculous nature is going to happen. And the crystal skulls seem to me to be acting like little mini-energy vortexes activating spiritual gifts, spiritual insights into people they have contact with."

## EXPOSING THE FEAR FACTOR IN UFOS –

## WICKED THIS WAY COMES

By Timothy Green Beckley

All is not as rosy in UFOland as it might appear on the surface!

Stories of encounters with the supposedly friendly "all-too-cute" ETs are NOT always the norm, and represent only one side of the coin (or disc since we are referring to flying saucers). Little Elliot may have befriended Steven Spielberg's cozy, cuddly alien, but all too often our almond-eyed visitors have their own agenda, which frequently puts them at odds with our earthly plans and aspirations. They have been known to abduct, dice and slice and put us through a world of utter discontent.

Not only can the Ultra-Terrestrials – my favorite term for any entity that comes out of or is associated with a UFO, since we cannot really determine their origin, be it interplanetary or more close to home, perhaps from a parallel universe – be  damned ornery, but they have the power to interfere with both our physical and mental states and put fear into our hearts. Thus the term "Fear Factor." Even the peace-loving contactees of the early days of UFOlogy were made aware of the Ultra-Terrestrials' shenanigans.

In our previously published book, *"Round Trip To Hell In A Flying Saucer,"* we documented the many instances of shape-shifting, levitation and the presence of transparent or translucent entities that can oftentimes wreak havoc on an entire household following what might seem like a benign close encounter but which ends up going well beyond a one night cosmic stand.

Likewise, in the book "Evil Empire Of The ETs and Ultra-Terrestrials," I pointed out how the occupants of the craft we have come to identify as Unidentified Flying Objects—UFOs! —have some of the same characteristics as spirits from the dark corridors of demonology and have been known to produce the same sort of phenomena at landing sites as you would find in a haunted house or at a séance. I've chatted for hours with "Coast to Coast AM" host George Noory about such eerie matters and most of the conversation has been preserved on You Tube, where you can find the interviews by simply typing in my name and "Coast to Coast AM" and all manner of links will pop up in a matter of mere seconds.

There are numerous aspects of this dark side of UFOs that we must examine closely, to include:

+ The connection between UFOs, demons and possibly Satan himself.

+ The fascination for and the link between Nazism, occultism and German-made flying saucers.

+ The ghastly exercise of blood draining and human sacrifice throughout antiquity and their relationship to animal and human mutilations and bloodletting in modern times, which align closely to the appearance of UFOs in specific theaters of operation on our planet.

+ The weird claims of John Lear that aliens are coming here to kidnap humans and not return them. That people are being used for food, and how "they" are experimenting with us – sadistic experimentations – and attempting to suck out our souls and place them in containers for their own use.

+ The Islamic belief in the normally invisible elementals identified in the Koran as the Jinn and how these malevolent spirits are able to misrepresent themselves by camouflaging their true identity and traveling around at fantastic speeds.

+ Shape-shifters who can turn into human-looking beings, animals, orbs, fireballs or manifest themselves even as physical "hardware" to fool us into believing they are mechanical devices.

+ The casting of magical spells, occult rituals and the ability to conjure up spirits and beings often mistaken for UFOnauts but more closely aligned with the elemental kingdom.

## THEIR ONGOING PLANS FOR US, WHICH INCLUDE RAPE, PILLAGE

## AND PLUNDER BOTH OF HUMANS AS WELL AS OF THE ENTIRE PLANET!

Witnesses tell tales of unbelievable aggression. "The creatures were hostile and went into attack modes several times, putting up dense fogs. One time when they stopped, it was like a backwards tornado coming from the mouth of the leader of the ships. It was like a ray that he was sending down a funnel. He did it five times, then he left…" One Navy Commander with strong CIA ties has stated: "Much if not all of the phenomenon is nefarious – a monstrous evil with occasional good." According to Dr. Karla Turner, whose work Sean Casteel examines later on in the newly released Global Communications book UFOs – WICKED THIS WAY COMES, there is evidence that the intelligence behind the mysterious discs can control what we think we see. They can appear to us in any number of guises and shapes. They can alter our perception of our surroundings. They can take over our consciousness, disable our control of our bodies, install one of their own entities, and use our bodies as vehicles for their own activities.

Unrecognized by most researchers is the fact that over the ensuing years, flying saucers have made themselves "known" in a variety of awesome and thought-provoking ways.

Well established are the instances in which unidentified airborne objects have been accused of causing blackouts and power failures. Lights in entire communities, down to the most modest single dwellings, have flickered out due to the approach of a "foreign" apparatus of unknown origin. Ample exposure has also been given to cases in which UFOs have brought automobiles and other mechanical devices to a complete halt. Several well-seasoned UFO researcher-writers have penned lengthy papers on this so-called EM (electromagnetic) effect. What of other, even more bizarre, irrational side effects, traceable to disturbingly close confrontations with UFOs and their many-faceted crew members?

There is a news story, reprinted as a lead-in to a chapter in the new book, that appeared more than 40 years ago, buried away on the inside pages of a widely circulated daily newspaper, in which a father tells of a strange transformation wrought on his daughter by UFOs in the vicinity of their home.

The mere thought that UFO activity might cause a young girl's hair to glow in the dark and change colors is staggering. Of course, it is impossible to check on the validity of this episode at this late date, but we do have other equally unusual tales which lead us to speculate that this experience was indeed not a hoax, a fabrication or a coincidence.

Doubtless this case must be placed in a category by itself – there are no others precisely like it on record. Yet, from the bulging files of clippings and personal eyewitness testimony I have amassed over the years, this particular incident by no means misrepresents the many strange after- and side-effects which can be directly attributed to flying saucer activity.

Despite a new respectability about this topic, there remain many factors deeply engrained as part of the UFO puzzle which have not been openly publicized. Nor has adequate research been done to explain them. It is a documented, well-established fact that UFOs have affected or been able to alter in some way:

>> The growth of plant life, insects and humans;

>> The forces of gravity;

>> The passing of time and anything remotely connected with it;

>> The placement of physical objects; and

>> The normal healing process.

The Warping of Time

*UFOS – WICKED THIS WAY COMES* covers all these diverse elements in complete detail. I am especially fond of the effect of "warping time" that has been noted in many instances where UFOs and human beings collide. These time distortions have been known to last for several seconds to several hours. Also, in a number of contact cases, time itself, as we know it, is extended or compacted way out of proportion.

It is almost as though UFOs and Earth time are incompatible.

Journalist Arthur Shuttlewood is convinced that the perplexing timepiece stopping phenomenon in England is a direct result of UFO activity over his hometown of Warminster – yet another strange effect we must contend with. On the night of September 9, 1969, a dozen residents of Potten End (a suburb near Warminster) had the singular and disturbing experience of having their timepieces remain motionless for about an hour. All the stories seem to coincide, although there was no direct relationship between the witnesses, nor did they know of anyone outside their own dwelling having the same experience.

One of those who found himself faced with such a situation is Norman Gilbert, an engineer who said, "I set my watch as usual and placed it on the nightstand before retiring. Upon awakening the next morning and seeing that it was still early, I dozed again, thinking I still had yet an hour more of sleep coming to me before getting ready for work. Arriving at my job, at what I thought was 7:00 AM, I was jokingly browbeaten by my fellow employees for being late." Gilbert then discovered that his watch was an hour slow.

Similarly, Mr. E.W. Rayment, a Potten End builder, had the unusual experience of having both his watch and bedside clock lose one hour on the same night. Another one of those who had the puzzling experience was Mr. John Booth of Dunbar Cottage. He described how his wife Kathleen's watch had stopped altogether on that same Saturday night. "We fiddled about with it for around an hour trying to get it to go again, but without success."

The following morning, Booth observed that the watch had started to work again without anyone touching it, and his wife has had no trouble with it since. Each watch-stopped individual could offer no explanation why their watches stopped on Saturday night and precisely at 8 PM. They were thoroughly convinced that it was not due to lack of winding.

A spokesman for the Science Research Council based at the Ministry of Defense, Navy Department's observatory at Hurstmonceux, near Eastbourne, said: "Nothing like this has ever been reported before."

However, Arthur Shuttlewood, author and UFO investigator, was told that at the instant the watches and clocks stopped working, a number of Berkhamsted people heard "odd humming sounds" and saw a peculiar shape in the sky – which experts determined to be an extraterrestrial ship.

Shuttlewood himself was involved in an episode where he had a 45-minute time disorientation while atop Cradle Hill watching a pair of UFOs through binoculars. The incident, which transpired in November of 1970, had Shuttlewood – who described in detail his multitude of experiences with flying saucers over this tiny English town in the Summer Issue of "Saga's UFO Report" – observing the celestial multi-hued lights, resembling a string of burning beads. Shuttlewood immediately noted the time on the luminous hands of his wristwatch, marking down the time of the sighting as 11:31 PM. At this point he attempted to signal one of the UFOs, which had descended to a point approximately 30 feet from where he stood. As the beam of its flash pierced the solemn darkness, he was able to distinguish the metallic gray outline of the ship's hull, straddled on top by a spherical dome.

"At this point, something odd and unworldly happened to me. To be honest, I cannot recall with any degree of clarity what transpired next. In short, I cannot remember if the object disappeared or if it continued to hover, or if indeed I walked away from Cradle Hill at all. What I do know is that an awful numbing sensation affected my limbs. I shut my dazzled eyes and felt desperately tired all of a sudden. The next thing I knew – I don't know how I got there – I was standing by a wooden fence at the bottom of Cradle Hill. Glancing at my watch, I was horror-struck. The time was now 12:35 AM. Despite the fact that it was a deadly-cold night and I was well wrapped against the bitter winter chill, my body was bathed in sweat. Moreover, tears were cascading down my face, and I could taste the salt in my mouth."

Shuttlewood says that he was upset because "my son was to have picked me up in my car at midnight at a nearby rendezvous point." Reaching the waiting auto, Shuttlewood apologized for being 40 minutes late. The editor's son, looking at his watch, remarked "You're not late, you're bang on time."

At this point, Shuttlewood realized that he had been the pawn of a bizarre time-distortion game. Checking his timepiece once again, he discovered that time had once more jostled, this time backward. It was now 12:07!

Made in the USA
Middletown, DE
22 September 2023

39076684R00099